BERLITZ®

FRANCE

1987/1988 Edition

D1115111

 By the staff of Berlitz Guides
A Macmillan Company

How to use our guide

These 256 pages cover the **highlights of France,** grouped into five regions. Although not exhaustive, our selection of sights will enable you to make the best of your trip.

The **sights** to see are contained between pages 44 and 191. Those most highly recommended are pinpointed by the Berlitz traveller symbol.

The **Where to Go** section on page 38 will help you plan your visit according to the time available.

For **general background** see the sections France and the French (p. 8), Facts and Figures (p. 16), History (p. 17) and Historical Landmarks (p. 36).

Entertainment and **activities** (including eating out) are described between pages 191 and 215.

The **practical information,** hints and tips you will need before and during your trip begin on page 216. This section is arranged alphabetically with a list for easy reference.

The **map section** at the back of the book (pp. 244–251) will help you find your way around and locate the principal sights.

Finally, if there is anything you cannot find, look in the complete **index** (pp. 252–256).

CONTENTS

CONTENTS

Cover photo: Château de Chenonceau

Text:	Jack Altman
Layout:	Doris Haldemann
Photography:	Monique Jacot
	pp. 10, 113, 115, 118, 119, 122, 209 Mireille Vautier;
	pp. 129, 130, 133, 135, 136, cover Claude Huber;
	p. 125 PRISMA/Schuster GmbH;
	p. 169 PRISMA/Etienne; p. 198 Loomis Dean;
	pp. 201, 213 Erling Mandelmann
Cartography:	Falk-Verlag, Hamburg
	pp. 44, 82, 112, 140, 170 Philippe Aquoise

Acknowledgements
We would like to express our warmest thanks to Claire Teeuwissen,
Geneviève Vincent, Pierre Carta, Nicholas Campbell and Gérard
Chaillon for their assistance in the preparation of this guide.

*Found an error or an omission in this Berlitz Guide? Or a change
or new feature we should know about? Our editor would be happy to
hear from you, and a postcard would do. Be sure to include your
name and address, since in appreciation for a useful suggestion,
we'd like to send you a free travel guide.*

*Although we make every effort to ensure the accuracy of all
the information in this book, changes occur incessantly. We cannot therefore take responsibility for facts, prices, addresses and
circumstances in general that are constantly subject to alteration.*

FRANCE AND THE FRENCH

Modest people, as Winston Churchill once said of a political opponent, often have much to be modest about—but nobody ever accused the French of modesty. Behind their carefully constructed grouchy façade, this race of perpetual malcontents clearly believes that France is the most splendid place on earth. Even their most fervent detractors have a hard time proving them wrong.

If the French do complain so much, it's perhaps because they feel they always deserve even better. In a modern world obsessed with being at the cutting edge of technology, the French still find it important to do a little polishing, too.

Not that they're duds in modern industrial achievement. Just in the field of public transport, for instance, sophisticated French subway systems are exported to major cities on every continent; Concorde, the supersonic plane they built with the British, has proved to be a great success; and their high-speed

The zest and sparkle of French life in a fountain at Paris's Palais-Royal.

Still the backbone of France, farmers like this have little time for frivolous Saint-Tropez.

and perfumes, their dashing art and monumental architecture. French civilization is essentially an exercise in enlightened self-indulgence.

They're always looking for some way to turn the ordinary into something special. And it's all for their own pleasure and the world's admiration. Amazing the magic a French girl can perform with a comb in her hair or a simple cotton scarf around her neck. Remember what happened when good old American blue jeans were taken up by the French and turned into a thing of high fashion.

Give them a couple of eggs and they won't just boil them, fry them or make an omelette (all of which they're quite prepared to do superlatively)—they feel obliged to produce a soufflé or a hollandaise sauce that makes an egg proud to be an egg. Even hamburgers have been stretched by one fast food chain into a more manageable long bun, apparently inspired by the traditional *baguette* sandwich.

The French just won't leave well enough alone, and occasionally overdo it. You may consider their formal, geometrically planned gardens a pompous

train, the TGV, is widely considered the best in the world.

The French are generally much more efficient than their international reputation. Service in hotels and restaurants is good; the road network is excellent. But Frenchmen cannot live by nuts and bolts alone. Quality of life remains their paramount preoccupation. No accident that they are best known for their food and wine, their clothes

distortion of nature, or their triumphal arches and grandiose palaces just a bit pretentious. However, this tendency to show off, frowned upon in more sober lands, and affectionately dubbed *la frime* in France, may be an irresistible desire to celebrate the riches with which nature has endowed the land.

France is blessed with an astonishing variety of landscapes. The stark, rough, dazzling ex-panses of naked rock and arid ruddy soil of some parts of Provence could be the setting for an American Western. But that's just as much France as the more conventional image of rolling green meadows bounded by straggling hedgerows beside an arrow-straight, shady avenue of plane trees, with a village clustering around its church on the horizon.

The country is a veritable

11

compendium of European geography, modified with a "French touch". The plains and plateaux of Picardy in the north and Alsace to the east are the logical conclusion of the central European steppes. The wide open spaces lend themselves to large-scale agriculture (and all-too-convenient battlefields) before ending in the gentler green fields of Normandy to the west or the vineyards of Burgundy that herald the south.

The Alps of Savoie and the Dauphiné extend the gigantic chain that rises from Austria across Germany and Switzerland to peter out in the rugged little *Alpilles* of Provence. The olive trees and vineyards, umbrella pines and cypresses of this Provençal countryside and the lazy beaches of the Côte d'Azur are a natural continuation of the classical Mediterranean landscape, until it gives way to the formidable mountain barrier of the Pyrenees at the frontier with Spain.

With those mountain ranges protecting the eastern and southern frontiers, the mild Atlantic winds penetrate deep inland, bringing all the rain and sun needed for a highly productive agriculture, while avoiding the extremes of a continental climate.

Inland from the Atlantic coast —Aquitaine, Dordogne, Périgord—the south-west is rich in farming and vineyards. It's the land of good duck and goose, of fine Bordeaux wines. At the country's western edge, Brittany's spectacular craggy shoreline has earned the region a reputation for rough weather. In fact it enjoys the mildest of climates, even in winter, and offers the surest of bets for its seaside resorts in summer.

The kings and counts and feudal lords have gone from the Loire Valley and the forests and marshes of Sologne, but the hunting and fishing country remains.

At the country's heart, slightly north of the geographical centre, Paris nestles in a basin ideal for industrial and commercial enterprise, comfortably surrounded by the forest and farmland of the Ile-de-France. And the Champagne country lies conveniently to the east to help celebrate its successes.

If the land itself is the most obvious source of a Frenchman's pride, the nation's cultural wealth is just as important. The fine arts do not intimidate the French as something to be confined to a small élite. For most people, "intellectual" is not the dirty word it seems to be in so many other countries. One of the most popular television shows devotes an hour and a half every week to talking, very entertaininingly, about nothing but books. The museums do better business than football stadiums, and crowds flock to theatre and music festivals in spring, summer and autumn all over the country. Even popular arts such as advertising, the cinema, fashion or comic strips are elevated to the level of high culture, with their own museums and festivals.

An active government cultural policy in recent years has preserved the architectural monuments of the "national patrimony" from the ravages of time, weather, war, revolution and the barbaric assaults of building speculation. The Palace of Versailles has been refurbished to sparkle as in the days of Louis XIV, the Louvre Museum reorganized for an ambitious expansion. The simplicity of Romanesque village churches or the grandeur of Gothic cathedrals can more and more be appreciated at their best. Even the ruins, of Roman towns or medieval monasteries, have come alive again as the sites of open-air concerts or theatre.

One major boon to the visitor has been the steady replacement of most of those boring uniformed guides, who recited their facts and figures about abbeys or palaces like melancholy parrots, by bright young art historians who actually like the places they work in. Their descriptions are fresh and informative, and they'll answer questions that go beyond the brochure or guide book.

The country offers plenty of outdoor enjoyment, too: water sports and plain old sunbathing on the beaches of Normandy and Brittany as well as the more famous resorts of the Côte d'Azur (the French would like to discourage that Italian word Riviera); first-class skiing in the Alps and the Pyrenees; hiking around the country's national parks and nature reserves. Proof that France is far from being a country of hidebound highbrows is the fact that the Walt Disney enterprise has chosen the Marne Valley east of Paris for Europe's first Disneyland.

The people are as varied as their landscapes, but don't let anybody tell you the cliché is a lie. The red-nosed, moustachioed fellow with a beret on his head, a crumpled cigarette drooping from his lip and a long *baguette* under his arm *does* exist. The French themselves have long acknowledged that all those who are not like that have a brother-in-law who is. But there's all the difference in the world between the prudent, close-mouthed Norman and the vociferous, easy-going Provençal, between the pious Breton and the pagan sophisticates of Paris.

For a people so fiercely proud of their identity, with all the recurrent waves of xenophobia that such nationalism encourages, the French are a marvellous mixture, another compendium of the European map, this time in an ethnic sense. Up in Picardy, the Flemish influence is unmistakable. Although Alsace may celebrate Bastille Day more proudly than any other French province, its cuisine, wines and dialect are profoundly Germanic. The Côte d'Azur and Corsica have a distinctly Italian flavour, and the people north of the Pyrenees are not so very different from their Spanish cousins to the south. Then there are the Celts of Brittany, the Norsemen of Normandy, the Basques of the Pays Basque....

As the land of the Declaration of the Rights of Man, France has never for long resisted welcoming political refugees. There were Polish, German, Italian, American and British deputies in the National Assembly of the French Revolution. Russians fled to France from the Tsar and Stalin, Spaniards from Franco, Jews from Hitler, Armenians from the Turks, Lebanese from the civil war of Beirut.

However, it's in the artistic world, as a pole of attraction rather than a refuge from fear, that France has happily made a mockery of its own suspicion of foreigners. Not by accident did Van Gogh come from the Netherlands, Picasso from Spain, Max Ernst from Germany or Chagall from Russia to make their home in France. One of France's greatest poets of the

The serious business of stoking up energy for Megève's slopes.

14

20th century, Wilhelm Kostrowitsky, better known as Guillaume Apollinaire, was born in Rome of a Polish mother and Italian father. Irishman Samuel Beckett happily writes in French. And Kenzo, Lagerfeld and Cerruti design in the international but inexorably Paris-based language of *haute couture*.

Despite occasional tensions, perhaps inevitable in times of economic uncertainty, Frenchmen increasingly recognize that immigrant workers from its former colonies—Algerians, Tunisians and Moroccans—enrich the national culture. And the cuisine.

Not least of all, they add even more flavour, colour and music to the greatest of French assets, the street scene, the sheer light and movement of life itself.

FACTS AND FIGURES

Geography:	With a land mass of 547,000 sq. km. (213,000 sq. mi.), France is by far the largest country in Western Europe, a hexagon neatly measuring 1,000 km. (620 mi.) from north to south and another 1,000 km. from east to west. It is bounded by three seas (the English Channel, the Atlantic and the Mediterranean) and three mountain ranges (the Pyrenees, the Alps and the Jura), with the Rhine river and Flanders plain to the north-east. The country's four main rivers are the Loire running west to the Atlantic from the plateau of the Massif Central, the Seine flowing north-west from Burgundy through Paris to the Channel, the Garonne which flows down from the Pyrenees, past Toulouse and Bordeaux, to the Atlantic, and the Rhône starting in the Swiss Alps to turn south at Lyon down to the Mediterranean.
	Highest mountain: Mont Blanc (Alps) 4,807 m. (15,800 ft.).
Population:	59,000,000 (including 4,000,000 non-French, principally North African, Portuguese, Italian and Spanish).
Capital:	Paris 2.2 million (metropolitan area 9 million).
Major cities:	Marseille (900,000), Lyon (450,000), Toulouse (380,000), Nice (340,000), Nantes (260,000), Strasbourg (250,000), Bordeaux (230,000).
Government:	Under the Constitution of 1958, France's Fifth Republic elects a president every 7 years, exercising executive power with a prime minister and cabinet of ministers. The legislature is divided between the National Assembly, elected by universal suffrage every 5 years, and a largely subordinate Senate, chosen every 9 years by an electoral body of deputies and regional councillors. At local level, the 1982 decentralization law reorganized the country's 96 departments into 22 regional councils.
Religion:	Predominantly Catholic, 43,600,000, while Muslims are estimated at 2,800,000, Protestants 2,000,000 and Jews 600,000.

HISTORY

Neanderthal man was a *homo sapiens*, literally a man who knows, but the most famous Stone Age Frenchman, Cro-Magnon, was what the anthropologists call a *homo sapiens sapiens*, a man who knows he knows. From that Stone Age caveman dug up by railway workers in the Dordogne, down to Charles de Gaulle with his "certain idea" of what France ought to be, the French have always wanted to know what it means to be a Frenchman.

Their history is a constant quest for national identity, a conflict between strong regional loyalties and the central authority of a Cardinal Richelieu, King Louis XIV, Emperor Napoleon, President de Gaulle—or his successors.

Round about 2000 B.C., Celtic tribes, probably from eastern Europe, came looking for greener pastures in Franche-Comté, Alsace and Burgundy. At the same time, migrants from the Mediterranean countries were trickling into the south.

The first recorded settlement was the trading post set up by Phocaean Greeks from Asia Minor at Massalia (Marseille) around 600 B.C., followed by other ports at Hyères, Antibes and Nice. But the Greeks developed few contacts with the interior beyond a little commerce in olives and wine with the Celts of Burgundy. When their position was threatened by Ligurian pirates at sea and bellicose tribes from their hinterland, the merchants of Marseille called on Rome for help.

From Gaul to France

In 125 B.C., the Romans came in force, conquered the "Gallic barbarians" and set up a fortress at Aquae Sextiae (Aix-en-Provence). They took advantage of this new stronghold to create Provincia (now Provence), stretching from the Alps to the Pyrenees, to guarantee communications between Italy and Spain.

When this province was endangered by new attacks from the north, Julius Caesar himself took charge, conquering practically the whole of Gaul by 50 B.C. Caesar drew Gaul's northeastern frontier at the Rhine, taking in present-day Belgium, and warned that the Germanic tribes across the river—Franks, Alamans and Saxons—would always mean trouble.

The Romanization of Gaul exiled the most energetic warriors to defend the outposts of the empire, while their families settled down to work the land, or build towns at Lyon, Orange, Arles and Nîmes—and the first great highways between them.

Merchants developed a thriving trade with the rest of the empire. The pattern for the peasantry and bourgeoisie of France was thus established.

Christianity was introduced to Gaul in the 1st century A.D., but it was not really accepted until 391 when it became the empire's official religion. Large-scale conversions were led by Martin de Tours, soldier-turned-bishop (sword and cross formed a regular alliance in French history). The new religion soon cemented national solidarity in the face of more barbarian invasions, this time by the Franks.

Gallic unity collapsed with the crumbling empire. King Clovis, the leader of the Franks, defeated the Roman armies at Soissons in 486 and won the allegiance of most Gallo-Romans by converting to Christianity ten years later. With Paris as his capital, he extended his rule to the Mediterranean. But the realm was divided up among his heirs and progressively fragmented by the rivalries of the Merovingian dynasty that battled for power over the next 300 years.

Spain's Arab rulers exploited this disunity to sweep north across Gaul, controlling Languedoc, Dordogne and a large part of Provence before being defeated at Poitiers in 732 by the army of Charles Martel, bastard son of King Pépin.

Even the mighty Charlemagne, king of the Franks from 768 to 814, did not create an enduring national unity, as his sons fought for the spoils of his empire.

This time it was the Normans from Scandinavia who took advantage of the Carolingian dynasty's divided kingdom, pillaging their way inland along the Loire and Seine, plundering Paris in 845. Saracens invaded the Provençal coast from North Africa, and Magyar armies attacked Lorraine and Burgundy.

To keep the support of the nobles' armies, the king had to give the nobles more and more land. The realm broke up into the fiefdoms of the feudal Middle Ages, precursors of the country's classical provinces—Provence, Burgundy, Normandy and Brittany, etc.

In the central region, from the Loire Valley to Belgium, Hugues Capet achieved a precarious ascendancy. He was crowned the first king of France in 987. As at the fall of the Roman Empire, it was the Christian Church that provided the essential element of national unity. Hugues was anointed at Reims with an oil said to be brought to earth by the angels. He established kingship by divine right for the French.

In Carcassonne's dungeons, the only things missing are dragons and damsels in distress.

Middle Ages

Alliance with the Church was the underpinning of royal authority. In exchange for the anointment, the Church was enriched with lands and the right of taxation by tithe, a fraction of the peasants' seasonal produce.

After the more sober spirituality of the Romanesque churches, the soaring Gothic cathedrals of Chartres, Paris (Notre-Dame), Bourges and Amiens were at once monuments to the glory of God and testimony to the sheer power, spiritual and temporal, of the Catholic Church.

France, dubbed by the pope "eldest daughter of the Church", took the lead in the Crusades against the "infidels" in Palestine, stopping off on the way across Europe to massacre Jews and heretics. Louis IX, the ideal of the Christian king for the justice he handed down to his subjects and for the Crusades he led to the Holy Land, was sainted after his death in Tunis in 1270.

When things grew too hot for the papacy in Italy, it was quite natural for it to move to Avignon in 1309, where it stayed some 70 years.

France's other major preoccupation was England. In 1066, as probably more British than

French schoolchildren know, Duc Guillaume of Normandy crossed the English Channel and became William the Conqueror. For the next 400 years, English and French monarchs fought over the sovereignty of various pieces of France—among them, Aquitaine, Touraine, Normandy and Flanders.

It's a tiresome tale of inextricable tangles of marital alliances or military victories more important to national morale than resolving the perennial conflict—Bouvines (1214) for the French, Crécy (1346) and Agincourt (1415) for the English. It took a teenager from Lorraine, Jeanne d'Arc (Joan of Arc), to pull the French into good enough shape to resist the English at Orléans. For her pains, the English burned her to death in Rouen in 1431, but her martyrdom stirred national pride enough, 20 years later, to boot the English out of France.

But the noble national cause was not the first concern of the ordinary Frenchman. Wars were just another hardship, taking sons away from the farm to fight, while the armies—French as much as foreign—ravaged the land or pillaged the towns.

During war or peace in this feudal age, Church and aristocracy continued to claim their respective portion of the peasants' labour, leaving barely enough for mere subsistence. But all too frequently, a cycle of drought, famine and plague would decimate the population. A Dordogne farmer rarely took time off to find out who his current monarch was.

In any case, large portions of France were independently controlled by powerful dukes whose allegiance to the king was only nominal. The unity of France was still a long way off.

Ancien Régime

Absolutism was the dominant feature of what post-Revolutionary France called the *Ancien Régime*. The monarchy began to come into its own with François I (1515–47). He strengthened the central administration and abandoned an initially tolerant policy towards the Protestants. Debonair Renaissance prince, he introduced a grand style at court.

François brought Leonardo da Vinci to work at Blois, and Rosso and Primaticcio to decorate Fontainebleau. He also commissioned paintings by Raphael and Titian for the royal collections that are now the pride of the Louvre. A new opulent architecture blossomed with the châteaux of the Loire and around Paris.

Joan of Arc remains a potent symbol of French nationalism.

On the international scene, after he had crushed the Duke of Milan's army at Marignano, and formed a showy alliance with Henry VIII of England, his European ambitions were halted by the German Emperor Charles V. François even suffered the indignity of a year's imprisonment in Madrid following a resounding defeat at Pavia in 1525.

The bloody 16th-century conflicts between Catholics and Protestants throughout Europe centred more on political and financial intrigue than questions of theology. The French Wars of Religion pitted the Catholic forces of the regent Catherine de Médicis against the Protestant (Huguenot) camp of Henri de Navarre. Their crisis came on August 24, 1572, with the Saint Bartholomew's Day Massacre. Two thousand Protestants, in Paris for Henri's wedding with Catherine's daughter Marguerite de Valois, were killed. The general massacre of Protestants spread to the countryside, and by October, another 30,000 had lost their lives.

The conciliatory policies which painfully emerged brought the prince of Navarre to the throne as Henri IV (1589–1610), but not before he had promised to convert to Catholicism.

The enormous personal popularity of the good-natured but tough king from the Pyrenees proved vital for healing the wounds from the bitter wars. The Edict of Nantes was signed in 1598 to protect the Protestants and, five years later, the Jesuits were allowed back into France. But Henri won the hearts of the people most by finding time to pursue his calling as an incorrigible womanizer, known to posterity as the *Vert Galant*. Until he was stabbed to death by a Catholic zealot.

France floundered in intrigue under the regency of Marie de Médicis, mother of young Louis XIII, until Cardinal Richelieu

---

Too Much Starch?

Executing a king's assassin was no simple business, least of all when the king was as beloved as Henri IV. For an ordinary capital offence during those pre-Revolutionary times, hanging did the trick—the more dignified decapitation by axe being reserved for those of noble blood. But a regicide, even when he had been found guilty and sentenced to public execution, had to be tortured and, still alive, "quartered" by four horses each attached to an arm or leg. His remains were then cremated by the executioner. In the case of Henri's murderer, François Ravaillac, the frenzied crowd in front of the Paris town hall set upon his remains, and only his shirt was left over for cremation.

took charge as prime minister in 1624.

Directing national policy until his death in 1642, he reasserted the authority of his king against both the conservative Catholics that surrounded the queen mother, and the Protestant forces who were fiercely defending the privileges granted them by the Edict of Nantes. With his successful siege of the Protestant stronghold at La Rochelle, the cardinal neutralized the threat of their military strength while guaranteeing their freedom of worship.

Richelieu's major achievement was the greater centralization of royal power, laying the foundations of that strong national identity that has characterized France ever since. He tightened the king's control over legislation and taxes, enraging the Vatican by daring to impose a new levy on the Church. More powerful royal stewards were sent out to diminish the autonomy of the regional *parlements*, councils with judicial rather than legislative functions, dominated by the high clergy and nobles. The Cardinal also created the *Académie française* in 1635 to ensure the purity and clarity of the French language through its *Dictionnaire* and its *Grammaire*.

Promoting overseas trade and the founding of a navy, Richelieu launched France somewhat be-lately on the road to empire with the colonization of Guadeloupe and Martinique, in the Caribbean. In Europe, the Catholic cardinal, master of *Realpolitik*, was not above supporting the Protestant Swedish, Danish and German forces in the Thirty Years' War against the Catholic Austrians, Italians and Spanish. All that mattered was that it serve France's interests.

Richelieu's protégé Mazarin, another cardinal, took over the job of prime minister during the minority of Louis XIV. The court and regional aristocracy were infuriated by the Italian-born churchman's intimate relationship with the king's mother, Anne of Austria. Nor did they like his astounding knack for amassing a vast personal fortune while managing, very efficiently, the affairs of state. But most of all, they despised the way he eroded the nobles' power and smoothed the path to an increasingly absolutist monarchy.

The revolts of the *Fronde* forced Mazarin, Anne and the boy-king to flee from Paris in 1649. However, the royal family's triumphant return three years later, with the rebellious nobles crushed, saw the monarchy stronger than ever.

Louis XIV drew his own conclusions from Mazarin's careful coaching in the affairs of state. When he began his personal rule in 1661, at the age of 23, there was no question of a new prime minister impinging on the royal prerogative. Adopting the unequivocal symbol of the sun, Louis was to be outshone by no one. Counsellors were wholly subservient. Louis never once convened the parliamentary assembly of the *Etats généraux*, even though its powers were minimal.

He moved the court to Versailles, not only to get away from the troublemakers of Paris, but to impoverish the nobility, by forcing them to contribute to the crippling luxury of his palace, with no other function than to support the king in time of war.

It's all too easy to be bedazzled by the brilliance of life at Versailles, by its architectural splendour, and most of all by the sheer hypnotic power of Louis XIV's cult of self-glorification. In his lifetime, many petty European princes tried to imitate his style with their own little Versailles, complete with court artists and sycophants. It took French historians a long time to resist the glitter for the less attractive realities of what that style cost the nation.

Royal Mistresses

Since royal marriage was an affair of state rather than of the heart, the king of France made no bones about having mistresses, too. One of them was given formal precedence as maîtresse en titre *(titular mistress). She wasn't always a giggle, as Louis XIV discovered with the sanctimonious pillow-talk of Madame de Maintenon.*

As the last person to see the king before he went to sleep, the royal mistress was ideally placed to whisper more than sweet nothings in his ear and inevitably acquired a taste for politics.

Ambitious families competed to get one of their daughters into the royal bed, and Louis XV entertained three Nesle sisters, one after the other, until the youngest, Madame de Châteauroux, got the titular job. She was succeeded by the most famous mistress of them all, Madame de Pompadour, née Jeanne Antoinette Poisson, from an important family of financiers involved in military contracts. With her famous high-flying hairdo, the extravagant Pompadour was a great patron of the arts, promoting the painting career of François Boucher and protecting Voltaire from his many court enemies.

Madame du Barry, who rose to royal favour literally from the streets, was Louis XV's last and loveliest maîtresse en titre, *and perhaps the only one reluctant to get involved in politics. Particularly in 1793 when she was carried screaming to the guillotine.*

To enhance his glory, the Sun King turned to foreign conquest. The devastating military expedition he launched across the Rhineland and Palatinate, the series of largely fruitless wars with Spain, Holland, England and Sweden, did not endear him to the European people. Moreover, they left France's once thriving economy in ruins.

At home, his authoritarian rule required a brutal police force. Taxes soared to pay for his wars, and more and more peasants had to abandon their fields when press-ganged into his armies. Influenced in later life by the Catholic piety of Madame de Maintenon, his mistress and

The gigantic palace of Versailles is a perfect expression of Louis XIV's ego.

subsequently secret wife, Louis put an end to religious freedom for Protestants by revoking the Edict of Nantes.

In the face of forced conversions, the Protestant Huguenots —many of them the most talented bankers, merchants and artisans of their generation—fled to Switzerland, Germany, the Netherlands, England and Scandinavia.

The reaction to Louis XIV's death in 1715, a sigh of relief, was almost inevitable. Having outlived his children and grand-children, he was succeeded by his five-year-old great-grandson, Louis XV. But government was in the hands of the late king's cultured, libertine and atheist brother, Philippe d'Orléans.

After the morose twilight years of the Sun King, life perked up with the satiric pen of Voltaire and the erotic fantasies of Watteau's paintings and Marivaux's comedies. The court moved back to Paris.

The generally lazy regent gave a bunch of incompetent nobles too much of a say in the running of the state. Regional *parlements* obtained the right to present remonstrances, thin end of a wedge to weaken the monarchy.

The easy-going Louis XV was called, at least in the first half of his reign, the *Bien-Aimé* (Beloved). The king seemed more interested in his mistresses than in running a tight ship of state. Despite this (or perhaps because of it) the economy recovered, the overseas empire expanded in the East and West Indies, arts and letters flourished in this age of enlightenment.

But the new voices were a clear threat to the established order. Diderot's *Encyclopédie* championed reason over traditional religion, Rousseau discoursed on the origins of inequality, Voltaire shot at everything that didn't move.

Revolution and Napoleon

Louis XVI, grandson of Louis XV, faced attacks on all sides. The intransigent aristocracy and high clergy were anxious to protect ancient privileges; a burgeoning bourgeoisie longed for reforms that would give them a larger piece of the national pie; the peasantry was no longer prepared to bear the burden of feudal extortion; and a growing urban populace of artisans groaned under hardships symbolized by the fluctuating price of bread.

At the assembly of the *Etats généraux*, convened for the first time in 175 years, it was clearly the king's enduring absolutism rather than the throne itself that was under fire. For reactionary nobles, the king was guarantor of their hereditary status. Liberal reformers wanted a constitutional monarchy similar to England's, not a republic. Even grievances drawn up by peasants and townspeople insisted on continuing devotion to the king himself.

Two months later, the blindness of the king's conservative advisors and his own weakness and vacillation led to the explosion of centuries of frustration and rage—the storming of the Bastille, the régime's prison-fortress in Paris. That July 14, 1789, the king went hunting near his château at Versailles and wrote

26

in his diary at the end of the day: *"Rien"* ("Nothing").

A National Assembly voted a charter for liberty and equality, the great Declaration of the Rights of Man and of the Citizen. The aristocracy's feudal rights were abolished, the Church's massive land-holdings confiscated and sold off.

Rather than compromise, the king fled Paris in a vain effort to join up with armed forces hostile to the Revolution. With Austrian and German armies massing on France's frontiers and the forces of counter-revolution gathering inside the country, the militant revolutionary Jacobins led by Maximilien de Robespierre saw the king's flight as the ultimate betrayal. A Republic was declared in 1792, and Louis XVI was guillotined in 1793. His son Louis XVII died in obscure circumstances under the Revolutionary government, probably in 1795.

Under pressure from the poorer classes, who did not want the Revolution appropriated for the exclusive benefit of the bourgeoisie, the Jacobin-led revolutionary committee ordered sweeping measures of economic and social reform, but also a wave of mass executions, the Terror, aimed at moderates as well as aristocrats. Despite his attempts to quell the extremists, Robespierre was overthrown and guillotined in the counterattack of the propertied classes.

During their *Directoire*, a new wave of executions—the White (royalist) Terror—decimated the Jacobins and their supporters. But the bourgeoisie, fearing both the royalists and their foreign backers, turned for salvation to a Corsican soldier triumphantly campaigning against the Revolution's foreign enemies—Napoleon Bonaparte.

In between his defeat of the Austrians in Italy and a less successful campaign against the British in Egypt, Bonaparte returned to Paris to crush the royalists in 1795 and, four years later, staged a coup against the *Directoire*. He was 30 years old.

In the first flush of dictatorship as First Consul, he created

---

Left and Right
The ideological divisions of "left" and "right", today adopted all over the world, derive from the seating arrangement of the National Assembly that legislated the French Revolution. Quite simply, supporters of the Revolution sat on the left and opponents on the right. Within the ranks of the Revolutionary left, what the British might now call the "militant tendency" sat up on the high benches, the montagne *(mountain), while the moderates sat down in the* marais *(marshes).*

the Banque de France, established state-run *lycées* (secondary schools) and gave the country its first national set of laws with the *Code Napoléon*. The centralization dear to Richelieu and Louis XIV was becoming a clearer reality.

The supreme self-made man, Bonaparte became Emperor Napoleon in 1804 at a coronation ceremony in which he took the crown of golden laurels from the pope and placed it on his own head.

He managed to pursue simultaneously foreign conquest in Germany and Austria, and domestic reforms—a modernized university and police force, proper supplies of drinking water for Parisians. During his disastrous campaign in Russia, he found time in Moscow to draw up a new statute for the *Comédie-Française* (the national theatre), which had been dissolved during the Revolution.

The nationalism that Napoleon invoked in his conquest of Europe's *Ancien Régime* turned against him in Spain, Russia and Germany. The monarchies regrouped to force him from power a first time in 1814. He

made a brilliant but brief comeback the following year, when an alliance of British, Prussian, Belgian and Dutch troops inflicted the final defeat at Waterloo.

Kings and Emperors Depart

More intelligent than his executed brother, Louis XVIII tried at first to reconcile the monarchy with the reforms of the Revolution and Napoleon's empire. But his nobles were intent on revenge and imposed a second, even more violent, White Terror against Jacobins and Bonapartists, including some of Napoleon's greatest generals.

Louis's reactionary successor, brother Charles X, was interested only in renewing the traditions of the *Ancien Régime*, even having himself anointed and crowned at the ancient cathedral of Reims. But the middle classes would no longer tolerate the curtailment of their freedom and the worsening state of the economy in the hands of an incompetent aristocracy. They reasserted their rights in the insurrection of July 1830—the purely liberal revolution they would have preferred back in 1789—paving the way for the "bourgeois monarchy" of Louis-Philippe.

This last king of France, heir of the progressive Orléans branch of the royal family, encouraged the country's belated exploitation of the Industrial

Napoleon's battles celebrated on the Arc de Triomphe have given way to the sweeter things of life.

29

Revolution and the complementary extension of its overseas empire in Asia and Africa (Algeria had been occupied just before the 1830 revolution). But the new factories created an urban proletariat, clamouring for improvement of its miserable working and living conditions. The response of fierce repression and other ineptitudes led to a third revolution in 1848, with the Bonapartists, led by Napoleon's nephew, emerging triumphant.

The Second Republic ended four years later when the man whom Victor Hugo called "Napoléon le Petit" staged a coup to become Emperor Napoleon III. Determined to cloak himself in the legend of his uncle's grandeur, he saw his role as champion of the people. But he used harsh anti-press laws and loyalty oaths to quell the libertarian spirit that had brought him to power.

The economy flourished with the expansion of a vigorous entrepreneurial capitalism in iron, steel, railways and overseas ventures such as the Suez Canal. Despite Napoleon's obsession with the new "Red Peril" (the 1848 Communist Manifesto of Marx and Engels was floating around Paris), he could not prevent such social reforms as the workers' right to form unions and even to strike.

With the excessive enthusiasm that characterized the age, Baron Haussmann's urban planning barrelled its way through old Parisian neighbourhoods to create a more airy and spacious capital. Similarly, architect Viollet-le-Duc often went overboard restoring the great Gothic cathedrals and medieval châteaux in ways their original creators had never imagined.

Hugo, in exile in Guernsey, was writing *Les Misérables* and Baudelaire his *Fleurs du Mal*, while Offenbach was composing acid but jolly operettas like *La Belle Hélène*. Courbet was painting his vast canvases of provincial life and Manet his *Déjeuner sur l'Herbe*.

Life was generally looking up. The bourgeoisie showed off its new prosperity with extravagant furnishings, silks, satins and baubles, and in 1852 Paris opened its first department store, Au Bon Marché. In this optimistic, forward-looking society, with a necessary accompaniment of social critique and constant pressure for improvement, France was assuming its true national identity.

But Germany had an account to settle. In 1870, Prussian Chancellor Bismarck exploited an abstruse diplomatic conflict with France to bring the various German principalities and kingdoms together into one fighting force for war. And after lightning victory over the ill-prepared French armies, the German nation or Empire (Reich) was founded under Kaiser Wilhelm I in the Palace of Versailles. The confiscation of Alsace and Lorraine avenged the old but unforgotten scars left by Louis XIV's devastation of the Rhineland and Palatinate, and Napoleon's more recent invasion.

The Third Republic

Defeat shattered the Second Empire. While the new Third Republic's government under Adolphe Thiers negotiated the terms of surrender, workers' communes refused to capitulate. They took over Paris and a few provincial cities in March 1871 for ten brave but desperately disorganized weeks. They were brutally crushed by French government troops, and order was restored.

France resumed its industrial progress, quickly paid off its huge war-reparations debt to Germany and expanded the overseas empire in North and West Africa and Indochina. Rediscovered national pride found its perfect expression in the great Eiffel Tower thrust up into the Paris skies for the international exhibition of 1889.

In 1874, the first exhibition of Impressionism had blown away the dust and cobwebs of the artistic establishment. Novelist Zola poured forth his diatribes against industrial exploitation. Rodin, more restrained, sculpted *le Penseur* (The Thinker).

Leading the "republican" hostility to the Church's entrenched position in the schools, Jules Ferry enacted in 1882 the legislation that has been the basis of France's formidable state education system ever since.

On the right, nationalist forces were motivated by a desire to hit back at Germany, seeing all contact with foreigners or any form of "cosmopolitanism" as a threat to national honour and integrity.

For many, the Jews were the embodiment of this threat—Edouard Drumont's vehemently anti-semitic *La France juive* (Jewish France) was a runaway national bestseller. It appeared in 1886, eight years before Captain Alfred Dreyfus, an Alsatian Jew in the French Army, was arrested on what proved to be trumped-up charges of spying for the Germans. In a case that pitted the fragile honour of the Army against the very survival of French republican democracy, the captain had to wait 12 years for full rehabilitation.

The desire for revenge against Germany remained. Germany's own imperial ambitions grew, competition for world markets became more and more intense. Most of France went enthu-

---

No Small Affair

Over and above a judicial error, the Dreyfus Affair crystallized the passions that had burst into the open with the French Revolution, the conflicts between order and justice, conservatism and progress. It was no accident that the association formed by the Dreyfusards was named the Ligue des droits de l'homme (League of the Rights of Man), still in existence today to defend the historic Declaration of 1789.

Not least of all, the peculiar prestige that intellectuals have enjoyed in French society derived directly from their contribution to the Jewish captain's vindication, epitomized by Zola's decisive newspaper article "J'accuse" ("I accuse"). Coming down from their ivory tower, writers and academics demonstrated they could have a direct influence on public events. Elsewhere, "intellectual" is often an insult hurled at an overeducated troublemaker by his opponents. His French equivalent may be heard unashamedly beginning his tirades: "Moi, intellectuel..." ("An intellectual myself...").

---

siastically into World War I and came out of it victorious and bled white.

With the 1919 Treaty of Versailles, France recovered Alsace and Lorraine; but 1,350,000 men had been lost in the four years of fighting. The national economy was shattered, and political divisions were more extreme than ever.

In face of the fears aroused by the Russian Revolution of 1917, the conservative parties dominated the immediate post-war period, while a new French Communist Party, loyal to Moscow, split with the Socialists in 1920. France seemed less aware of the threat from Nazi Germany, allowing Hitler to remilitarize the Rhineland in 1936 in breach of the Versailles Treaty, a step Hitler later said he had never dreamt of getting away with.

In the 1930s, extreme right-wing groups such as *Action française* and *Croix-de-Feu* (Cross of Fire) provided a strong antidemocratic undercurrent to the political turmoil of financial scandal and parliamentary corruption. The bloody 1934 riots on Paris's Place de la Concorde offered a disturbing echo to the street fighting of Fascist Italy and Nazi Germany.

The left-wing parties responded by banding together in a Popular Front, which the Socialists led to power in 1936. In the first few weeks, Léon Blum's government nationalized the railways and instituted a 40-hour week and the workers' first paid holidays (two weeks, today five). But the Communists broke the alliance after Blum first failed to support the Republicans in the Spanish Civil War and then—faced with financial difficulties—put a brake on the reforms.

War and Peace

Blum's government collapsed in 1938, and the new prime minister, Edouard Daladier, found himself negotiating the Munich agreements with Hitler, Mussolini and Britain's Neville Chamberlain. A year later, France was once again at war with Germany.

Relying too complacently on the defensive strategy of the fortified Maginot line along the north-east frontier with Germany (but not facing Belgium), the French army was totally unprepared for the German invasion across the Ardennes in May 1940. With fast-moving tanks and superior air power, the Germans were in Paris 30 days later. Marshal Philippe Pétain, the old hero of World War I, capitulated on behalf of the French on June 16. Two days later, on BBC radio's French service from London, General de Gaulle issued his appeal for national resistance.

Compared with other occupied countries such as Belgium, Holland or Denmark, France's collaboration with the Germans is an inglorious story. Based in the Auvergne spa of Vichy, the French government often proved more zealous than its masters in suppressing civil liberties and drawing up anti-Jewish legislation. It was French police who rounded up the deportees for the concentration camps, many of them denounced by French civilians seeking to profit from the confiscation of property.

The underground Resistance fighters were heroic but a tiny minority; a few of them conservative patriots like de Gaulle, most of them socialists and communists, and also a handful of refugees from Eastern Europe.

Deliverance came when the Allies landed on the Normandy beaches on June 6, 1944. De Gaulle, with his canny sense of history, took an important step towards rebuilding national self-confidence by insisting that French armed forces fight side by side with the Americans and British for the liberation of the country, but, above all, that the French army be the first to enter Paris itself.

After the high emotion of de Gaulle's march down the Champs-Elysées, the business of reconstruction, boosted by the generous aid of the Americans' Marshall Plan, proved more arduous. The wartime alliance of de Gaulle's conservatives and the Communist Party soon broke down. The General could not tolerate the political squabbles of the Fourth Republic and withdrew from public life.

Governments changed like musical chairs, but the French muddled through. Intellectuals dressed all in black debated in Paris's Left-Bank cafés whether Albert Camus was correct in writing that it was less important to be happy than to be merely conscious of what's going on. And anyway, as Jean-Paul Sartre argued at the next table, "There's nothing in heaven, neither Good nor Evil, nor anybody to give me orders."

The French empire was collapsing. After a fruitless last stand in Vietnam, Pierre Mendès France wisely negotiated an Indochinese peace settlement. He gave Tunisia its independence and handed Pondicherry over to India, but was ousted from office as hostilities broke out in Algeria.

De Gaulle returned from the wilderness in 1958, ostensibly to keep Algeria French. But he'd seen the writing on the wall and brought the war to an end with Algerian independence in 1962. His major task was to rescue France from the chaos of the Fourth Republic. The new constitution, tailor-made to de Gaulle's authoritarian requirements, placed the president above parliament, where he could pursue his own policies outside the messy arena of party politics.

De Gaulle's visions of grandeur, independent of America's NATO and the Soviet Union's Warsaw Pact, gave France a renewed self-confidence. One of his great achievements was the close alliance with West Germany, overcoming centuries of bloodshed between the two peoples.

With self-confidence came smugness, and the French bourgeoisie was given one of its periodic frights with the massive student rebellions of 1968. The "events of May" that erupted in Paris's Latin Quarter and spread through the country disturbed de Gaulle enough for him to fly off to seek reassurance with his troops stationed in West Germany.

But people were reluctant to make a complete change until 1981, when the forces for reform gathered enough strength to elect François Mitterrand, the Fifth Republic's first Socialist president.

Like the Popular Front in 1936, the new government began with a quick-fire set of reforms—a broad programme of nationalization, abolition of the death penalty, raising the minimum wage, and a fifth week of holiday-with-pay—until the world economic crisis imposed a necessary brake. Special emphasis was placed on cultural programmes, increasing subsidies for theatre, cinema, pro-

The vanity of political leaders—
left, right or centre—
makes them ideal fashion models.

vincial museums and libraries, but also for scientific research.

Probably the most important reform was the least glamorous: the decentralization that increased regional autonomy and reversed the age-old trend of concentrating political, economic and administrative power in the national capital. By allowing the local pride of such historic regions as Provence, Normandy, Brittany or Languedoc to

reassert itself, France demonstrated it was at last secure in its national identity.

The political scene took on a new and intriguing complexity in 1986 with the election of a conservative government, thrust into unprecedented *"cohabitation"* with President Mitterrand.

HISTORICAL LANDMARKS

Prehistory	28,000 B.C.	Cro-Magnon man in Dordogne.
	2000	Celts invade France from east.
Gaul	600	Phocaean Greeks found Marseille.
	125–121	Romans establish colony of *Provincia* (Provence).
	59–50	Julius Caesar conquers Gaul.
	486 A.D.	"Barbarians" end Roman control.
	496	Clovis, King of Franks, converts to Christianity to rule Gaul.
Middle Ages	732	Arabs halted by Charles Martel at Poitiers.
	768–814	Charlemagne King of Franks.
	987	Hugues Capet first king of France.
	1066	Duke William of Normandy conquers England.
	1096	French lead First Crusade.
	1209	Pope orders wars against "heretics" in south-west.
	1337–1453	Hundred Years' War.
	1431	Joan of Arc executed.
Ancien Régime	1515–47	François I marks ascendancy of absolutist monarchy.
	1572	St. Bartholomew's Day massacre of Protestants in Wars of Religion.
	1598	Henri IV protects Protestants with Edict of Nantes.
	1624–42	Cardinal Richelieu governs for Louis XIII.
	1642–61	Cardinal Mazarin takes over.
	1648	France seizes Alsace.
	1661–1715	Sun King Louis XIV moves court to Versailles.
	1685	Revocation of Edict of Nantes.

Revolution and Napoleon	1789	Fall of Bastille (July 14); Declaration of the Rights of Man.
	1793	Louis XVI guillotined.
	1794	Robespierre guillotined.
	1804	Bonaparte crowns himself Emperor Napoleon.
	1805	Trafalgar lost, Austerlitz won.
	1812	Retreat from Moscow.
Kings and Emperors Depart	1815	Napoleon defeated at Waterloo, Louis XVIII restored to throne.
	1830–48	"Bourgeois monarchy" of Louis-Philippe.
	1848	Liberal Revolution overthrows monarchy.
	1852	Napoleon III proclaimed emperor.
Third Republic	1870–71	Franco-Prussian War. Germans seize Alsace-Lorraine. Napoleon III deposed.
	1914–18	World War I.
	1919	France regains Alsace-Lorraine.
	1936–37	Socialist-led Popular Front.
War and Peace	1939–45	World War II. Germany occupies France, de Gaulle heads Resistance.
	1944	Allies invade Normandy (June 6).
	1945–46	De Gaulle heads 4th Republic's first government.
	1954	Mendès France decolonizes Indochina and Tunisia.
	1958	De Gaulle president. End of 4th Republic.
	1962	France gives up Algeria.
	1968	Student rebels shake government.
	1981	Mitterrand 5th Republic's first Socialist president.

WHERE TO GO

It's perhaps natural when planning a trip to France to think of it as a meal. If you're not travelling with the set menu of a package tour, but prefer to choose your destinations *à la carte*, you may at first be daunted by the sheer variety.

We've divided the country up into just five regions: Paris and its vicinity (known to the French as the Ile-de-France); North-East (Picardy, Champagne, Lorraine,

Get away from the madding crowd on a winding Jura mountain road.

Alsace, Burgundy and the Jura); North-West (Normandy, Brittany and the Loire Valley); South-East (the Alps, Provence, Côte d'Azur and Corsica); and South-West (Périgord, Atlantic coast and the Pyrenees).

Since we aim at a representative rather than encyclopaedic survey of the country, our selection of places within those regions is by no means exhaustive.

Experienced visitors to France may feel a few of their own favourite corners of the country have been given short shrift, even though they may find others they have never heard about, but newcomers will have more than enough to choose from.*

Depending on how much time you have available, you can combine at least two or three of the regions to get a sense of that great diversity of French life: the big city and the wine country, the mountains as well as the Atlantic or Mediterranean coasts.

Any itinerary you draw up should naturally include Paris. Ideally, divide your stay there in two: sightseeing at the beginning, before you grow lazy at a seaside resort or in some sunny village in the hills, and then shopping at the end, so that you don't have to carry your purchases around with you for the rest of the trip.

For a "green" vacation, for example, you might want to combine Paris and the Ile-de-France with Normandy and Brittany. For stark contrasts—of climate, countryside and temperament—combine the capital with Provence or Corsica.

But the mix should not just be geographic. The cultural monuments of France, its cathedrals,

---

* You'll find more detailed information to specific regions in the Berlitz Travel Guides to *Paris, Brittany, Normandy, Loire Valley* and *French Riviera*.

palaces and museums, deserve your attention, but they'll be much easier to digest and appreciate if you alternate them with lots of time at the beach or on country walks. France does not lack places where it's a simple joy to do absolutely nothing at all. And museum-going itself can be more fun if you vary the diet with some of the more off-beat collections devoted to comic-strips, toys, balloons, bread, graffiti, fire engines.

Many people do not have the choice of going to France outside the major holiday periods—Easter, July and August. But if it's at all possible, think of the spring, autumn or even the winter, when the big sightseeing destinations are blessedly easier to visit. The island church of Mont-Saint-Michel on the Normandy coast in the mists of December can be pure magic.

A passing tip for visiting the big museums in peak seasons: go at dinner time on a late-closing day, when at least the French feel they have something more important to do.

Getting Around

Even if you're the adventurous kind of traveller who likes to improvise, don't turn your nose up at the tourist offices. In France, tourism being a major factor in the country's balance of payments, the organization for for-

> **Not By Bread Alone**
> *Museum opening hours vary from season to season and year to year, so check the current situation with the local tourist office. You can be sure that most museums are closed on Tuesday, a day dictated by the French need to reconcile food and culture. It enables butchers, bakers and grocers, whose day off is usually Monday, to start their week with a little fine art, while the next day, museum-guardians can get their meat, bread and potatoes.*

eign visitors is very efficient. For general information, the *office de tourisme*, both in your own country and in the regional capitals throughout France, is worth a visit.

Even the smallest towns with only one monument, vineyard or pile of prehistoric fossils to boast of have a *syndicat d'initiative*. These friendly local tourist offices offer free maps, brochures, advice about sporting and cultural events, camping facilities. The ones in the bigger towns can often provide, with advance notice, an English-language guide for local sightseeing tours.

The Berlitz-Info section at the back of the book (p. 216) gives detailed practical guidance on the technicalities of travel through France, but here are some general thoughts to help you plan the trip.

First of all, *how* are you going to travel? The excellent system of roads and public transport (soon to be reinforced by the tunnel under the English Channel) makes it a good idea to use both car and train together. Take the train for long journeys, and rent a car at your destination to explore the back country. Several special rail cards include reduced rates for car rentals.

With the high-speed TGV *(Train à Grande Vitesse)* from Paris, you can be in Dijon heading for the Burgundy vineyards in an hour and a half, Lyon in two hours, and Avignon, for your Provençal adventure, in under four. A similar service is opening up to Bordeaux.

The one disappointment of French trains is the relatively uninspired dining-car service. Don't despair, make up your own picnic hamper from the market before you get aboard—cold meats, salad, Camembert, grapes, *baguette* and wine add a terrific sparkle to the countryside flashing past your window.

For drivers in a hurry, the network of toll motorways (expressways) is first class, linking up most of the major cities and still expanding. Otherwise, it's more fun to explore the country along the good-quality secondary roads. If you're afraid of getting lost, follow the green arrows, indicating the route of *Bison futé*

(Wily Buffalo—a Red Indian invented by the Ministry of Transports), which proposes alternative itineraries to avoid traffic jams.

French drivers are adventurous, even aggressive, less spectacular than, say, the Italians, but not unskilful. Defensive driving is always a good idea, but timidity will get you into an unholy mess in the Paris rush hour. In fact, try to drive as little as possible inside the cities. The *métro* (subway) is the fastest way around Paris, but the buses, both in the capital and the other big towns, are best for taking in the sights. Unless you feel really safe in French metropolitan traffic, keep your cycling—you can rent a bike at the railway station—for the villages and country roads.

If you have plenty of time at your disposal, consider renting a sail-it-yourself barge or cabin cruiser, and coast sleepily along the Canal de Bourgogne from Dijon, the tributaries of the Loire or the Canal du Midi from Toulouse down to the sea at Sète. It's great fun helping the keepers open the locks. With a couple of bikes on board, you can always stop along the way to explore inland. Larger hotel-boats for up to 20 people, plus crew, are organized for gourmet cruises from one gastronomic port of call to another.

41

GETTING AROUND

Try to vary the kind of places you stay in. Depending of course on your budget, it's worth splashing at least one night for the exquisite comfort and service of a great hotel, either what the French call a *palace*, which usually refers to an old-fashioned luxury hotel, or a converted château, abbey or mill house. On holiday, you owe it to yourself to be treated occasionally like a monarch and, in the right place, the French still know how to do it.

Too many modern hotels tend to be highly efficient, comfortable, well situated in the big towns, and totally characterless. It's not what you came to France for. But even if you can afford a *palace* every night, don't miss out on the great charm of a simple country inn *(auberge)*. More frugal, but with the bonus of good country cooking, are the *gîtes ruraux*, often a converted farmhouse where the farmer's wife cooks your meal—ideal when hiking.

However and wherever you travel around France, one last piece of advice: even if you can't speak French, do try to make a tiny effort to speak just a couple of words. You've probably heard horrendous stories about how impatient the French can be with people who can't speak their language. In fact it's often been a case of the foreigner's not making even the slightest attempt to say a *Bonjour, S'il vous plaît* or *Merci beaucoup* to break the ice.

It can be very disconcerting for an ordinary Frenchman to be suddenly confronted with a torrent of English (imagine someone in Houston or Huddersfield trying to cope with a Frenchman who spoke no English). Despite their reputation, the French are a very courteous people, calling

You're captain of your own destiny when drifting peacefully along the Burgundy Canal, which begins in Dijon.

each other *Madame* or *Monsieur* and always saying an appropriate *Bonjour* or *Au revoir* when entering or leaving a shop or café. It may well be the inadvertent absence of such courtesies that raises the hackles of that touchy fellow who barks at you. But at least he doesn't bite. With the right smile, an *Excusez-moi, Monsieur* can melt the coldest Gallic heart.

Being Berlitz, we'll try to help you with some of the simplest phrases, at the back of the book. The rest is up to you and your own desire to play the French game. *Amusez-vous bien!*

PARIS AND VICINITY

Anyone seeking a rapid sense of the country must inevitably start in Paris and its immediate surroundings.

With France's heavily centralized civilization, Paris, more than most national capitals, dictates the country's tastes and style of life. All ambitious French people "go up" to Paris to make their fortune, and so people from every region—with every local cuisine to feed them—are represented there. The Parisian's traditional contempt for the "provinces" is matched only by his fierce loyalty to the distant home of his ancestors, most often just one generation removed.

Before it was the national capital, Paris was the home of the medieval dukes of the region still known as the Ile-de-France, which, gradually asserting itself over other duchies like Burgundy or Normandy, imposed its name on the whole country.

The Paris basin is a treasury of national monuments. Roughly bounded by four rivers—the Seine, Oise, Aisne and Marne —the Ile-de-France was the birthplace of the first great Gothic cathedrals, such as Saint-Denis, Senlis, Chartres and Beauvais. It was the cradle of the French monarchy; its surrounding greenery and dense forests also provided good sites for later kings and nobles to build their palaces away from the troublesome mob of Paris, at Fontainebleau, Chantilly and, of course, Versailles.

All the interesting sights around the capital are an easy day trip by car or local train, so that you can keep your Paris hotel if you wish (but you'd probably find the local country inns a lot cheaper).

PARIS

The city and the people of Paris share a boundless self-confidence that exudes from every stone in its monuments and museums, bistrots and boutiques, from every chestnut tree along its avenues and boulevards, from every street-urchin, mannequin, butcher and baker, from every irate motorist and every charming maître d'hôtel.

You readily forgive the bombast of some of the monumental architecture when you see what makes this the City of Light.

Stand on the Pont Royal in late afternoon and look down the Seine to the glass-panelled Grand Palais, bathed in the pink and blue glow of the river. That unique light brings a phospho-

---

From Bog to Beaubourg
The fishing village of the Celtic Parisii on an island in the Seine (today's Ile de la Cité) was conquered in 52 B.C. by the Romans, who called it Lutetia (Marshland). In the early Middle Ages, the town expanded to the left bank with the monastery of Saint-Germain-des-Prés, the right bank being unmanageably boggy.

Although Hugues Capet, first king of France (see p. 18), made it his capital in 987, Paris did not become the permanent seat of royal government for another 600 years. Crusader Philippe Auguste took time off to build the Louvre as a fortress in 1190. Fifty years later, the Sorbonne was founded as a theological college.

It was Henri IV who made Paris a truly royal capital. He built the splendid Place des Vosges and Place Dauphine, beautified the river banks and completed the grand Pont-Neuf. Fashionable Paris evolved in the 17th century with the first elegant houses of the Faubourg Saint-Honoré and the Cours-la-Reine built for Marie de Médicis as precursor to the Champs-Elysées. Cardinal Riche-

lieu enhanced its intellectual standing by creating the Académie française, *while bequeathing his magnificent home, the Palais-Royal.*

After the humiliations of the Fronde *revolts (see p. 23), Louis XIV abandoned Paris for Versailles, but the town's cultural life reasserted itself under his successors. Cafés sprang up around the Palais-Royal as centres of the intellectual ferment preceding the Revolution. Place de la Concorde became Place de la Révolution for the time of the guillotine. The Louvre became a national museum.*

To celebrate his battles, Napoleon built the Arc de Triomphe and Place Vendôme, but he himself felt his most important achievements were those of a mayor rather than a conqueror—water purification, food markets (les Halles), slaughterhouses (la Villette), a new police force and streamlined municipal administration. Under his nephew, Napoleon III, troublesome working-class neighbourhoods were razed to make way for wide boulevards and avenues, giving Paris its modern airy look —and a clear line of fire for the artillery in case of revolt.

If the Eiffel Tower was a fetish of the triumphant 19th century, the Centre Pompidou, better known as Beaubourg, is the brash symbol of today's modernism—both celebrating Paris's eternal gall.

rescence to the most commonplace little square or side street. In case the message isn't clear, Paris offers golden nighttime illumination of its major historical buildings. To celebrate Bastille Day (July 14) or the 1944 Liberation (August 25), blue, white and red laser beams are bounced off the Eiffel Tower, Arc de Triomphe and Town Hall.

Despite the inevitable erosion of social change and urban renovation, the jargon of Paris's topography still evokes not just a place but a state of mind. The Right Bank conjures up an image of bourgeois respectability. Historically the stronghold of merchants and royalty, it remains today the home of commerce and government. Faubourg Saint-Honoré offers the luxury of jewellery shops and *haute couture*, and the more imperial than republican authority of the president's palace, while the Champs-Elysées claims the first-run cinemas, airline companies and car showrooms.

The Left Bank, on the other hand, has always had a bohemian and intellectual image, dating back to the founding of the university and monasteries. Today, the Sorbonne, the *Académie française*, the publishing houses and myriad bookshops continue to exercise an intellectual magnetism.

But a constant flow and interchange of citizenry from one bank to the other takes place across the bridges of the Seine, a narrower and so much more "manageable" river than, say,

Get your first view of Paris from the Seine, here passing under the new Pont des Arts.

London's Thames or New York's Hudson.

Paris is one of the world's most densely populated capitals. Its non-stop street scene derives from the fact that nearly every one of its 20 *arrondissements*, or districts, has shops, offices and apartments side by side and on top of each other. There's always someone out there moving around. Join them.

The Seine

The river is by far the best place to begin to take the measure of Paris. Its mixture of grandeur and intimacy is the very essence of the city.

Again and again the Seine provides a spectacular vantage point for the city's great landmarks. The Eiffel Tower, the Palais de Chaillot and Trocadéro Gardens, the Grand and Petit

Palais, the Palais Bourbon, the Louvre and Notre-Dame all take on a near enchanting, dreamlike quality if you see them first when floating by in a boat. The **guided boat trip** is well worthwhile.

But this is also a river to be walked along, despite the traffic on rapid *voies express* along the banks. You can take delightful strolls between the Pont Sully, at the eastern end of the Ile Saint-Louis, and the Pont de la Concorde. Stop to rest occasionally on a bench beneath the poplar and plane trees along the Seine, ideally early morning or late afternoon, when that pink Paris light is at its best.

The river's bridges are a major attraction; four of them especially worthy of your attention. The **Pont-Neuf** (*neuf* means "new") is in fact Paris's oldest standing bridge, completed by Henri IV in 1606. It was a favourite of street-singers, charlatans, amateur dentists, professional ladies, pickpockets and above all *bouquinistes* selling their old books and pamphlets out of boxes. Established booksellers on the Ile de la Cité were enraged and drove them off to the banks of the Seine, where they've been ever since.

The centrally situated **Pont Royal**, built for Louis XIV in 1685, commands some splendid panoramas: the Tuileries Gar-

---

Paris by Boat

The river cruises are accompanied by multilingual commentaries on all the landmarks. Times vary, but they usually go from around 10 a.m. to 10.30 p.m. If you love boats, take a daytime trip at the beginning of your stay and a romantic night-time cruise at the end to enjoy the illuminations.

Bateaux-Mouches have open-air or covered seating according to the weather. The year-round standard 75-minute tour starts from the Quai de la Conférence, goes west to the Pont Mirabeau, then turns back upriver as far as the Pont Sully at the end of the Ile Saint-

Louis. The special lunch (1 p.m.) and dinner cruises (8.30 p.m., jacket and tie for men) last 150 minutes. Telephone 42.25.22.55.

The cheaper vedette or motorboat tours take 60 minutes. Vedettes Paris-Tour Eiffel (Easter to autumn) start by the Pont d'Iéna (Left Bank) and the Quai de Montebello, going west to the Pont de Bir-Hakeim and east to the Pont Sully and back. Telephone 45.51.33.08.

Vedettes du Pont-Neuf leave from the Pont-Neuf, Square du Vert-Galant, to the Eiffel Tower and back around the islands. Telephone 46.33.98.38.

dens and the Louvre immediately over on the Right Bank, the Musée d'Orsay on the Left, the Grand and Petit Palais downriver and the Palais de l'Institut de France, home of the *Académie française*, up.

The **Pont de la Concorde**, truly the bridge of the French Revolution, went up between 1787 and 1790. Its support structure used stone from the demolished Bastille prison—galling for Royalists, since it had originally been named Pont Louis XVI.

On moonlit nights, lovers head for the **Pont Alexandre III**, undoubtedly the most kitschily romantic of all with its *Belle Epoque* lanterns and melodramatic statues of Fame and Pegasus. They really don't care to know it once honoured the tsar for some obscure military treaty.

Right Bank

Etoile–Concorde–les Halles

Start at the **Place de l'Etoile** (officially Place Charles-de-Gaulle, but nobody calls it that), preferably on top of the **Arc de Triomphe.** One reason for climbing up Napoleon's gigantic triumphal arch—50 metres (164 feet) high, 45 metres (148 feet) wide—is to get a good view of the 12-pointed star, formed by 12 avenues radiating from the arch in a *tour de force* of geometric planning. The vast sloping mound of the *place* cannot be taken in properly at ground level.

Over the years the Arc de Triomphe has taken on a mythic quality as succeeding régimes have invested it with the spirit of the nation. Napoleon himself saw only a life-size wooden and canvas model. Louis-Philippe inaugurated the final version in 1836, complete with bas-reliefs and statuary celebrating victories of the Revolution and Napoleonic Empire. The Etoile's monumental ensemble was completed for Napoleon III by Baron Haussmann.

Victor Hugo was given a positively pharaonic funeral ceremony at the Arc de Triomphe in 1885. The Unknown Soldier of World War I was buried here in 1920, and three years later the Eternal Flame was lit.

When Hitler came to Paris as conqueror in 1940, this was the first place he wanted to see. But General de Gaulle gained his revenge by starting his march of Liberation here in 1944.

Avenue Foch, leading away from the Etoile to the Bois de Boulogne, is the grandest of the city's residential avenues, somewhat democratized these days by the *boules* players on its gravelled side paths.

The **Champs-Elysées** remains the town's, perhaps the world's, most glamorous avenue. It stretches in an absolutely straight line from the Arc de Triomphe to the Place de la Concorde, lined with chestnut trees all the way. The first two-thirds, as you walk down, are devoted to cinemas, shops and café terraces. You'll

Last vestige of the past, at the new shopping centre of les Halles, is the church of Saint-Eustache.

find the best vantage points for people-watching between Avenue George V and Rue Lincoln on the "shady" side and at Rue du Colisée on the "sunny" side.

After the Rond-Point, a pleasant park (stamp-collectors' market every Thursday) takes you down to the **Place de la Concorde.** The gigantic square has had a hard time earning its name. More than 1,000 people were

guillotined here during the Revolution and the counter-revolutionary White Terror that followed. In 1934 it was the scene of bloody fascist rioting against the government and, ten years later, the Germans' last hold in Paris. Today, with floodlit fountains and elegant lamps, it is a night-time romance and a daytime adventure, both for the pedestrian pausing to enjoy the vast opening of the Paris sky and for the driver daring to make his way around it.

Smack in the centre you'll see Paris's oldest monument, the 23-metre (75-foot) pink granite Obelisk of Luxor from the temple of Ramses II, dating back to 1300 B.C., erected here in 1836. For a change, it's not something Napoleon plundered on his campaigns but a gift from Mohammed Ali, viceroy of Egypt.

After the bustle of the Champs-Elysées and Place de la Concorde, take refuge in the cool shade of the chestnut trees in the **Jardin des Tuileries**. Fragments of the royal palace destroyed in the 1871 Commune are still standing by the Jeu de Paume museum in the north-west corner. The gardens are now a favourite with children watching marionette shows, riding donkeys or sailing and sinking their boats on the circular ponds.

At the eastern end of the Tuileries stands the pink **arc de triomphe du Carrousel**, roughly contemporary with its bigger brother at the Etoile, visible in a straight line beyond the Obelisk. This imposing effect was originally planned for Napoleon to see from his bedroom in the Louvre. Today, the vista is somewhat spoiled by the modern skyscrapers of la Défense looming on the horizon.

Leaving the Louvre museum for a separate visit (see p. 69), cross the Rue de Rivoli to the **Palais-Royal**, built as Cardinal Richelieu's residence in 1639 (and originally named the Palais-Cardinal). This serene arcaded palace with its garden of limes and beeches and a pond where the young Louis XIV nearly drowned has always been a colourful centre of more or less respectable activity.

In the days of Philippe d'Orléans, Regent of France during Louis XV's minority, it was the scene of notorious orgies. To meet the family's extravagant debts, ground-floor rooms were turned into boutiques (today still selling coins, medals, engravings and antiques) and cafés that attracted a fashionable society. And some shady hangers-on: artists, charlatans, prostitutes, pickpockets—and intellectuals. On July 13, 1789, a young firebrand orator, Camille Desmoulins, stood on a table at the Palais-Royal's Café de Foy to make the call to arms that set off the French Revolution the next day. After Waterloo, Prussian General Blücher arrived to blow 1,500,000 francs in one night at one of the many rambunctious gambling dens.

East of the Palais-Royal, the old food markets of les Halles (moved to the more hygienic, inevitably less colourful suburb of Rungis) have been replaced by gardens, new apartment buildings and the **Forum des Halles**, a rather garish shopping centre. Around it, the lively neighbourhood of cafés, boutiques and art galleries linking up with the Centre Pompidou (Beaubourg, see p. 70) is very popular with the young crowd. The liveliest meeting-place is around the handsome Renaissance **Fontaine des Innocents** (once part of a cemetery).

On the north side of les Halles, another monument of the Renaissance period, but decidedly Gothic in silhouette, is the church of **Saint-Eustache**, remarkable for its stained-glass windows over the choir.

Vendôme–Opéra–Madeleine

The airy octagonal **Place Vendôme** still exudes the opulence of its original conception under Louis XIV, when only his financiers could afford the rents. Three centuries later, little has changed—a score of international banks have their offices here, along with celebrated jewellers, the Ministry of Justice and the Ritz Hotel.

The spiral of bronze bas-reliefs on the Vendôme column, commemorating Napoleon's victories and topped by a statue of the emperor himself, was cast from 1,250 cannons captured from the Austrians at Austerlitz.

Window-shop your way past the goldsmiths and furriers of the Rue de la Paix to the **Opéra**, massive Neo-baroque monument to the gorgeous pretensions of Napoleon III's Second Empire. Completed in 1875, four years after his downfall, it is claimed to be the world's largest theatre though seating only 2,000 people.

The Boulevard des Capucines and the Boulevard des Italiens, known as the **grands boulevards**, meet at the Place de l'Opéra. They are perhaps less fashionable now than in their heyday at the end of the 19th century, but you can still recapture some of the atmosphere. On the Boulevard des Capucines, you retrace the footsteps of Renoir, Manet and Pissarro taking their paintings to the house of photographer Nadar, at number 35, for the historic 1874 exhibition of Impressionism. Today the boulevards house some of the town's most popular cinemas—appropriately, because here, at the Hôtel Scribe, the Lumière brothers staged the first public moving-picture show in 1895.

Variously conceived as a stock exchange, the Bank of France or a theatre, the **Madeleine** doesn't look like a church, but that's what it is. Napoleon wanted to turn it into a *Temple de la Gloire* for his Great Army, but his architect persuaded him to build the Arc de Triomphe instead. The restored monarchy opted for a church, as originally planned under Louis XV. The huge Greco-Roman edifice, consecrated only in 1842, was left without transept, aisles, bell-tower or even a cross on the roof. Parisians like it most for the flower market at its base and the grand **view** from the top of the steps down the Rue Royale to the Place de la Concorde.

Down on the right is Maxim's restaurant, which began as an ice-cream parlour and is now a monument more venerable than the Madeleine. Cutting across the Rue Royale, the **Rue du Faubourg-Saint-Honoré** is the city's most luxurious shopping street. At number 55, peek through the heavily guarded gates of the French president's Elysée Palace.

Montmartre

Long famous as the home of artists and bohemian crazies, who call it "la Butte" ("the Mound"), Montmartre is an essential piece of Paris mythology. It claims a fabled past as Mons Martyrum where, after being decapitated, the town's first bishop, Saint Denis, picked up his head and walked away. Scholars insist it was really named Mons Mercurii, site of a pagan Roman temple. Difficult to decide in a neighbourhood

Crowds flock to Sacré-Cœur mainly for its great view of Paris.

that includes the Sacré-Cœur and Pigalle.

Topographically, Montmartre is still the little country village of 400 years ago—narrow, winding, hilly streets and dead-ends. Leave the car behind and take the *métro,* Porte de la Chapelle line from Concorde to Abbesses.

Do *not* get off at Pigalle; however attractive you may find its lurid glitter at night, by day it might depress you into not visiting the rest of Montmartre.

From the Place des Abbesses, take Rue Ravignan to 13, place Emile-Goudeau. This was the site of the **Bateau-Lavoir** studio, an unprepossessing glass-roofed loft reconstructed since a 1970 fire. Here, if in any one place, modern art was born: Picasso,

Braque and Juan Gris developed Cubism, while Modigliani painted his own mysteries, and Apollinaire wrote his first surrealistic verses. Nearby, the illustrious predecessors of these "upstarts"—Renoir, Van Gogh, Gauguin—lived and worked in the Rue Cortot, Rue de l'Abreuvoir, Rue Saint-Rustique (site of the restaurant A la Bonne Franquette where Van Gogh painted his famous *La Guinguette*).

Coming a long way down in the artistic scale, street painters still throng the **Place du Tertre**, Montmartre's historic village square where marriages were announced and criminals hanged.

On the Rue Saint-Vincent at the corner of the Rue des Saules, look out for Paris's own vineyard, the Clos de Montmartre, whose wine reputedly "makes you jump like a goat".

At the other end of the Rue Saint-Vincent, you come around the back of the **Sacré-Cœur** basilica. You have probably spotted it a hundred times during the day, so its back view will make a welcome change. This weird Romano-Byzantine church has a dubious reputation. Aesthetes scorn its over-ornate exterior and extravagant interior mosaics; working-class people of the neighbourhood resent the way it was put up as a symbol of penitence for the insurrection of the 1871 Commune and defeat in the war against the Prussians. The miraculously white façade derives from its special Château-Landon stone that whitens and hardens with age. For many, the most attractive feature is the **view** of the city you get from the dome or from the terrace below.

Marais

The Marais district, north of the two river islands, has bravely withstood the onslaught of modern construction to provide a remarkably authentic record of the development of Paris from Henri IV at the end of the 16th century to the Revolution. Built on land reclaimed from the marshes, as the name suggests, some of Europe's most elegant Renaissance houses *(hôtels)* now serve as museums and libraries.

Take the *métro* to Rambuteau and start at the corner of Rue des Archives and **Rue des Francs-Bourgeois**, named after the poor people allowed to live there tax-free in the 14th century. The National Archives are kept here in an 18th-century mansion, **Hôtel de Soubise**. Across a vast horseshoe-shaped courtyard you rediscover the exquisite rococo of Louis XV's times in the apartments of the Prince and Princess of Soubise. Up on the first floor is the Musée de l'Histoire de France with the only known portrait of Joan of Arc painted in her lifetime and the diary of

PARIS

Louis XVI noting for July 14, 1789: *"Rien"* ("Nothing").

A garden (not always open to the public) connects the Hôtel de Soubise with its twin, the **Hôtel de Rohan** on Rue Vieille-du-Temple. Look out for Robert le Lorrain's fine sculpted horses of Apollo over the old stables in the second courtyard.

Two other noteworthy mansions on the Rue des Francs-Bourgeois are the **Hôtel Lamoignon** at the corner of Rue Pavée and the **Hôtel Carnavalet**, home of the illustrious 17th-century lady of letters Madame de Sévigné, now the Musée historique de la Ville de Paris.

At the end of the Rue des Francs-Bourgeois is what many consider to be the city's most handsome residential square, **Place des Vosges**. Henri IV had it built in 1605 on the site of a horse-market. The square achieves a classical harmony with subtle diversity of detail in the gables, windows and archways of its stone and red brick façades. The gardens, once a favourite spot for the aristocratic duel, are now a pleasant children's playground. Strangely enough, the best time to see the square as a whole is in winter, when the lovely chestnut trees are bare and don't obscure the façades. Victor Hugo used to live at number 6, now a **museum** of his manuscripts, artefacts and drawings.

Finish your visit to the Marais with a walk through the old **Jewish quarter** (or *shtetl*, as Paris Jews call it) around the Rue des Rosiers. Jews have lived there continuously, apart from recurrent persecutions, since 1230, and Rue Ferdinand-Duval was known as Rue des Juifs (Jews' Street) until 1900. The other main street of the *shtetl*, Rue des Ecouffes (a medieval slang word for moneylender) completes the lively shopping district. Jews from North Africa are gradually replacing the Ashkenazi of Eastern Europe, who themselves took over from the original Sephardim. Delicatessens and *falafel* shops keep the district nicely "ecumenical".

Cimetière du Père-Lachaise

Such is the city's perpetual homage to the great of its past that cemeteries enjoy a special, not at all lugubrious, place in Paris life. In a haven of calm, the grounds are beautifully kept, the avenues of tombs a fascinating walk through history. Largest of Paris's "cities of the dead", Père-Lachaise has a population estimated at 1,350,000 buried here since its foundation in 1804. A little map available at the entrance will help you locate the famous tombs, which include Rossini and Chopin, La Fontaine and Molière, Sarah Bernhardt and Oscar Wilde.

56

Some of the métro *entrances are masterpieces of Art-Nouveau design.*

The Islands

Ile de la Cité

Shaped like a boat, the Square du Vert-Galant as its prow, the Ile de la Cité is the veritable cradle of the city of Paris, the original dwelling place of the fishermen and bargees of early Lutetia. In the middle of the 19th century, it fell victim to the over-ambitious urban planning of Baron Haussmann. The much praised but often insensitive prefect of Paris swept away most of the medieval and 17th-century structures, leaving only the Place

Dauphine and Rue Chanoinesse as testimony to the island's rich residential life.

The baron was also thinking of replacing the triangular **Place Dauphine's** gracious gabled and arcaded red brick architecture with neo-Grecian colonnades; fortunately he was forced out of office for juggling his books before the wreckers could move in. The *place* was built in 1607 by Henri IV, whose equestrian statue can be seen on the nearby Pont-Neuf. Today, its sidewalk cafés shaded by plane trees enjoy an intimacy worlds away from the big city.

The massive **Palais de Justice**, housing the law courts of mod-

Lucrative Sacrilege

After 1789, the Sainte-Chapelle remained intact, unlike many other churches. The destruction it narrowly avoided would not have been, as is too often believed, at the hands of violent, God-hating Revolutionaries. It would have been undertaken by peace-loving, profit-minded entrepreneurs who made a fortune during and long after the Revolution by dismantling churches and monasteries to build factories and houses from their masonry. Such, for instance, was the fate of the great abbeys of Jumièges in Normandy (see p. 119) and Cluny in southern Burgundy (p. 106).

Undeniably, Revolutionary crowds did plunder the church's treasury, venting their spleen on a Church that had for centuries taxed and exploited them, more for the clerics' personal benefit than for the spiritual welfare of their flock. The aesthetic considerations of later generations did not count for much during a revolution, either for the have-nots or for the haves.

The delicate walls of 13th-century stained glass (Paris's oldest) and harmonious proportions confer an ethereal quality upon the chapel, in startling contrast to the ponderous palace surrounding it. It was completed in 1248 by the sainted King Louis IX to house relics such as Christ's crown of thorns. The **15 stained-glass windows** depict 1,134 scenes from the Bible.

Between 1789 and 1815, the chapel served variously as a flour warehouse, a clubhouse for high-ranking dandies and finally as an archive for Bonaparte's Consulate. That saved the chapel from projected destruction, because the bureaucrats didn't know where else to put their mountains of paperwork. These days they find space in the endless corridors of offices around the courtrooms of the Palais and the "Maigret country" of the *police judiciaire*. The great *Salle des pas perdus* is worth a visit for a glimpse of the lawyers, plaintiffs, witnesses, court reporters and hangers-on waiting nervously for the wheels of French justice to grind into action.

But their anxiety is nothing in comparison to those condemned to bide their time in the prison of the **Conciergerie** during the Revolutionary Terror (1793–94). Named after the royally appointed *concierge* in charge of common-law criminals, this "an-

ern Paris, holds echoes of the nation's earliest kings, who dwelt here, and of the aristocrats and Revolutionary leaders who in turn were imprisoned here before execution.

It also conceals a Gothic masterpiece, the **Sainte-Chapelle**.

techamber of the guillotine'' welcomed Marie-Antoinette and Robespierre, Madame du Barry and Saint-Just, Danton and 2,500 others. Take the guided tour of the Galerie des Prisonniers. The Salle des Girondins displays a guillotine blade, the crucifix to which Marie-Antoinette prayed before execution and the lock of Robespierre's cell. Look out on the Cour des Femmes, where husbands, lovers, wives and mistresses were allowed one last tryst before the tumbrels came.

The site of the cathedral of **Notre-Dame de Paris** has had a religious significance for at least 2,000 years. In Roman times a temple to Jupiter stood here, followed in the 4th century by the first Christian church, Saint-Etienne. A second church, dedicated to Our Lady, joined it 200 years later. Both were left derelict by Norman invaders until bishop Maurice de Sully authorized construction of the cathedral to replace them in 1163. The main part of Notre-Dame took 167 years to complete and, in its transition from Romanesque to Gothic, it has been called a perfect expression of medieval architecture. Few remain unimpressed by its majestic towers, spire and breathtaking flying buttresses.

Despite its gigantic size, the cathedral achieves a great balance in its proportions and harmony in its façade. The superb central **rose window**, encircling a statue of the Madonna and Child, depicts the Redemption after the Fall. Look for the **Galerie des Rois** across the top of the three doorways. The 28 statues representing the kings of Judah and Israel have been remodelled after the drawings of Viollet-le-Duc; the originals were pulled down during the Revolution because they were thought to be the kings of France. (The 21 heads discovered in 1977 are displayed in the Musée de Cluny, see p. 74.)

Inside, the marvellous lighting is due in part to two more outsize rose windows dominating the transept. On the right of the entrance to the choir is a lovely statue of the **Virgin and Child**.

As with many Gothic masterpieces, the first architect is unknown, but the renowned Pierre de Montreuil is credited with much of the 13th-century work. In the 18th century, more damage was done by the ''improvements'' of redecorators of the *Ancien Régime* than by Revolutionary iconoclasts. For the present structure, we must be grateful to the great restorer-architect Eugène Viollet-le-Duc, who worked centimetre by centimetre over the whole edifice from 1845 to 1863. He was working in response to the public outcry started by Victor Hugo's novel, *Notre-Dame de Paris*.

The only original bell left is the South Tower's *bourdon*, whose much admired purity of tone was achieved by melting down its bronze to mix it with gold and silver donated by Louis XIV's aristocracy. Today, the bells are operated not by a hunchback but by an electric system installed in 1953.

Ile Saint-Louis

Very much a world apart, the Ile Saint-Louis is an enchanted self-contained island of gracious living, long popular with the affluent gentry of Paris. President Georges Pompidou lived here (on the Quai de Béthune), much preferring it to the Elysée Palace. In the 17th-century **Hôtel Lambert**, on the corner of Rue Saint-Louis-en-l'Ile, Voltaire carried on a tempestuous affair with the lady of the house, the Marquise du Châtelet.

The island's church, **Saint-Louis-en-l'Ile**, is as elegant as the mansions, bright and airy with a golden light illuminating an attractive collection of Dutch, Flemish and Italian 16th- and 17th-century art and some superb tapestries from the 12th century.

Something disturbing about that sardonic smile of the gargoyles up on Notre-Dame Cathedral.

One of the most notable mansions is the **Hôtel Lauzun** (17, quai d'Anjou), built in the 1650s by the great architect of Versailles, Louis Le Vau. Its highly ornamental interiors provided a perfect setting for the fantasies of the Club des Haschischins founded by Charles Baudelaire and Théophile Gautier.

Today, they've been replaced by a veritable club of ice-cream eaters, for whom the island's greatest attraction is to buy a cone from the local merchant and stroll along the poplar-shaded streets to the western end of Quai d'Orléans. There, you have the most wonderful **view** of the apse of Notre-Dame, much more romantic than the cathedral's "front".

Left Bank

Latin Quarter

Perfectly simple: from the 13th century, when the city's first university moved from the cloisters of Notre-Dame to the Left Bank, the young came to the *quartier* to learn Latin.

In those days *l'université* meant merely a collection of people—students who met on a street corner, in a public square or courtyard to hear a teacher lecture them from a bench, an upstairs window or balcony. Today there are classrooms, overcrowded, but the tradition of

open-air discussion continues, often over an endlessly nursed coffee or glass of wine on a sidewalk café on the Boulevard Saint-Michel, in the streets around the faculty buildings or in the ever-present cinema queues.

Begin at the **Place Saint-Michel**, where Paris students come to buy their textbooks and stationery, and the young of other countries come to sniff the Latin Quarter's mystique (and other more heady stuff) around the bombastic Second Empire fountain. Plunge into the narrow streets of the Saint-Séverin quarter—to the east, Rue de la Huchette, Rue de la Harpe and Rue Saint-Séverin—into a medieval world updated by the varied exotica of Turkish pastry shops, smoky Greek barbecues and stuffy little cinemas. A moment's meditation in the exquisite 13th–15th-century Flamboyant Gothic church of Saint-Séverin, where Dante is said to have prayed, and you are ready to confront the Latin Quarter's citadel, the **Sorbonne**.

Founded in 1253 as a college for poor theological students by Robert de Sorbon, Louis IX's chaplain, it took shape as an embodiment of the university under the tutelage of Cardinal Richelieu. In the *grand amphithéâtre*, which seats 2,700, you can see the Cardinal's statue along with

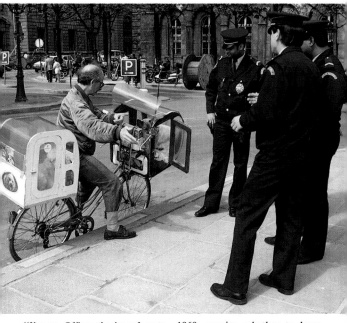

"You see, Officer, the dog refuses to pay his fare and won't budge."

those of Descartes, Pascal and Lavoisier.

As you look at Puvis de Chavannes' monumental painting on the back wall, allegorizing Poetry, Philosophy, History, Geology and the other disciplines, try to imagine 4,000 students packed into that hall in May 1968, arguing whether to have the whole thing plastered over. The student revolt against over-crowding, antiquated teaching and bureaucracy as the symbols of a dehumanized social system made the Sorbonne a focal point of the movement. When police invaded its precincts—which for centuries had guaranteed student immunity—the rebellion erupted into the streets.

Around the corner is the huge

Neo-classic domed **Panthéon**, originally intended as a church for Louis XV but now a secular mausoleum of some of the nation's greatest heroes. In the crypt are interred the remains of Voltaire and Rousseau, Hugo and Zola, assassinated Socialist leader Jean Jaurès, and Louis Braille, the inventor of the alphabet for the blind. The most recent hero to be so honoured

---

Right Moves
The neighbourhoods of the Left Bank trace from east to west the inexorable career of a successful Parisian intellectual—heart on the left, wallet on the right. The forces of protest and outright revolt have traditionally been nurtured in the Quartier latin, before subsiding into the lifelong scepticism voiced in the cafés of Saint-Germain-des-Prés. The rebels graduate from the university and move, if they prosper, west to the more genteel Faubourg Saint-Germain, closer to their publishers. If they hit the jackpot—a bestseller, their own law practice, even a ministry—they can move on to the more spacious apartments around the Champ-de-Mars, with a view of the Eiffel Tower for the kids. Without crossing the river to the notoriously snobbish 16th arrondissement, they can enjoy the same comforts and claim that they're still on the Left Bank.

---

was the World War II Resistance fighter, Jean Moulin.

Time for a break in the **Jardin du Luxembourg**. If you want to picnic in the park (sorry, not on the grass), make a detour first to the old street market behind the Panthéon on the **Rue Mouffetard**, old hunting-ground of Rabelais and Rabelaisians ever since. Despite their 17th-century origins, the Luxembourg Gardens avoid the rigid geometry of the Tuileries and Versailles. The horse chestnuts, beeches and plane trees, the orangery and ornamental pond were a major inspiration for the bucolic paintings of Watteau.

Montparnasse
In the twenties, Montparnasse took over from Montmartre as the stomping ground of the capital's artistic colony, or at least of its avant-garde. American expatriates such as Hemingway, Fitzgerald, Gertrude Stein, John Dos Passos and Theodore Dreiser also contributed to the free-living mystique.

Other quarters are known for their palaces and churches; Montparnasse (named after a 17th-century gravel mound since removed) has cafés and bars for landmarks, most of them along **Boulevard du Montparnasse**. The Closerie des Lilas, a centre for French Symbolist poets at the turn of the century, served as a meeting-place for Lenin and Trotsky before World War I and for Hemingway and his pals after the war; the Select, first all-night bar to open in Montparnasse, in 1925, quickly became a Henry Miller hang-out and continues resolutely to resist efforts to spruce it up; la Coupole, favourite of Sartre and Simone de Beauvoir, is still going strong, more living theatre than restaurant; breakfast was taken at the Dôme, for a change of air; and the Rotonde, favoured by Picasso, Vlaminck and Modigliani, is back as a restaurant after a spell as a cinema. Around the corner, on Boulevard Raspail, is a splendid Rodin bronze of Balzac.

Habitués just pretend not to see the monstrous 58-floor Tour Maine-Montparnasse office block by the railway station.

Saint-Germain-des-Prés

Saint-Germain-des-Prés is the literary quarter par excellence, home of the major publishing houses, the *Académie française*, bookshops and literary cafés. But it's also a charming neighbourhood for day-long people-watching, antique-hunting and gallery-hopping.

The cafés around the **Place Saint-Germain-des-Prés** are the "village centre". On the north side is the Café Bonaparte, on the west the famous les Deux Magots (funny Chinese statues). Both provide ringside seats for the street theatre of mimes and musicians, who pass around the hat, and for the neighbourhood eccentrics, who do it for free.

The Café de Flore up the boulevard has more intellectual aspirations, with a rather confusing ideological history. During the Dreyfus Affair it was headquarters for the extreme right-wing *Action française*; in 1914 the home of Surrealists Apollinaire and André Salmon, who liked provoking brawls; and, in the fifties, Sartre's more peaceful left-wing existentialists, who never got enough sleep to find the energy to fight.

The **church** of Saint-Germain-des-Prés is an attractive mixture of Romanesque and Gothic, with an 11th-century clocktower.

North of the church, the Rue Bonaparte takes you to the prestigious **Ecole des Beaux-Arts**. Incorporated in its structure are fragments of medieval and Renaissance architecture and sculpture. On the Rue des Beaux-Arts is the hotel (now simply but expensively called l'Hôtel) where Oscar Wilde died in 1900. He complained about the "horrible magenta flowers" of his room's wallpaper, saying "one of us has to go". Now both have.

The august and handsome **Institut de France**, home of the *Académie française*, is on the

Quai Conti by the Pont des Arts. It was built by Louis Le Vau in 1668 to harmonize with the Louvre across the river. The *Académie* was founded by Richelieu to be the supreme arbiter of the French language. Periodically decried as a bunch of prestigious old fuddy-duddies, the 40 lifetime members are chosen in hotly contested elections to update the Academy's French dictionary, but are distinguished mostly for their acceptance speeches and obituaries. Guides to the Institut like to point out the east pavilion, site of the 14th-century Tour de Nesle. They say Queen Jeanne de Bourgogne used to watch from there for likely young lovers whom she summoned for the night and then had thrown into the Seine.

Invalides–Eiffel Tower

The massively monumental **Hôtel des Invalides** was founded by Louis XIV as the first national hospital for soldiers. Housing today the Musée de l'Armée, it is also the supreme celebration of Napoleon, since his body was brought here in 1840 from the island of Saint Helena.

Awesomely elaborate, **Napoleon's tomb** is set in the crypt directly under the Invalides' golden dome. His body, dressed in the green uniform of the Chasseurs de la Garde, is encased in *six* coffins, one inside the other Chinese-box-fashion. The first is

The long and the short of it, at the Trocadéro and Eiffel Tower.

67

of iron, the second mahogany, then two of lead, one of ebony and the outer one of oak. The monument of red porphyry from Finland rests on a green granite pedestal, encircled by 12 colossal Victory pillars sculpted by Pradier.

Also in the crypt are the remains of the Emperor's son, brought to France from Vienna in 1940 by Adolf Hitler.

The military complex continues with the Ecole militaire and the spacious gardens of the **Champ-de-Mars**, once the site of military exercises and parades and more recently the series of World's Fairs held between 1867 and 1937.

There are monuments and there is the **Eiffel Tower**. Some celebrate heroes, commemorate victories, honour kings and saints. The Eiffel Tower is a monument for its own sake, a proud gesture to the world, a witty structure that makes aesthetics irrelevant. Its construction for the World's Fair of 1889 was an astounding engineering achievement—15,000 pieces of metal joined together by 2,500,000 rivets, soaring 300 metres (984 feet) into the air on a base covering only 130 square metres (1,400 square feet).

Like many other World's Fair exhibits, the tower was slated for destruction in 1910, but nobody had the heart to go through with it. Though many writers hated it. Guy de Maupassant signed a manifesto against "this vertiginously ridiculous tower". Verlaine rerouted his journey around Paris to avoid seeing it.

Today, everyone seems to love it. It has a splendid new inner illumination at night, a popular *brasserie* on the first platform, elegant gourmet restaurant on the second, and a **view** from the top stretching over 60 kilometres (40 miles) on a pollution-free day.

Bois de Boulogne

These 900 hectares (2,224 acres) of parkland on the western edge of the city constitute one of the happier achievements of Baron Haussmann. He transformed the old Rouvray forest, left completely wild until 1852, into the closest thing Paris has to a London-style park: roads and paths for cycling and rambles, horse-trails, boating lakes, restaurants and cafés with open-air dancing, plus the grand race course at Longchamp.

One of the main attractions is the **Parc de Bagatelle**, a walled garden with the city's most beautiful display of flowers. For the children, the **Jardin d'acclimatation** offers a miniature railway, Punch and Judy show, house of distorting mirrors, pony-rides and a miniature farm of pigs, goats and chickens.

Museums

The Louvre

The Louvre museum is so huge that people are sometimes frightened to go in at all. But you do not have to be an art fanatic to realize that to come to Paris without setting foot inside this great and truly beautiful palace would be a crime. No other museum has such a comprehensive collection of painting and sculpture. If you do it right, it can be an exhilarating pleasure.

First of all, get up very early on a sunny day and walk across the gardens of the Place du Carrousel. Admire Maillol's nubile statues and then sit on a bench to take in the sheer immensity of this home of France's kings and monumental showcase of a world's treasures.

At the east end is the Cour Carrée, covering the original fortress built by Philippe Auguste in 1190 to protect Paris from river attack while he was away on a crusade. Stretching out from the Cour Carrée (of which you should see Perrault's marvellous colonnade on the east façade) are the additions of François I, Henri IV, Catherine de Médicis, Louis XIV, Napoleon and Napoleon III. President Mitterrand's great glass pyramid in the Cour Napoléon completes eight centuries of construction.

The latest addition is designed by American architect I. M. Pei to provide a spectacular modern entrance, together with underground bookshops and cafés, at the centre of corridors leading to the various wings of the museum.

François I, the Louvre's first major art collector, acquired four Raphaels, three Leonardo da Vincis and one Titian (portrait of the king himself). By 1793, when the leaders of the Revolution declared the palace a national museum, there were 650 works of art in the collection; at the last inventory, in 1933, there were 173,000. So don't be depressed if you don't see everything.

If you're planning several visits, you might like to concentrate on just one section at a time—the Italian, the French, the Spanish, the Flemish and Dutch, but also the ancient Egyptian, the Greek and Roman.

For an overall view of the collections, we've attempted a first selection:

Egyptian: lion-headed goddess *Sekhmet* (1400 B.C.) and the colossal *Amenophis IV* (1370 B.C.).

Greek: the winged *Victory of Samothrace* and the beautifully proportioned *Venus de Milo*.

Italian: the sculpture of *Two Slaves* by Michelangelo; Leonardo da Vinci's fabled *Mona*

Lisa (La Joconde), but also his sublime *Virgin of the Rocks*; Titian's voluptuous *Woman at Her Toilet* and sombre *Entombment of Christ*; the poignant *Old Man and His Grandson* of Ghirlandaio.

French: Poussin's bittersweet *Arcadian Shepherds*; Watteau's hypnotically melancholy *Gilles* and graceful *Embarkation for Cythera*; Delacroix's *Liberty Guiding the People* and Courbet's piercing study of provincial bourgeoisie, *Funeral at Ornans*.

Dutch and Flemish: Rembrandt's cheerful *Self-Portrait with a Toque*, his beloved *Hendrickje Stoffels*, also portrayed nude in *Bathsheba Bathing*; Van Dyck's gracious, dignified *Charles I* of England; among the scores of "official" Rubens, his tenderly personal *Helena Fourment*; Jordaens' *Four Evangelists* as diligent Dutchmen.

German: a gripping *Self-Portrait* by Dürer; Holbein's *Erasmus*.

Spanish: the uncompromising Velázquez portrait of ugly *Queen Marianna of Austria*; El Greco's powerfully mystic *Christ on the Cross*; Ribera's gruesomely good-humoured *The Club Foot*.

English: Gainsborough's exquisite *Conversation in a Park*; Turner's *Landscape with River and Bay*; and **Americans** will be delighted to contemplate Whistler's *Mother*.

Beaubourg

The official name of Europe's most spectacular cultural centre is Centre d'art et de culture Georges-Pompidou, shortened to Centre Pompidou (after the French president whose pet project it was). But somehow Parisians have an aversion to naming their major monuments after their political leaders, and so this bright and dynamic monster will probably always be known quite simply as Beaubourg, after the 13th-century neighbourhood surrounding it.

The combination of public library, modern art museum, children's workshop, *cinémathèque*, industrial design centre, experimental music laboratory and open-air circus on the front plaza is the most popular show in town.

After an initial reaction similar to the delight and rage originally provoked by the Eiffel Tower, people have grown accustomed to the construction's resemblance to a multicoloured oil refinery. The comparison is readily accepted by its architects, Italians Renzo Piano and Gianfranco Franchi and Englishman Richard Rogers, who deliberately left the building's service system visible and colour-coded:

Beaubourg's avant-garde sculpture continues the Paris tradition of playful fountains.

red for the transportation, green for the water pipes, blue for the air-conditioning ducts and yellow for the electrical system.

One of Beaubourg's simplest pleasures is just going up the escalators in the long glass tubes that run diagonally from the bottom-left to the top-right-hand corner. Watch Paris unfold in front of your eyes with a stunning **view** of the city's rooftops—best on the *fourth*, not the fifth, floor.

Other Major Museums

Though physically part of the Louvre, the **Musée des Arts décoratifs** is a separate museum with its own entrance at 107, rue de Rivoli. The rich permanent collection includes tapestries, furniture and porcelain, but look out for the fascinating temporary exhibitions featuring great styles and eras of design history such as Jugendstil, Bauhaus and the American fifties. Next door is the new **Musée national des Arts de la mode**, devoted to the decorative art of which Paris is still the world capital, high fashion.

Right across the river, the 19th-century Orsay railway station has been transformed into the **Musée d'Orsay**. This exciting new museum embraces France's tremendous creativity from 1848 to 1914 in the domains of painting, sculpture, architecture and industrial design, advertising, newspapers, book publishing, photography and the early years of the cinema. It also displays the collection of Impressionists and their followers transferred from the Jeu de Paume museum, now used for temporary exhibitions.

On the river side of the Tuileries, the **Orangerie** is best known for its ground-floor rooms decorated with Monet's beautiful *Nymphéas* murals, offering a moment of repose after a hard day's sightseeing. But you should also take a look upstairs at the excellent Walter-Guillaume collection of Cézanne, Renoir, Utrillo, Douanier Rousseau and Picasso.

Another recent addition is the long-awaited **Musée Picasso** (5, rue de Thorigny in the Marais, *métro* Saint-Paul). From the private collections of Picasso's heirs, the museum has received over 200 paintings and 158 sculptures, in addition to hundreds of drawings, engravings, ceramics and models for theatre décors and costumes. It also exhibits the artist's personal collection of masterworks by fellow painters Braque, Matisse, Miró, Degas, Renoir and Rousseau.

Housed in the Hôtel Salé, a beautifully restored 17th-century mansion, the museum offers a moving portrait of the man, his family, his mistresses and friends, with letters, manuscripts, photo albums, notebooks, his French Communist Party membership card, bullfight tickets and holiday postcards.

La Villette (on the north-east corner of town, *métro* Porte de la Villette) has been converted from the world's biggest slaughterhouse to a striking futuristic complex of cultural and scientific activities.

Refusing to call itself a museum, La Villette's **Cité des sciences et de l'industrie** puts the accent on public participation in all phases of space technology, computers, astronomy and marine biology. The unabashed functionalism of its architecture carries the Beaubourg principle

Time for reflection beneath the deflecting facets of the Géode sphere.

73

to a logical conclusion. Its most attractive symbol is the shining stainless steel **Géode** sphere containing a revolutionary cinema with a hemispheric screen 36 metres (118 feet) in diameter. There's also a giant rock-concert hall, **le Zénith**, alongside a projected avant-garde musical counterpart to the scientific museum, sorry, city: **Cité de la musique**.

In the Palais de Chaillot (Trocadéro): **Musée de l'Homme**, devoted to man's prehistory, and the fascinating **Musée du Cinéma**, with reconstructed sets and studios, historic posters, original scripts, costumes of Greta Garbo and Catherine Deneuve, John Wayne's hat and Rudolf Valentino's jellaba.

And: **Musée de Cluny** (6, place Paul-Painlevé, *métro* Maubert-Mutualité), for the great *Lady with the Unicorn* tapestry, but also sculpture of Paris's Roman and Gothic past; **Musée Guimet** (6, place d'Iéna), a superb collection of Indian, Japanese and Chinese art; **Musée de l'Affiche** (18, rue de Paradis), advertising posters of the past and present.

Many museums are devoted to the work and life of just one artist, the best of these being **Rodin** (77, rue de Varenne), with its lovely sculpture garden; but look, too, for the home of **Balzac** (47, rue Raynouard) and **Delacroix's** studio (6, rue de Furstenberg).

ÎLE-DE-FRANCE

Versailles

This most popular of excursions from Paris is an easy day trip, just 21 kilometres (15 miles) from the capital, but to do it justice, calculate a full day, with a very early start.

Organized bus tours start at the Tuileries Gardens on the Rue de Rivoli side. However, the palace and gardens are so enormous that you may prefer to do them at your own pace, leaving out what your head and feet can't take.

With a little planning, an otherwise tiring day can be a delightful treat. Try the following agenda: early start at a Paris street market to buy a picnic (better than the Versailles tourist traps); morning tour of the palace; stroll through the palace gardens to lunch beside the Grand Canal; siesta and tea in the gardens of the Petit Trianon; wander back across the palace gardens for a last sunset view of the great château.

The Palace

If you don't already have a clear idea of what kind of man Louis XIV was, take a long, hard look at his palace. Never did a piece of architecture more exactly express the personality of its builder than the Château de Versailles—extravagant, pompous, dazzling, formidable, glorious and vainglorious.

Louis XIII had hoped to turn his favourite hunting ground into a modest retirement home. For his son, Versailles became the centre of a universe, proclaiming his own grandeur in a sprawling edifice of stone and brick, marble, gilt and crystal.

The palace has been splendidly restored since World War I with private contributions, most notably of that transatlantic Sun King, J. D. Rockefeller. Wherever the original furnishings and decoration are missing, superb appropriate equivalents have been installed.

As you make your way through the gilded gates and cross the vast Cour des Ministres where the state secretaries worked, past the imperious statue of Himself to the main entrance on the right of the Cour Royale, you realize it wasn't Mussolini who invented the Long Walk to intimidate his underlings seeking an audience.

Inside, the self-guided tour is instantly more reassuring. You begin at the intimate little **Royal Chapel**, a gem of High Baroque, a harmonious décor of white marble with gilded altar and balustrades. You get the king's-eye-view looking down into the nave where the courtiers worshipped.

In the rooms of the **Grands Appartements,** named after the gods and goddesses whom Louis felt to be his appropriate com-

---

Statistics of Grandeur

Not just a whim of megalomania, building Versailles was Louis XIV's cold political decision to force his hitherto obstreperous nobles into submission by impoverishing them with permanent attendance at his court. To lodge the 3,000 courtiers and servants, the palace took 50 years to build, spanning the whole of his reign and still incomplete at his death.

Louis Le Vau and Jules Hardouin-Mansart were the architects, Charles Le Brun directed the interior design and monumental sculpture, while André Le Nôtre laid out the gardens. Of the 36,000-strong work force (plus 6,000 horses), 227 men died on the job.

The 115 hectares (280 acres) of gardens and parkland are only a tenth of what had to be tended for the Sun King—including 150,000 flower plants that were changed 15 times a year.

And it all cost 65 million livres (French pounds). Exorbitant, says any self-respecting anti-royalist, but, to put it into perspective, it's been calculated as the equivalent of what republican France spends on just one aircraft carrier and was in any case a spit in the ocean compared with the 3,000 million that Louis XIV spent on his wars.

panions, the king entertained his courtiers three times a week: Monday, Wednesday and Thursday. The **Salon de Diane** was a billiard room—not many people could beat Fast Louis. The table's gone, but Bernini has left a superb bust of the champion at 27. The ceiling painting of the Sun King in his chariot and pictorial references to Alexander the Great and Augustus Caesar make it clear the **Salon d'Apollon** was Louis XIV's throne room.

But the most astonishing of these royal apartments is the glittering **Galerie des Glaces**, 73 metres (240 feet) long, built to catch every ray of the setting sun in the 17 tall arched panels of mirrors. This was the palace's grandest reception hall, where the king gave his wildest parties and received his most important foreign envoys. Le Brun's paintings depict Louis XIV's wars in Holland and his more peaceful achievements at home.

In the **Queen's Bedroom**, 19 royal children were born, many of them—as was the custom—with members of the public looking on.

On a separate guided tour, you can visit the marvellous **Royal Opera** of Louis XV, and the king's private apartments. The **King's Bedroom**, with two fine portraits by Van Dyck, is set at the exact centre of the sun's path

from east to west. The court was encouraged to come every day to witness the monarch's rising from bed and moment of retirement. Louis XIV died here in 1715 of gangrene of the leg.

The Gardens

If English and Japanese gardens attempt, in their different ways, to enhance nature by "tidying it up" while imitating a "natural" landscape, the French garden, of which Versailles is the supreme expression, quite deliberately imposes a formal pattern.

Resuming a tradition of classical Rome, André Le Nôtre used the paths and avenues of trees and statuary to divide flowerbeds, ponds and fountain basins into intricate geometric patterns. Pause at the palace's western terrace along the Galerie des

---

Fountains and Fireworks
Beginning at 3.30 p.m. on three Sundays a month, from May to September, the grandes eaux *of the Apollo, Neptune and Dragon fountains are turned on. The spectacular display recaptures some of the splendour of festivities at the court of the Sun King. There are also several special night-time floodlit shows with fireworks. Details (and reservations for the fireworks) from the Versailles Office de tourisme, 7, rue des Réservoirs, telephone 39.50.36.22.*

Glaces for a first view of his harmonious, subtly asymmetrical arrangement of the grounds.

As you make your way through the gardens, look back occasionally at the changing perspectives of the palace. Directly beyond the western terrace is the Axe du Soleil (Path of the Sun) leading down to the **Bassin d'Apollon** (Louis XIV's solar obsession is unavoidable). Adorned with classical sculptures of Greek mythology, this and the great **Bassin de Neptune** and **Bassin du Dragon** in the north-east corner were centrepieces of the royal garden parties.

Beyond the Bassin d'Apollon is the **Grand Canal**, on which the King kept his Venetian gondolas. Today, small boats are available for you to row yourself.

North-west of the château, the **Grand Trianon** palace, surrounded by pleasantly unpompous gardens, was the home of Louis XIV's mistress, Madame de Maintenon, where the aging king increasingly took refuge.

The **Petit Trianon**, where Marie-Antoinette tried to hide from that nasty Revolution, has the allure of a doll's house in comparison with the rest of Versailles. Its gardens, with ponds, mounds and shady woods, are English in style; a relaxing change from the formality of the château. The childlike playfulness of the doomed queen's hideaway is reinforced by her **Hameau**, a hamlet of thatched cottages where she and her retinue pretended to be milkmaids and farmboys.

Chartres

One of the most moving experiences on a journey across France is to drive through the wheat fields of the fertile Beauce plain, and see, looming suddenly on the horizon, the silhouette of **Chartres cathedral**.

This unquestionable masterpiece of French civilization marks the transition in the 12th century from the solid, sober Romanesque style of the Church's beginnings to the more airy, assertive Gothic of its ascendancy. Apart from a few decapitated statues, it came miraculously unscathed through the Wars of Religion and the Revolution. As you face the harmoniously asymmetrical western façade, the southern tower, **Clocher Vieux**, is a supreme expression of Romanesque simplicity while the taller northern tower, **Clocher Neuf**, is already lighter, with its slender, more ornate steeple.

On the central porch, **Portail Royal**, note the stately, deliberately elongated sculptures of Old Testament figures, compared with the freer, more vigorous statues round on the northern and southern porches.

Inside, the glory of the church is its 173 **stained-glass windows**; that unique "Chartres blue" and deep red bringing an ethereal light into the nave, especially from a late afternoon sun through the western rose-window, depicting the Last Judgment. Among the oldest and most famous of the windows, on the southern side of the choir, is an enthroned Mary with Jesus on her lap, **Notre-Dame de la Belle Verrière**. The church is dedicated to Mary, representing her 175 times in the various sculptures and windows.

In the paving of the nave's centre aisle, you'll notice a large circular **labyrinth**; medieval worshippers traced its path from the circumference to the centre as part of a mystic spiritual exercise.

Back outside, from the Episcopal Garden *(Jardin de l'Evêché)* at the rear of the cathedral, a stairway takes you down to the **old town**. Its streets of attractive 16th- and 17th-century houses along the Eure river afford a pretty view of the cathedral.

Fontainebleau

The great forest south of Paris was popular hunting country for François I and Henri IV; their **palace** is an elegant monument to their Renaissance tastes. Napoleon cherished it as a place for reflection, and it was there that he abdicated in 1814 to go into a first exile on the Isle of Elba.

Allegorical paintings in the **Galerie de François Ier** bear testimony to the king's preoccupation with war and death, and also to the sanctity of kingship. **Napoleon's apartments** are still decorated with the furnishings of his empire. A new Napoleonic museum has been installed in the Louis XV wing.

But save most of your time for the majestic **Forest of Fontainebleau**, 25,000 hectares (over 60,000 acres) of oak, beech, silver birch, pine, chestnut and hornbeam *(charme)*. Apart from the lovely walks and indeed lengthy hikes over well-marked paths, a great attraction is the miniature "mountain range" of sheer rocks and cliffs, much appreciated by apprentice climbers for trying out their equipment and technique before tackling the Alps. The most popular are the rugged Gorges de Franchard, due west of the palace. The Gorges d'Apremont, near the little town of Barbizon famous for its 19th-century landscape painters, are less crowded.

Chartres' stained-glass windows have miraculously survived centuries of war and revolution.

Chantilly

Fifty kilometres (30 miles) north of Paris, Chantilly is celebrated for its château, its elegant race-course and stables, and *crème chantilly* (whipped cream), served at the château gates on hot waffles.

The **château**, which belonged to the powerful Condé dynasty in the 17th century, joins a not ugly but somewhat bastard reconstruction of the great edifice destroyed in the Revolution to the charming, authentic Renaissance building known as the Petit Château.

The main body of the château houses the **Musée Condé**, a superb collection of Italian, French

A royal treat at Fontainebleau, even if not quite the kind of carriage that François I used.

and Dutch masters, including Raphael, Veronese and Fra Angelico, Poussin, Watteau, exquisite portraits by Clouet, Van Dyck and Teniers. One of the charms of the collection is that the paintings are hung, not in any classical order by school, but according to the personal whim of their last owner, the Duke of Aumale.

The palace grounds make a pleasant walk, especially the English Garden behind the Petit

> ### Skewered
> One day in April, 1671, Louis XIV visited Chantilly with 5,000, yes, 5,000 friends for a three-day stay. The Condé family's brilliant but highly sensitive master chef, Vatel, went berserk earning his title of Contrôleur général de la Bouche de Monsieur le Prince (General Supervisor of the Prince's Mouth). Bad enough on the first night when three tables had to go without their roast. When the fresh fish failed to arrive the next day, Vatel went up to his room and ran himself through with his sword.

Château. Louis XIV was very jealous of the Grand Canal, ponds and waterfalls designed by André Le Nôtre and insisted the master gardener do even better in Versailles. You may prefer the more intimate scale of Chantilly.

In June, the Hippodrome west of the château is host to the prestigious Prix du Jockey Club horse race. But all year round, you can visit the monumental 18th-century **Grandes-Ecuries** (stables), now a horse museum, with live horses munching hay next to wooden statues.

Senlis

For your first taste of unspoiled village life just a quick 50-kilometre (30-mile) drive north from Paris, try the charming little town of Senlis, with its imposing Gothic **cathedral** and handsome 15th- and 16th-century houses, still partly encircled by Gallo-Roman ramparts. The finely sculpted porch on the western façade inspired the design for Chartres cathedral and Paris's Notre-Dame.

Compiègne

Some 80 kilometres (50 miles) up the autoroute du Nord, Compiègne is another classical Ile-de-France royal hunting forest and palace. Besides being the last home of Marie-Antoinette, the **palace** was a favourite of Napoleon III and his wife Eugénie, whose extravagant memorabilia constitute the **Musée du Second-Empire**.

Also in the palace is a fascinating **Musée de la Voiture**. It displays all kinds of vehicles, from the coach that carried Napoleon to and from Moscow in 1812 to a splendid 1900 4-horsepower Renault and other turn-of-the-century classics.

The **Forest of Compiègne** offers plenty of good walks; or you can hire a horse at the village of Saint-Jean-aux-Bois. The forest is famous for its **Clairière de l'Armistice**, where the Germans signed the Armistice of their defeat in 1918 in Marshal Foch's private train coach. Twenty-two years later, Hitler obliged the French to sign their capitulation in the same place.

NORTH-EAST

The invaders pouring over the northern and eastern frontiers these days tend to be peaceful —tourists from Britain, the Netherlands, Belgium and Germany. But the plains and plateaux of Flanders and Picardy, Alsace and Lorraine have historically been the arenas of bloody war.

In the Hundred Years' War, England knew its days of glory on the Picardy fields of Crécy and Azincourt (Agincourt). For Louis XIV's wars against the Netherlands, the great military architect Vauban built a line of fortifications in the frontier towns, at Calais, Dunkirk, Douai, Valenciennes and, still visible today, the great citadel at Lille. More recently, Flanders and the river valleys of the Somme and Marne were the major battlefields of World War I. Alsace and Lorraine suffered humiliating conquest at Wissembourg and Metz in 1870 and again in 1940, but wit-nessed the resurrection of the French Army at the Liberation.

The windswept countryside is dotted with poignant memorials and military cemeteries. The villages have a hardy charm, and the larger towns, Arras and Amiens to the north, Nancy and Strasbourg to the east, exude great civic pride. Linking north and east, the fields of Champagne and its royal city of Reims have also known their wars, but today prefer, for our greater joy, to bask in bubbly.

Deeper into the interior, Burgundy is a more solidly implanted heartland. Most famous today for its vineyards, it was historically the stronghold of the dukes of Dijon, alongside the ecclesiastical empires of the Cluny and Cistercian monasteries and their great Romanesque churches. To the east, the Jura mountains of Franche-Comté offer visitors invigorating hikes through dense forests and along the rivers of the valley landscapes celebrated by the paintings of Gustave Courbet.

PICARDY
If you're coming into France from the English Channel or across the Belgian border, don't just rush straight down the *autoroute* to Paris. Picardy has plenty of interesting stops and even some worthwhile short detours for a more leisurely journey.

Saint-Omer

Prosperous from the textile industry since the Middle Ages, the town emerged from bombardment in two world wars with a gentle serenity unusual for the austere north.

Formerly a cathedral, the 13th-century **Basilique Notre-Dame** dominates the town with an imposing grandeur. Note the fine stone sculptures of the Virgin and a Last Judgment over the south porch. Inside, the marble and alabaster treasures evoke the wealth of the diocese in the 16th and 17th centuries, particularly the elaborate chapel screens and, in the north arm of the transept, an intricate astronomical clock. Nearby, the 13th-century sculpted figures of the *Grand Dieu de Thérouanne* are strangely foreshortened because they were originally seen from below (on another church).

The **Hôtel Sandelin** museum is well worth a visit, both for the splendid 18th-century mansion, with its Louis XV furnishings, and for its rich collections of porcelain from all over the world. The Saint-Omer decorative glazed earthenware *(faïence)* is a major feature, and the Delft collection is outstanding, not only for its celebrated blue ware but also for some exquisite polychrome pieces. Tobacco fanatics and non-smokers alike will love the display of over 2,000 terra-cotta pipes. The enamelled bowls depict demons and dogs, Napoleon and Jesus and quite a few naughty scatological and erotic scenes.

Le Touquet

Perhaps to attract a clientèle from the capital, this breezy seaside resort added the name Paris-Plage. It might more aptly have called itself Knightsbridge-Plage, being a pure creation of London's smart set at the end of the 19th century, when swimming became all the rage.

Today, it's something of a nicely faded museum piece, but the sailing and windsurfing are good, the riding, golf and tennis simply splendid.

In the lovely **forest,** you'll find elegant Tudor-style timbered villas that it's more diplomatic to call "Anglo-Norman".

Arras

This is the place celebrated among British schoolchildren for the tapestry through which Hamlet stabbed poor old Polonius. The town, just off the *autoroute* from Calais, has two of the most beautiful city squares in France. The classical Flemish style of the 17th- and 18th-century arcades and gabled façades on the **Grande Place** and **Place des Héros** invites comparison with the great squares of Brussels and Bruges.

Amiens

The majestic **cathedral** of Picardy's capital is without doubt an authentic masterpiece of French Gothic architecture. It was almost completed in just 44 years in the middle of the 13th century, and thus preserved a homogeneous style, a noble silhouette miraculously unharmed by the heavy air raids of World War II.

Its glory is the oak carving of the 110 **choir stalls**, the work of 16th-century cabinet-makers whose names—Jean Turpin, Alexandre de Heudebourg, Arnould Boulin—deserve mention alongside their more celebrated contemporaries of the Italian Renaissance. Dramatically depicting over 400 scenes from the Old and New testaments, 3,650 figures present a magnificent pageant of the customs and costume of the people of François I. Among the panels of Cain and Abel, Abraham and Isaac, Jesus and Mary, all very Flemish figures, are carvings of a Picardy baker, dairymaid, fruitmonger and laundress.

The **Musée de Picardie** (48, rue de la République) has a good collection of paintings, most notably a couple of Van Goyen landscapes, El Greco's *Portrait of a Man*, a witty self-portrait of Quentin de La Tour, and François Boucher's erotic pink nymphs.

CHAMPAGNE

In the great French lexicon of good living, no word is more loaded with magic than Champagne. Magic, in the miraculous conjunction of geology, topography and climate that have produced the world's most celebrated wine. In this northernmost of France's wine-producing regions, with a bright mellow summer and mild winter, the Champagne country around Reims and Epernay has ideal south-facing slopes to exploit every last ray of sun, together with just the right chalky soil to store and release the requisite heat and humidity among the vines. Add the ingenuity of the cellar masters who concoct the magic potion, and you have the makings of a very good party. The great manufacturers will be glad to give you a glimpse of how they do it.

Reims

If Champagne is the wine of kings, Reims is the town that consecrated the divine right of kingship. It was here, at the end of the 5th century, that Saint Rémi is believed to have baptized the pagan Clovis and here again that Hugues Capet was anointed and crowned first king of France in 987. It was a major achievement of Joan of Arc to have Charles VII crowned at Reims cathedral in 1429. Charles X, last of the Bourbons, sought the same divine legitimacy in 1825 with a Reims coronation.

The magnificently proportioned 13th-century **cathedral** was badly damaged by fire in World War I, but it has been well restored and remains one of the country's great Gothic edifices. Try to see its lovely buff stone façade in the late afternoon sun, with a pair of binoculars to study the rich sculpture of the Gallery of Kings high above the windows.

In the interior, the most noteworthy of the surviving 13th-century **stained-glass windows** are the rose window above the western entrance, illustrating the life of the Virgin Mary, and one devoted to the Creation in the north arm of the transept. Directly beyond the altar is the **Chagall chapel,** in which the Russian artist connects his Jewish origins to the Christian religion with a window depicting Abraham and Jesus.

The originals of the cathedral's major sculptures are on display next door in the museum of the archbishop's residence, the **Palais du Tau**. The most famous pieces are the Smiling

Of Reims cathedral's sculptures, the Smiling Angel is famous as symbol of the town's hospitality.

Joy from Trouble with Bubbles

Ever since Roman times, the wine growers of Champagne knew they had a good product—in the Middle Ages they got into violent fights over it with rivals in neighbouring Burgundy. But until the end of the 17th century, they had a "problem" with bubbles, which they had the devil of a time getting rid of. Then a monk named Dom Pérignon, cellar master at the abbey of Hautvillers, decided he liked this bubbly stuff and found a way of stabilizing it by blending it with other wines and adding an exact dose of sugar. This is roughly what today's Champagne producers do, prior to the vital second fermentation.

Mere technique, the méthode champenoise of getting the bubbles into the wine is not enough to make real Champagne.

There are only 23,000 hectares (57,000 acres) of true Champagne vineyards—1.5% of the national total—and their grapes alone, black and white, are authorized to go into a Champagne bottle. The white chardonnay grapes growing south of Epernay on the Côte des blancs bring the light, fresh note; the black pinot noir on the Montagne de Reims add body; and pinot meunier west of Epernay add a dash of fruitiness. You'll find these grapes all over the wine-growing world, but only the Champagne region has that special chalky soil, not only for the vineyards, but also for the vaults of the gallery cellars.

The wine growers harvest their grapes in October and bring them to the underground galleries of the major producers for pressing and a first fermentation that turns the sugar into alcohol. By the New Year, a clear wine, usually 75% black and 25% white grapes, is ready for the all-important cuvée, the cellar master's secret blend with up to 30 other wines that gives each "label" its distinctive taste. Natural yeasts and a small amount of cane sugar are added prior to bottling and a second, slower fermentation, which lasts about three months. The wine is then left to age. Every day the bottles are turned alternately one-eighth to the left or to the right, to remove the deposits that attach to the sides. This takes at least a year—or three for a vintage, millésime, after an outstanding harvest when older wines are not needed for the cuvée. From time to time the bottles are carefully shaken to bring the deposit up to the top. This is removed by freezing, before the liqueur de dosage is added: a mixture of cane sugar in vintage Champagne, which determines the degree of "dryness" —extra sec, demi sec or brut.

Topped with a fresh new cork, wire muzzle and shiny little seal, that, at last, ladies and gentlemen, is Champagne. Cheers!

Angel, symbol of Reims hospitality, and the allegorical figure of the Synagogue, blindfolded because it was felt the Jews were too stubborn to behold the truth of Christianity.

For an hour's tour of the city's **Champagne cellars**, you can get details at the Office de tourisme, 1, rue Jadart, 51100 Reims, telephone: 26.47.25.69. The cellars are in fact 250 kilometres (155 miles) of galleries quarried out of the city's chalk foundations back in the days of Roman Gaul. Practically all the major Champagne "labels" offer tours. Piper-Heidsieck has a little train; Ruinart, the oldest, is organized on three levels; Taittinger is partly installed in the crypt of a demolished abbey.

Epernay

The town's advantage over Reims is that you can combine a visit of its cellars—Moët & Chandon or Mercier—with a drive south along the great **Côte des blancs** vineyards that produce the white *chardonnay* grapes. The prettiest view of the vines and the Marne valley is just 10 kilometres (6 miles) down the D 10 at **Cramant**.

You can see a reconstitution of Dom Pérignon's famous 17th-century cellar and laboratory in the abbey museum of **Hautvillers**, 6 kilometres (4 miles) north of Epernay.

LORRAINE

A region of strategic importance guarding the eastern approaches to Paris, Lorraine has long been a pawn in France's perennial conflicts with Germany. Amid the resulting devastations of war and the more recent depression of the region's declining coal, iron and steel industries, the historic town of Nancy stands out as a gleaming survivor. Its golden 18th-century architecture makes it a rewarding stopover on any journey between Paris and Alsace.

Nancy

Head straight for **Place Stanislas**. Surrounded by elegant Classical mansions and gilded wrought-iron grilles with ornamental gateways framing the marble fountains of Neptune and Amphitrite, the square is one of the most harmonious urban spaces in Europe.

Visit the **hôtel de ville**, in the largest of the mansions, for its fine staircase, designed by the same Jean Lamour who created the wrought-iron grilles, but above all for the marvellous view of the square. In the centre stands a statue of the man responsible, King Stanislas Leszczyński of Poland.

Deposed by the Russians in 1736, he had the good fortune to be Louis XV's father-in-law and was given the Duchy of Lorraine as compensation. He expressed his gratitude by devoting the rest of his life to refurbishing a town devastated by the Thirty Years' War of the previous century.

The square's grand, spacious effect is completed to the north by an **arc de triomphe** (dedicated to Louis XV) at the entrance to the long **Place de la Carrière**, also graced by 18th-century mansions and Jean Lamour's iron grilles.

At the end of the *place,* in the Grande Rue, a splendid Renaissance doorway is all that remains to remind us of the former glory of the old ducal palace. Inside the palace, the **Musée historique lorrain** offers a fascinating glimpse of Nancy before Stanislas. Jacques Callot's horrifying engravings of the Thirty Years' War have their antidotes in the more serene paintings of Georges de La Tour.

Stroll back to Place Stanislas through the **Pépinière** gardens. In the north-west corner is Rodin's statue of the painter whom the French know by his pseudonym, Claude Lorrain, and the British as Claude Gellée.

The **Musée des Beaux-Arts** at 3, place Stanislas has a good collection of European art, notably Tintoretto, Ruysdael, Van Goyen, Ribera and Rubens, with the French represented by Delacroix, Courbet, Bonnard and Manet.

ALSACE

One of the reasons the Germans and French have always fought for the possession of this province is very simply that it's such a good place to live. Rich farmland, vineyards and dense forest, with the solidly protective Vosges mountain range on one side and the great Rhine river on the other, make it a nicely self-contained region.

The turmoils of history have left a dialect and an architecture of unmistakably Germanic origin, a political tradition indelibly marked by the French Revolution, and a cuisine that subtly mixes the two. The people seem to feel neither more German nor more French, just Alsatian—the best of both worlds.

Very appropriate for a region which houses the European Parliament in its capital, Strasbourg. Make your base there or in Colmar for excursions into the surrounding wine country and its spotless medieval villages.

Strasbourg

The city has emerged handsome, if not unscathed, from its troubled past. Gothic and Renaissance buildings have been lovingly restored. The *Winstuben* (wine bars) of its old neighbourhoods are hospitable gathering places for university students whose predecessors include Goethe and Bonaparte.

Strasbourg's petite France is a haven of peace in the modern city.

It's a good town for walking the narrow streets, or for taking a **boat cruise** on the river Ill, which divides into two branches to loop the historic centre. Launches start from the Pont Sainte-Madeleine behind the Château des Rohan.

The celebrated asymmetrical silhouette of the Gothic **cathedral**, with its single tower and steeple rising on the north side of its façade, gives your visit an inspiring start.

When Goethe arrived in Strasbourg, he just dropped his bag at his hostel, *Zum Geist*, and rushed off to the cathedral. The stout-limbed can follow his example, and start by climbing the 300-odd stairs to the platform

ALSACE

Alsace or Elsass?
*In the perennial tug-of-war be-
tween French and Germans, the
Alsatians themselves have often
been more concerned with their
own livelihood than espousing one
cause over the other.*

The French base their historical
claim on the lands of their Gallic
ancestors for whom, with Julius
Caesar's blessing, Germany began
on the other side of the Rhine.
The Germans claim the territory
as an inheritance of the German-
controlled Holy Roman Empire
after the death of Charlemagne.

Nominally under the Germans
throughout the Middle Ages,
Alsace was submerged among
hundreds of petty German principalities until it became a vital
buffer zone in the Franco-German
rivalry.

After the butchery of the Thirty
Years' War had halved its population, Alsace was more than happy
to accept French protection—consecrated by Louis XIV's formal
acquisition of Strasbourg in 1681.
The Revolution of 1789 was decisive in injecting the French language and customs into Alsatian
life. The Marseillaise was com-
posed in Strasbourg in 1792 for the
French Army of the Rhine (later it
was adopted by the volunteers of
Marseille). Alsace provided some
of Napoleon's most distinguished
generals—Kléber, Kellermann and
Rapp.

When the Germans seized
Alsace (and Lorraine) in the war
of 1870, thousands of Alsatians
preferred exile in Algeria, or elsewhere in France. But the province
of Elsass prospered under Kaiser
Wilhelm, and not everybody was
delighted in 1918 by the welcome
back to France's chaotic Third
Republic.

The Third Reich helped most
of them change their mind. Under
the Nazis, the French language
was outlawed. Names had to be
changed from Charles to Karl,
Jean to Hans, French-style wreaths
were forbidden in cemeteries,
along with a ban on baguettes and
berets—"this ridiculous headgear,
totally un-Germanic". Alsace was
supposed to disappear as a distinct
cultural entity and become part
of an administrative district of
"Oberrheingau".

This time, there was no reason to
regret the return to French rule,
and today no province waves the
French flag more fervently than
Alsace. But Alsatian workers don't
hesitate to commute across the
border into Germany for the
higher salaries; and the great
two- and three-star restaurants of
Ammerschwihr, Strasbourg and
Illhaeusern are overflowing with
German customers.

just below the steeple for a fine **view** over the city.

Combining the architectural style of Ile-de-France Gothic with Rhenish German sculpture, the church is an apt symbol of Alsatian culture. The original designer, Erwin von Steinbach, began the magnificent pink Vosges sandstone façade in 1277 but only got as far as the splendid **Gallery of Apostles** over the central rose window.

Ulrich von Ensingen, master builder of the great cathedral of Ulm, began construction of the octagon of the north tower in 1399. The graceful openwork spire was added in the 15th century by Johannes Hültz of Cologne. The French Revolutionaries threatened to tear the steeple down, as it offended their principle of equality, but were reassured when a local townsman coiffed it with a patriotic blue, white and red bonnet. All traces of an ugly 19th-century attempt to "balance" it with a second tower have been removed.

The Revolutionaries did destroy most of the cathedral's statues, but 67 were saved (many of the originals now housed in the Musée de l'Œuvre Notre-Dame next door). The central porch is still intact, depicting Jesus' entry into Jerusalem, the Crucifixion and other scenes from the New and Old testaments.

Inside, there's a formidable Flamboyant Gothic **pulpit**, built for preacher Geiler von Kaysersberg to match his terrifying fulminations against the Protestant Reformation. Among the admirable 12th–14th-century **stained-glass windows** in the nave and northern aisle are portraits of medieval German emperors.

The "popular attraction" of the south arm of the transept, approached through the Portail de l'Horloge, is the 19th-century **astronomical clock** in which Death and all kinds of other jolly little figures parade around the dial to announce 12 noon. For some reason, this happens at 12.30 p.m., but in the summer, get there at noon anyway or you won't see a thing. Then after everyone's gone, stay on to see in peace the marvellous 13th-century sculpted **Angel's Pillar** *(Pilier des Anges)*.

A sound and light show *(Son et Lumière)* is held at the cathedral in summertime, in German and in French, recounting 2,000 years of the city's history.

On the Place de la Cathédrale, at the beginning of the Rue Mercière, stands the 13th-century **Pharmacie du Cerf** (Stag Pharmacy), older than the cathedral and reputedly the oldest pharmacy in France. The other venerable house of the square, now a restaurant, is the **Maison Kammerzell**. The ground floor dates from 1467; the beautifully sculpted wooden façade of the superstructure from 1589.

Guardian of the city's medieval and Renaissance treasures, the **Musée de l'Œuvre Notre-Dame** is itself made up of a superb group of 14th-, 16th- and 17th-century houses around a secluded Gothic garden on the Place du Château south of the cathedral. Besides sheltering the most vulnerable of the cathedral's statuary and some stained-glass windows from the earlier 12th-century Romanesque building, the museum has a fine collection of Alsatian medieval painting by Konrad Witz, Martin Schongauer and Hans Baldung Grien.

In the middle of the predominantly Germanic old city centre, the **Château des Rohan,** the classical 18th-century residence of Strasbourg's princes and cardinals, makes an emphatically French statement.

The furniture collection of the château's **Musée des Arts décoratifs** offers interesting comparisons between Parisian and Alsatian aristocratic and bourgeois tastes of the 17th and 18th centuries. But the museum's pride and joy is its great ceramics collection, displaying beside Europe's finest porcelain and faïence the astonishing Rococo craftsmanship of the Strasbourg Hannong family, most remarkably a huge tureen in the form of a turkey. If you didn't get enough of the astronomical clock in the cathedral, you can have a close-up view here of figures from the original 14th-century model.

The château also houses the **Musée des Beaux-Arts**, noteworthy for a Giotto Crucifixion, Raphael's *La Fornarina,* and the unusual sombre realism of Watteau's *L'Ecureuse de cuivre.*

Behind the château, cross the Pont Sainte-Madeleine over the Ill and stroll along the Quai des Bateliers, past the remnants of old Strasbourg, to the bizarre 14th-century **Place du Corbeau** near the bridge of the same name. Continue along the Quai Saint-Nicolas to the **Musée alsacien** at number 23, a group of 16th- and 17th-century houses appropriate to the colourful collections of Alsatian folklore. Kids love the ancient toys and dolls. Instruments of worship and ritual illustrate the life of the province's important Jewish community.

Goethe marvelled at the silhouette of Strasbourg cathedral.

Make your way west to the Pont Saint-Martin for a first view of the city's most enchanting quarter, the old tannery district known as **la petite France**. At a point where the Ill divides into four canals, the tanners shared the waterways with millers and fishermen. Their sturdy gabled houses line the Rue des Dentelles and Rue du Bain-aux-Plantes. The timbered façades and immaculate balconies festooned with geraniums are the most delightful part of Strasbourg's German past. On an uncrowded day, splash out on an expensive meal at one of the waterside restaurants.

The **Barrage Vauban**, remains of the fortifications Vauban built for Louis XIV, spans the Ill to the west. Its roof affords a splendid panoramic **view** across the canals and *la petite France* to that soaring silhouette of the cathedral. At sunset, it makes the perfect finish to a day's walk. But many like to start out from here with an early morning view of the ensemble and then reverse the order of the walk we have proposed, reserving the cathedral for a triumphant climax.

Route du Vin

Sheltered from the cold, damp, north-west winds by the Vosges mountains, the vineyards of Alsace enjoy a microclimate ideal for a majestic white wine

that confidently holds its own against the more internationally renowned wines of Burgundy and Bordeaux.

The vineyards hug the gentle slopes between the Vosges and the Rhine valley along one narrow 120-kilometre (75-mile) strip, stretching from Marlenheim, just west of Strasbourg, down to Thann, outside Mulhouse. The winding "wine route" is well signposted; its charming medieval and 16th-century villages and castles (Haut-Koenigsbourg and Kaysersberg, for example) make it the prettiest vineyard tour in the country, best of all during the October wine harvest.

Tasting and purchases are possible at many of the properties. Inquire at the local *syndicat d'initiative* or Colmar's Maison du vin d'Alsace about specific vineyard tours organized from Obernai and Turckheim, among others.

A walk around the lovely lime-shaded ramparts of **Obernai** will convince you of the perennial prosperity of its wine growers and farmers. Among the elegant, spotless timbered houses of the 16th-century Place du Marché, note the fine **Halle aux blés** (Corn Market) and **hôtel de ville**, as well as the handsome Renaissance **Puits aux six seaux** (Six Pails Well) between the town hall and the parish church.

As famous for its Riesling wines as for its Renaissance houses, **Riquewihr** is almost too "picturesque" to be believed and so too often overcrowded. Cars must be left at the southern end of town. If you can get there on a quiet day, have a good look at the stately **Maison Liebrich** (1535) and **Maison Preiss-Zimmer** (1686) on the main street, Rue du Général-de-Gaulle. Just before you reach the main gate and town symbol, the 13th-century **Dolder**, turn off to the right to take a peep at the little **ghetto** in the wooden-galleried Cour des Juifs. For people who like instruments of torture, there is also a medieval chamber of horrors in the **Tour des Voleurs** (Thieves' Tower).

Nestling at the foot of its ruined castle, the pretty medieval town of **Kaysersberg** is famous as the birthplace of the Nobel Peace Prize winner Dr. Albert Schweitzer (1875–1965). His parents' house has become the **Centre culturel Schweitzer** (124, rue du Général-de-Gaulle) devoted to the life of the humanitarian, who was also a great performer of Bach's organ works. The parish church, **Eglise Sainte-Croix**, is worth a visit for its splendid 16th-century **altarpiece** by Jean Bongartz of Colmar. It is a polychrome sculpted wooden triptych of 18 panels portraying in moving detail the last days of

Jesus. A 10-minute walk up the wooded hill to the **castle tower** gives you a delightful view of the town and surrounding valley of the Weiss river.

To flee the madding crowds, seek out the unspoiled little town of **Turckheim**, epitome of the shiny bright Alsatian village. Its 16th- and 17th-century charm is preserved within a triangular rampart.

Colmar

Some people make a pilgrimage to this town just to visit the great Musée d'Unterlinden. But the town itself, with a miraculously preserved old city centre, has much else to offer and makes a quieter alternative to Strasbourg as a base for your vineyard excursion.

Converted from a 13th-century convent of Dominican nuns, the **Musée d'Unterlinden** provides the perfect setting for one of the world's undisputed masterpieces of religious art, Matthias Grünewald's awe-inspiring **Issenheim Altarpiece,** displayed in the chapel. Created for the Issenheim convent of Saint Anthony between 1512 and 1516, the altarpiece originally folded out in three panels which are now mounted for exhibition in separate sections.

To appreciate the climactic impact of the whole work, view it in the reverse order, starting at the far end with the stately sculpted polychrome wooden panel of Saints Augustine, Antony and Jerome, carved by Niklaus Hagenauer. The first of Grünewald's painted panels depicts on one side the conversion and temptation of Anthony and, on the other, the birth of Jesus and a chorus of angels. The second panel is devoted to the Annunciation and Resurrection and, on the reverse side, what is perhaps the most pain-filled and exalted Crucifixion ever realized. Grünewald's illuminated colour and uncompromising realism achieve an almost terrifying emotional intensity.

When you've recovered your composure, be sure to see the superb altarpiece of Martin Schongauer, Hans Holbein's portrait of a woman and, a proud new acquisition, Lucas Cranach's exquisite *Mélancolie*. The modern collection of Braque, Bonnard and Picasso offers an interesting counterpoint.

The old town centre is closed to traffic. Keep an eye open for the many handsome gabled houses of the Renaissance period: the **Ancienne Douane** (Old Customs House, Grand-Rue), **Maison des Arcades** (Grand-Rue), **Maison Pfister** (Rue des Marchands) and **Maison des Têtes** (Rue des Têtes).

As soon as a town has a couple of canals with quaint bridges over them, likely as not the neighbourhood will be called Little Venice. Colmar is no exception. Its **petite Venise** is south of the Old Town. From the Saint-Pierre bridge, you have a lovely view of its flowery banks, weeping willows and timbered houses, with the tower of Saint Martin's church in the distance, none of it remotely Venetian but still very pretty. The district on the opposite bank of the river was once a fortified enclave, inhabited mainly by market gardeners who used to sell their wares from barges on the river. It holds on to its original, colourful name of *Krutenau* (Vegetable Waterway).

Because it was recently vandalized, the **Eglise des Dominicains** is open only in the summer months, when it exhibits its great treasure (stolen and recently recovered), Martin Schongauer's altar-painting *Vierge au buisson de roses* (Madonna in the Rose Bower). Take a look, too, at the remarkable 14th- and 15th-century **stained-glass windows**.

Americans may be pleased to note that Colmar is the birthplace of Auguste Bartholdi, designer of the Statue of Liberty. His 17th-century house (30, rue des Marchands) is now the **Musée Bartholdi**, displaying his models and drawings. His statue of Napoleon's general Jean Rapp, another local boy, can be seen on the Place Rapp.

BURGUNDY

Burgundy has a marvellous variety of attractions: the wines, of course, and the fine gastronomy that goes with them, lazy days on the Canal de Bourgogne drifting past green meadows, the grand ducal palace of Dijon, its museums and its mustard.

While the Ile-de-France is the cradle of the great Gothic cathedrals, the major jewels of French Romanesque architecture

Luckily for bikers, Burgundy's vineyards are not too hilly.

are to be found in Burgundy, from Vézelay to Autun and south to the noble ruins of Cluny. The special joys of Burgundy are in the tiny villages, some of which we'll tell you about, but more that you'll be delighted to discover for yourself. Their manor farms and mill-houses, exquisite parish churches and open-air stone laundries *(lavoirs)* down by the stream are the rural soul of France.

If you're driving down from Paris, you'll get the best out of Burgundy by leaving the *autoroute* at the Courtenay or Auxerre exit and touring the rest of the way on the perfectly good, but above all beautiful secondary roads. The TGV goes through to Montbard, Dijon and Beaune. Auxerre makes a good stop for your first excursions into the Burgundy interior, particularly if you want to stock up for a picnic. It is the main distribution point for the famous Chablis white wines, but you may prefer to drive out to the vineyards in delightful undulating country east of the *autoroute*.

Vallée du Serein

This is just one of a score of lazy backroad excursions you can make through northern Burgundy's meandering green valleys. Either cutting across from Tonnerre or starting out from the village of Chablis, follow the

---

The Good, the Bad and the Ugly
From 1363 to 1477, the dukes of Burgundy amassed great wealth and power, to the envy of most of the kings of Europe, but what they really liked was fancy nicknames.

Philippe le Hardi (the Bold) won his when, at the age of 14, he slapped an English soldier in the face for insulting the king of France, Philippe's father. He was equally slap-happy with the enormous dowry he got from his wife Marguerite de Flandres, bringing the greatest Flemish artists to his court, covering himself in gold, silver, jewels and ostrich feathers and, 20 years before his death, ordering the most magnificent tomb in France. He died broke and his sons had to hock the family silver to pay for the funeral.

Jean sans Peur, notoriously ugly but *Fearless*, earned his name by slaughtering Turks, but it's more difficult to explain what, from a French point of view, was so *Good* about *Philippe le Bon*, who sold Joan of Arc to the English for 10,000 pieces of gold.

The last of the four great dukes got the name he deserved. He sought to consolidate the veritable empire that the family estates had become by invading Lorraine to link up Burgundy and Franche-Comté with possessions in Luxembourg, Picardy, Flanders and Holland. Proclaiming himself a latter-day Alexander the Great, he lost everything at the Siege of Nancy and went down in history as *Charles le Téméraire*—the *Fool-hardy*.

---

little Serein river, tributary of the Yonne, towards Avallon.

Notice as you go the massive farmhouses, veritable fortresses, characteristically roofed with *laves*, flat volcanic-stone tiles, that add to the landscape a marvellous patina of colour and texture. The finely arched front doors are often at the top of a sturdy staircase over the street-level cellar. You can spot, set in the stone walls, little sculpted heads of angels or demons, floral motifs or the scallop shell *(coquille Saint-Jacques)* marking the route of medieval pilgrims.

Noyers is a fortified medieval village with 16 towers in its ramparts. Many of its timbered and gabled houses date back to the 14th and 15th centuries, particularly on the Place de l'Hôtel-de-Ville and the Rue du Poids-du-Roy. From the little Renaissance church, there's a pretty view over the winding river.

At **L'Isle-sur-Serein**, the river divides momentarily to encircle the tranquil little town and the ruins of its 15th-century château.

Leave the river briefly to loop east around Talcy and its Romanesque church and the 13th-century château of Thizy, before ending the excursion at **Montréal**. This medieval town boasts a Gothic church with a Renaissance interior; note the carved oak choir stalls and Nottingham alabaster altarpiece.

Abbaye de Fontenay

This venerable Cistercian abbey, 6 kilometres (4 miles) east of TGV-station Montbard, turns its back on the world, standing behind high walls in a lovely valley at the edge of a forest. The abbey has been rescued from its humiliating 19th-century conversion into a paper-mill, and the cloisters present once more the calm and simplicity that were the ideals of its 12th-century founder, Saint Bernard de Clairvaux.

As you go through the gate decorated with the arms of the Cistercian order, you'll notice a niche for a guard dog below the staircase. On the right is an austere hostel and chapel for the few pilgrims that passed this way, and beyond it is the forge of the hard-working Cistercians. Left of the entrance is the monks' bakery and an imposing pigeon loft.

Paid for by Bishop Everard of Norwich, for whom Fontenay was a refuge from the hostility of Henry II of England, the **abbey church** has a sober unadorned beauty—no bell-tower, as there were no distant faithful to be called to worship, but harmonious proportions in the interior, and fine acoustics because Saint Bernard was a great lover of music. A serene statue of the Virgin Mary (13th century) stands in the north arm of the transept.

Vézelay

An exquisite centre of spirituality in a beautiful rustic setting, home of one of the major churches on the pilgrims' route from Germany and the Netherlands to Santiago de Compostela in Spain, Vézelay is today the target of new pilgrims—tourists in search of quintessential Burgundy.

If you're travelling at high season, this is one of those places where you should make a really early start to get in ahead of the crowd.

To recapture something of the experience of the medieval pilgrim, park your car (or get out of the bus) down at the Place du Champ-de-Foire. Pass through the turreted Porte Neuve and follow the **Promenade des Fossés** along the ancient ramparts lined with walnut trees. At the Porte Sainte-Croix, you have a fine view over the Cure river valley and the path which leads to the place where, in 1146, Saint Bernard exhorted King Louis VII to lead the French on the Second Crusade. It was also the starting point of the Third Crusade in 1190, when England's Richard the Lion-Heart joined forces with Philippe Auguste.

The **Basilique Sainte-Madeleine**, originally under the obedience of Cluny and repository of the relics of Mary Magdalen, remains a masterly achievement of French Romanesque architecture, despite suffering from natural disasters, wars and revolution. The restorations of Viollet-le-Duc have maintained its majestic harmony.

The bizarre monsters sculpted at Autun cathedral were supposed to scare believers away from sin.

The narthex, or entrance hall to the nave, is crowned by a magnificent sculpted **tympanum** of Jesus enthroned after the Resurrection, preaching his message to the Apostles. On the central supporting pillar is a statue of John the Baptist, beheaded not by Herod but by Huguenot vandals.

The nave is a wonder of light and lofty proportions, enhanced by the luminous beige stone and splendid ribbed vaulting. In contrast to the exalted quality of the tympanum's sculpture, the robust carvings of the **capitals** in the nave are lively and down-to-earth, making a clearly popular appeal to the church's pilgrims. The themes are from the Bible and the legends of the saints. Beside David and Goliath, Daniel in the Lion's Den, the building of Noah's Ark, one curious sculpture shows Saint Eugenia, tonsured and disguised as a monk, opening her robe to convince a sceptical friar that she's a woman. Although the church is dedicated to Mary Magdalen, she is surprisingly absent from the sculpture.

On the tree-shaded **terrace** beyond the church, relax on one of the benches and enjoy the view over the forested plateau of the Morvan. Then explore the old houses, wells and courtyards in the town's narrow lanes leading back down to the Place du Champ-de-Foire.

Autun

At the other end of the densely wooded Morvan plateau, Autun's 12th-century **Cathédrale Saint-Lazare** makes a natural point of comparison with Vézelay's Basilique Sainte-Madeleine.

While the Autun **tympanum** may lack the elevated spiritual impact of its counterpart at Vézelay, its rich carving of Jesus presiding at the Last Judgment is full of vitality. On the left, you see the happy few being welcomed by Peter. Immediately to the right of Jesus is the weighing of the souls, with Saint Michael trying to stop Satan cheating. On the far right, a cauldron is boiling a few of the unlucky ones.

Below Jesus' feet is a Latin inscription suggesting the tympanum to be the work of one man, Gislebertus (Gilbert). It says: "Gilbert did this. May such terror terrify those in thrall to earthly error, for the horror of these images tells what awaits them."

Gilbert is also believed to have carved the superb **capitals** on the pillars of the nave and aisles. Some of the more fragile pieces are exhibited in an upstairs **chapter room**, worth a visit for a close-up view of his magnificent workmanship. The sculpture places a graphic emphasis on the ugliness of sin (hanging of Judas, devil tempting Jesus) and the simple beauty of virtue (flight to Egypt or Mary Magdalen).

The nearby **Musée Rolin** shows a fine collection of Burgundian and Flemish sculpture and painting. The museum is partly housed in the elegant 15th-century mansion of Nicolas Rolin, a wealthy dignitary and benefactor of the famous Hôtel-Dieu at Beaune (see p. 106).

Dijon

Dijon is Burgundy's stately capital. It's the ideal gateway for the vineyards to the south and a drive around the pretty Val-Suzon to the north. It's also a starting point for barge cruises on the Canal de Bourgogne (see p. 41).

Not the least of the town's attractions is the shopping centre around the Place Darcy and Rue de la Liberté where you can hunt for such regional delicacies as the famous mustards, *pain d'épices* (gingerbread) and *cassis*, the blackcurrant liqueur that turns an ordinary white wine into a refreshing *kir*. For wines other than your immediate picnic needs, you're better off waiting for your tour of the vineyards or the wider selection available at Beaune.

To evoke the town's past glories, you must head for the semi-circular Place de la Libération (formerly Place Royale),

designed by Jules Hardouin-Mansart, architect of the Château de Versailles. The elegant 17th- and 18th-century façades of the **Palais des Ducs** conceal the Renaissance structures of the dukes' heyday, but many of their treasures remain to be seen in the interior, as part of the **Musée des Beaux-Arts**.

You get a notion of the magnificence of Burgundian court life by starting your visit at the **ducal kitchens**, built in 1435. Imagine the banquets prepared in the six huge walk-in cooking hearths, blackened now by a couple of centuries of barbecue smoke, arching over in a soaring Gothic vault into the central ventilation.

The ground-floor rooms of the museum have a model of the old palace and a collection of Burgundian sculpture from the 15th century to the present day. In the upstairs painting galleries, the dukes' close links with the Flemish masters of their day are illustrated by the fine *Nativité* of the anonymous Maître de Flémalle and Dierick Bouts' *Tête de Christ*. The collection also includes important works by Rubens, Frans Hals, Veronese, Konrad Witz and Martin Schongauer.

But the museum's greatest treasures are the dukes' tombs in the **Salle des gardes** (brought there from the Charterhouse of

There's a fortune in these fingers checking progress at the Clos de Vougeot vineyards.

Champmol, destroyed in the Revolution). It took the artists Jean de Marville, Claus Sluter and Claus de Werve 26 years (1385 to 1411) to complete the intricate marble and alabaster sculpture for the **mausoleum of Philippe le Hardi**. On the sides of the tomb bearing the recumbent statue of the duke are carved 41 marvellously expressive figures of mourners cloaked in monastic capes, variously praying, meditating, lamenting. The double tomb of Jean sans Peur and wife Marguerite de Bavière is also lavishly sculpted, but more stylized.

Near the tombs is Rogier van der Weyden's portrait of the third great duke, Philippe le Bon with the Golden Fleece, symbol of the chivalrous order he founded in 1429.

North of the palace, along the Rue de la Chouette and Rue Verrerie, you'll find some attractive late Gothic and Renaissance houses with picturesque inner courtyards, transformed into antique shops. In the Rue des Forges, note the **Hôtel Chambellan** at number 34 and the **Hôtel Aubriot** at number 40, home of the Provost of Paris who built the accursed Bastille prison.

Côte d'Or

The kingdom of wine, the power of legend. For some people, this destination is *the* reason for coming to France.

Delightful as the Burgundy vineyards may be, the landscape and villages of some other *routes des vins* may be considered prettier—Alsace, for instance. And other wine growers, such as those around Bordeaux, may have more handsome châteaux.

But none can compose a true connoisseur's poem like this, just by citing a few names on the map.

First verse, strictly red wine, *Côte de Nuits*: Gevrey-Chambertin, Chambolle-Musigny, Vougeot, Vosne-Romanée, Nuits-Saint-Georges. Second verse, where the whites follow the reds, *Côte de Beaune*: Aloxe-Corton, Beaune, Pommard, Volnay, Meursault, Puligny-Montrachet, Chassagne-Montrachet, Santenay. The two together make up the *Côte d'Or*, the most expensive and delicious poem in the world.

From Dijon down to Santenay, the Côte d'Or is just 60 kilometres (37 miles) long. Nothing to do with "coast", "côte" here means the hillside. As you drive south from Dijon, be sure to get off the main road, N 74, on to the parallel D 122, signposted as

Route des grands crus (Route of the great vintages), rejoining the N 74 at Vougeot.

You may notice a sign at the edge of the vineyards: "*Grappillage interdit*", which means just what it says—don't pinch the grapes (referring more particularly to those you might think were free for all, left hanging at the end of the harvest). Don't even try: Burgundians are ardent hunters.

Many of the famous vineyards are open to visitors, but tasting is strictly for serious customers with the clear intention of buying. The village of **Gevrey-Chambertin** makes a good first stop. The medieval château shelters the wine harvest in its great cellars. But the best cellars open to the public are in the château at **Clos de Vougeot**, owned by the Cistercian monks until the Revolution, now the property of the Chevaliers du Tastevin (fraternity of wine tasters). The grand old vats and winepresses are worth the visit, and the guides will tell you more than you ever wanted to know about wine.

For the beginner (and most others, too), **Beaune** is the place to buy. It's the centre of the industry, and practically all the great wines are represented here. You won't get a better bargain at the vineyard unless you know the owner. A little **Musée du Vin**

(Rue d'Enfer) tells the history of wine-making, with all its paraphernalia, from Roman times to the present day.

Of more artistic interest, the **Hôtel-Dieu** is a beautifully preserved 15th-century hospital (only recently converted to an old folks' home) founded by Chancellor Nicolas Rolin. Be sure to see the masterpiece of Flemish art commissioned by Rolin for the hospital chapel, Rogier van der Weyden's **altarpiece** of the Last Judgment, now on display in the museum, along with tapestries that adorned the walls of the unheated hospital wards to keep the patients warm.

Cluny

The abbey that today stands in ruin at the southern tip of Burgundy ruled its medieval world the way Louis XIV's Versailles dominated 17th-century France. Imagine the Sun King's palace reduced to rubble, with a few isolated but noble structures left standing to bear the weight of the vanished splendour, and you can appreciate something of the exquisite melancholy that rises from the stones of Cluny.

The 12th-century **Abbatiale Saint-Pierre-et-Saint-Paul** was the biggest church in Christendom until the completion of Saint Peter's in Rome in the 17th century. Only the right arm of one of the two transepts and the octagonal bell-tower, the **Clocher de l'Eau-Bénite**, remain. But even this truncated edifice imposes its grandeur, and Cluny's excellent young guides (English-speaking in summer)

help us conceive the rest. There used to be five naves, two transepts, five bell-towers, 225 choir stalls.

The elegant classical 18th-century **cloisters** make a poignant contrast with the Romanesque church.

The 13th-century **granary**, beside an even older flour mill, has been turned into an admirable **museum** for the abbey's sculpted

The rich decoration of the old Hôtel-Dieu hospital testifies to Beaune's historic prosperity.

capitals displayed on reconstructed pillars.

To see some of Cluny's impact on the surrounding countryside, visit a few of the villages whose Romanesque churches were built by Cluny's architects and craftsmen: among them, Saint-Vincent-des-Prés, Taizé, Berzé-la-Ville and Malay, each a little gem.

The shell of its ancient abbey is all that's left of Cluny's mighty monastic empire.

JURA

The Jura mountains cover several eastern *départements* making up the region of Franche-Comté. The area relies on the geography of its rampart-like mountains and dense pine forests to stay remote and blessedly unspoiled for nature-lovers.

Besançon

A useful base for your excursions, the capital of Franche-Comté has an attractive town centre around the pedestrian zone of the **Grande-Rue**.

The **Musée des Beaux-Arts** (Place de la Révolution) claims to be the oldest in France (1694). Of the Italian paintings, Bellini's *L'Ivresse de Noé* (Drunkenness of Noah) and Giordano's *Philosophe cynique* are outstanding. Look, too, for Cranach's *Lucrèce* and *Le Repos de Diane* and fine French works by Ingres, Courbet and Bonnard.

Arc-et-Senans

The 18th-century **Saline Royale** (saltworks), now abandoned, is surely one of the most elegant factories in the world, in fact the nucleus of a utopian city conceived by Claude-Nicolas Ledoux. He had the outlandish idea of making working conditions for the salt-labourers pleasant. In green surroundings, the buildings of the saltworks are set in a semicircle around administrative offices, each with easy access to the other and all in simple classical style.

A **museum** is devoted to Ledoux's plans, models and avant-garde theories, and seminars are held on urban and industrial planning for the future.

The Loue river inspired Gustave Courbet, but modern art adorns the Arc-et-Senans saltworks.

Vallée de la Loue

A favourite excursion is to trace the Loue river and its tributary, the Lison, back to their cascading **sources** through landscapes that inspired the paintings of Gustave Courbet.

His home town was **Ornans**. Stand on the Grand Pont for the celebrated view of the town's strange old timbered houses reflected in the calm waters of the

river. Close by the bridge is the **Musée Courbet** in the artist's house, with the old walking stick depicted in his famous *Bonjour monsieur Courbet*.

Les Reculées

These horseshoe-shaped valleys nestle like narrow amphitheatres against abrupt rocky cliffs, making rewarding destinations for a day's hike.

One of the best is the **Cirque de Baume**, between Lons-le-Saunier and Baume-les-Messieurs. South-east of Arbois, the **Reculée des Planches** takes you to the fairytale waterfalls of the Cuisance and ends at the dramatic **Cirque du Fer à Cheval.** By then you'll be ready to sample some heady Arbois wine; try the *vin jaune* with a chunk of Comté cheese.

NORTH-WEST

The sea played an important role in the history of the north-western corner of France. The Scandinavians came in their long-ships, landing on the Normandy coast and penetrating as far as Angers and Tours in the Loire Valley. Brittany has ever been a seafaring province, populated by Celts fleeing from the Anglo-Saxons across the Channel.

Today, Normandy offers a

Getting the Ants Out of Their Pants
It took a long time to stop the Normans (Norsemen, or Northmen) moving around. The Scandinavian seamen made their first isolated incursions into France while exploring the northern Atlantic in the 2nd and 3rd centuries. But they found nothing to hold their attention until prosperous Christians along the Seine valley began building monasteries and churches with a treasure of gold, silver and jewels.

In 820, the Norsemen staged their first major invasion in their dragon-headed longships, subsequently plundering their way up the river to Paris. Masters of guerrilla warfare and ambush, they had horses aboard for lightning raids into the interior. Chartres was one of their prime targets. To cut his losses, the French king Charles le Simple had the simple idea in 911 of giving these madcaps some land to settle down on: the Duchy of Normandy.

Duke Rollo and his men made their capital at Rouen. They converted to Christianity and happily set about organizing towns and farms and trade, just like any other civilized people. Those who couldn't take to the sedentary life went off on Crusades to the Holy Land, to devote their bloodthirsty pillaging and pirating to a Good Cause.

Conquest and exploration, often amazingly far from home, were always a useful safety valve for the Normans' natural aggressive energies: England and Sicily in the 11th century, Sierra Leone in 1364, Brazil in 1503, Canada in 1506, Florida in 1563. Chicagoans to this day honour the passage of a great sailor from Rouen: the financial district of the Middle West's "Wall Street" bears the name of La Salle, who passed that way on his exploration of Lake Michigan and the Mississippi River in 1682.

patchwork landscape of rich green hedgerowed farmland, and a rich dairy cuisine to go with it; lazy days at the elegant old seaside resorts; the timeless wonder of the Mont-Saint-Michel; the monumental reminders of medieval Norman warriors at Bayeux and the latterday liberators of World War II on the D-Day beaches.

Brittany's is a wilder, less civilized countryside, with a jagged coastline to match. Its oysters and mussels are as fresh as the sea breezes, its people as weatherbeaten as their granite houses. But nestling in the hollows of the windswept heaths are havens of pious calm among the parish

No French farmer is as cheerful as the prosperous Normandy breed.

closes, and you'll find plenty of peaceful sandy beaches in sheltered coves along the otherwise buffeted coastline.

From its aristocratic past, the Loire Valley has preserved not only its countless châteaux. The good life is there in abundance for anyone with the leisure to enjoy it. Its wines are more than respectable accompaniments for the game from the forests of Sologne and the freshwater fish of the Loire's tributaries.

NORMANDY

The region divides into an eastern half, Haute-Normandie, along the Seine valley, similar in scenery to the Ile-de-France; and the more rugged Basse-Normandie to the west, more akin to neighbouring Brittany. Vast expanses are cultivated for agribusiness; the more traditional orchards and lush meadowland cattle pastures produce strong cider and pungent cheeses.

The settled, tranquil existence of the solid bourgeoisie of Rouen or Caen and the even more solid farmers surrounding them makes you wonder whether the tumultuous history of their murdering, raping, pillaging ancestors isn't all a jolly myth.

Cantering at sunset on Normandy's Channel coast, the horse is king.

114

Dieppe

France's oldest seaside resort and the closest beach to Paris is a popular gateway to Normandy for those crossing the English Channel from Newhaven. To stretch your legs before starting out on the road, cross the drawbridge from the ferry port to the **port de pêche** (fishing port). At the early morning market, the phlegmatic Dieppois fishermen are as lively as they ever get.

The **Musée de Dieppe**, in a 15th-century château (Rue de Chastes), has a good collection of model ships and some fine scrimshaw, sculptures in ivory, dating from the 18th century when elephant tusks were a major import from Africa and Asia.

The courageous but abortive Canadian raid on Dieppe in World War II is commemorated in the **Musée de la guerre et du raid du 19 août 1942**, 2 kilometres (about 1 mile) west of town on the D 75 road (route de Pourville).

Rouen

The Norman capital's historic civic pride breathes from every stone, every timber frame lovingly restored or reconstructed after the crippling bomb damage of 1944. After all, this is the ancient centre of Normandy's thriving textile industry, and the place of Joan of Arc's martyrdom—a symbol of national resistance to tyranny.

Hugging a loop in the Seine, the town did draw at least one advantage from the war—the factories on the left bank were destroyed, leaving room for a modern residential area. The industries were rebuilt on the outskirts. On the right bank, the charming medieval and Renaissance centre around the cathedral has been renovated and reserved for pedestrians.

Start your walk, not at the cathedral, but at the western end of the historic district, on the **Place du Vieux-Marché**. Old and new Rouen come together around the bright and airy market halls and the attractive modern **Eglise Sainte-Jeanne-d'Arc**. Nearby is a monument to mark the spot where Joan was burned at the stake in 1431. Some stones have been excavated from the rostrum of her judges. Only a few Frenchmen still bear a grudge against the British, but ironic remarks should be avoided—the French take their freedom fighters seriously. Inside the church are some fine 16th-century **stained-glass windows** salvaged from an older church bombed in 1944.

Leading east from the market is Rouen's most celebrated street, the **Rue du Gros-Horloge**, now as always the city's bustling commercial centre. Its timber-framed houses of the 15th, 16th and 17th centuries are splendid examples of sturdy Norman architecture, achieving a very pleasing irregularity in the way the plaster is set in oblique forms between the solid oak posts and collar beams supporting the balconies. The elegant Renaissance arched clock-tower of the **Gros Horloge** is the town's emblem, its Eiffel Tower. The ornamental gilded clock face has only one hand, for the hours.

Beside the clock is a 14th-century belfry which still rings its bell at 9 p.m., time of the old curfew. Take the spiral staircase to the roof for a lovely view of the city and its circle of hills around the Seine valley.

East of the Gros Horloge stands the great **cathedral**, made famous in the modern age by Claude Monet's many Impressionist studies of its façade. The asymmetry of the two towers embracing the delicate tracery of the slender spires creates a highly original silhouette among France's best-loved cathedrals.

The façade offers a remarkably harmonious anthology of Gothic architecture. The north tower, **Tour Saint-Romain**, has the sober simplicity of the cathedral's early Gothic beginnings in the 12th century, while the taller, more elaborate south tower, **Tour de Beurre**, is Flamboyant Gothic of the 15th century. According to local belief, this "Butter Tower" was paid for by Catholic burghers in exchange for the privilege of eating good Normandy butter during Lent. The austerely sculpted porches flanking the main entrance are from the early period, and the more ornamental elongated central porch and the gabled upper windows were added in the 15th and 16th centuries. The main spire is neo-Gothic of the 19th century.

The rather severe interior contrasts with the elaborate exterior, but the impact of the double-storeyed nave is lightened by the tall arches of the choir. In the Chapelle de la Vierge beyond the choir is the monumental Renaissance **tomb of the Cardinals of Amboise**, with superbly sculpted allegories of the cardinal virtues. On the south side of the choir is the more modest tomb of the most heroic of medieval English kings, portrayed recumbent above the inscription in Latin: "Here is buried the heart of King Richard of England, known as the Lion-Hearted."

Behind the cathedral, cross over the Rue de la République to the 15th-century **Eglise Saint-Maclou**, the richest example of Flamboyant Gothic in the country. Note the masterful Renaissance carving of the oak doors on the central and north portals.

Sweet gentility at Cabourg, a moment of calm on Trouville beach.

In the interior, the same exuberant artistry can be admired in the sculpted wood **organ frame** and the stone tracery of the **spiral staircase**.

Turn north on **Rue Damiette**, graced by some of the town's handsomest old houses. The street leads to the elegant 14th-century Gothic abbey church, **Abbatiale Saint-Ouen**, best observed from the little park east of the chancel and its splendid flying buttresses.

The last great monument of the old town, in the Rue aux Juifs, is the grand **Palais de Justice**, a jewel of Renaissance and Flamboyant Gothic architecture built on the site of the medieval ghetto. Recent excavations uncovered a 12th-century

synagogue (visits by arrangement with the Office de tourisme, Place de la Cathédrale).

The prosperous town has a well-endowed **Musée des Beaux-Arts** (Square Verdrel), with important works by Velázquez, Caravaggio, Perugino, Veronese and Rubens. French artists include François Clouet, Delacroix and a series of dramatic paintings of horses by the Rouen-born Géricault.

Jumièges

The D 982 leading west from Rouen is the beginning of the **Route des Abbayes** that winds through woodland and meadows around the medieval Norman abbeys—most of them enjoying their heyday under William the Conqueror—at Saint-Martin-de-Boscherville, Jumièges, Saint-Wandrille, Le Bec-Hellouin and Caen, culminating in their masterpiece, the Mont-Saint-Michel.

Among them, the grandiose ruins of the **abbey** of Jumièges occupy a special, inevitably romantic place. The white granite shells of its two churches, the Romanesque Notre-Dame and smaller Gothic Saint-Pierre, with trees and grass growing in and around the nave and chancel, survive their troubled end with moving dignity.

Duke William returned from his conquest of England to attend the consecration of Notre-Dame in 1067. Seven centuries later, the Benedictine monastery was disbanded by the Revolution, and the buildings were blown up with explosives by a local wood merchant who had bought them cut-price in an auction. But the sturdy edifices resisted total destruction and are still dominated by Notre-Dame's two soaring square towers (minus their original spires).

Honfleur

On the Seine estuary, this pretty little port has witnessed the beginning of nearly all of Normandy's great seafaring adventures—and is still a mecca for sailing-enthusiasts. Towering over the sheltered yachting harbour of the **Vieux Bassin**, the tall slate- and timber-façaded houses gleam in the sun or, even more striking, glisten in a thunderstorm. Explore the old shipbuilders' quarter along the **Rue Haute** run-ning west from the Lieutenance, 16th-century remains of the royal governor's house at the harbour mouth.

Deauville

Cleverly blending old-fashioned elegance with modern comforts, the most prosperous of Normandy's seaside resorts is also the most expensive. But even if your budget doesn't extend to one of those seafront *palaces*, as the French call their luxury hotels, stop off on the wooden promenade of the celebrated **planches** for some of the most amusing people-watching in France. This is where a company director takes his secretary for weekend business conferences and runs into his wife with the chairman of the board. The white sandy **beach** with its colourful canvas sun shelters is a delight and the swimming perfectly good, but amazingly few people turn away from the spectacle on the *planches* long enough to go into the water.

Horse-lovers come for the summer racing, flat and steeple, and the prestigious yearling sale. What they win on the racing, they lose at the casino. The tennis and golf are first class; yachtsmen should bear in mind a Deauville proverb: if you can see the port of Le Havre, it will rain in the afternoon, and if you can't, it's already raining.

Côte Fleurie

Between the estuaries of the Touques and Dives rivers, 20 kilometres (12 miles) of sandy beaches, handsome villas and beautifully weather-beaten old hotels have great appeal for nostalgics of Napoleon III's Second Empire and the *Belle Epoque* of the 1900s.

The oldest of this coast's resorts, **Trouville** is now a slightly down-market Deauville, but just as lively, with an excellent beach where people seem less frightened of swimming, and bistrots on the port serving much better seafood.

The charm of **Houlgate** is in the trees and flowers of its gardens and the fine sands of its beach. Take the long walk at low tide east to the cliffs of the **Vaches Noires** (Black Cows).

Cabourg is the most stately of the old resorts. Take tea at least at its splendid **Grand Hôtel**, a true national shrine in which Marcel Proust wrote part of his *A la recherche du temps perdu*. It is the custom to fall asleep over a leather-bound copy in your deckchair.

Across the river is the little town of **Dives-sur-Mer** where, as they like to remind English visitors, William embarked in 1066. To rub it in, there's a Rue d'Hastings and a list of the Conqueror's companions on a wall of the parish church.

Pays d'Auge

A delightful excursion inland from either end of the Côte Fleurie takes you to the very essence of the popular image of Normandy, its orchards, rolling green valleys and massive timbered manor houses, the land where the apples become cider and Calvados and the dairies churn out the pungent, creamy Camembert, Livarot and Pont-l'Evêque.

You can buy the best Camembert, for instance (labelled VCN, *Véritable Camembert de Normandie*) at the Monday-morning market in **Vimoutiers**, 55 kilometres (35 miles) south of Deauville. But local tourist offices will guide you to farms where you can sample and buy the regional cheeses on the spot—more fun than in the unexceptional towns of Camembert, Pont-l'Evêque and Livarot themselves. Drivers should be wary of the cider—in longer draughts, it can pack as much punch as the Calvados.

Caen

Little remains of Caen's historic centre, but its good hotels and excellent seafood restaurants make it, with Bayeux, a useful starting-point for visits to the D-Day beaches.

Caen was the first major objective of the D-Day landings. It took two months to capture and

This Norman manor has seen better days, but the cows seem clearly contented.

was devastated by Allied bombs and the shells of the Germans as they retreated.

Luckily, the noble silhouette of the **Abbaye aux Hommes** has survived (best seen from the Place Louis-Guillouard). Its church, **Eglise Saint-Etienne**, harmoniously combining Ro-manesque towers and nave with Gothic steeples, choir and chancel, was begun in the momentous year of 1066, and William the Conqueror made its first abbot his archbishop of Canterbury. The elegant 18th-century monastery buildings have now become the town hall.

The remains of William's 11th-century castle house an excellent collection of European painting in the town's **Musée des**

Beaux-Arts. Highlights include Poussin's *Mort d'Adonis*, Tiepolo's *Ecce Homo*, Veronese's *Tentation de saint Antoine* and Rubens' *Abraham et Melchisédech*. The nearby **Musée de Normandie** makes a handsome introduction to regional folklore.

Bayeux

Proudly the first French town to be liberated in World War II, the day after D-Day, Bayeux was blessedly preserved from destruction. Its Gothic cathedral dominates a charming **old town** *(vieille ville)* of medieval and Renaissance houses on the Rue Saint-Martin, Rue Saint-Malo and Rue Bourbesneur.

But the town's most cherished treasure is the magnificent **Bayeux Tapestry** (or more correctly *embroidery*) created for Bayeux Cathedral in 1077 to tell the story of Duke William's conquest of England. It is lovingly mounted in the Centre Guillaume-le-Conquérant (Rue de Nesmond) and accompanied by a fascinating film (in an English and French version) explaining the work's historic background.

No dry piece of obscure medieval decoration, the beautifully coloured tapestry gives a vivid and often humorous picture of life at William's court, with insights into medieval cooking, lovemaking and the careful preparations for war. These and the climactic Battle of Hastings are depicted with all the exciting action and violence of a modern adventure film, with a cast of 626 characters, 202 horses, 55 dogs and 505 other animals.

Adding insult to injury, it was a group of defeated Anglo-Saxon artisans who had to do the wool-on-linen embroidery, 70 metres (230 feet) long and 50 centimetres (20 inches) high, under the supervision of William's half-brother, Odon de Conteville, Bishop of Bayeux.

Getting it in the Eye
The story told in the tapestry from the Norman point of view may come as a bit of a shock to the average patriotic British schoolchild. English King Harold is shown as a treacherous weakling who cheated noble, generous William out of the throne promised him by King Edward the Confessor.

Some scenes to watch out for: a unique view of Mont-Saint-Michel without, of course, its later Gothic additions (panel 17); Halley's Comet (April 1066) flies over the newly crowned Harold: a bad omen (panels 32–33); Battle of Hastings, William raises his visor to reassure his men that he's still alive (panels 53–55); Harold Rex Interfectus Est—Harold gets it in the eye (panel 57).

D-Day Beaches

Until June 6, 1944, the peaceful stretch of coast west of Cabourg, from Ouistreham to the Cotentin peninsula, was known simply as the Côte du Calvados, a flat, undramatic shoreline broken by a few unspectacular chalk cliffs and sand dunes. Then, at 6.30 a.m. came the first of a fleet of 4,266 vessels to turn the beaches into beachheads with their now illustrious code names of **Sword, Juno, Gold, Omaha** and **Utah.**

Today, with the flames and dust of battle long gone, the coast has retrieved its calm. At a site so charged with the emotion of death and war, the atmosphere of rather bleak serenity is in itself as evocative as the few remaining hulks of the Allies' rusty tanks and boats, the Germans' concrete bunkers and blockhouses, some simple monuments on the sites of the action and the miles of crosses at the military cemeteries.

To see where the British and Canadians, with the support of the Free French forces, attacked on the eastern half of the beaches, start out at the port town of **Ouistreham-Riva-Bella.** A museum (Place Alfred-Thomas) details the combined Anglo-French operation to capture this stretch of Sword Beach, with uniforms and weapons used during the action, including a pocket submarine and Goliath tank.

Drive west along the D 514 to **Bernières** and **Courseulles,** where the Canadians staged their Juno Beach landings, marked by monuments on the beaches, and the Canadians' cemetery 4 kilometres (2½ miles) to the south at Reviers.

At **Arromanches,** you can see the most fascinating monument to British ingenuity in the Allied landings—the remains of the artificial **Mulberry harbour.** The floating steel and concrete jetties and pontoons, hauled across the English Channel, were the only way of unloading tanks and heavy artillery on a coastline (Gold Beach) without natural harbours. The **Musée du Débarquement** on the seafront includes an exciting film explaining the whole heroic action.

The Americans' **Omaha** and **Utah beaches,** from Colleville to La Madeleine, are now official map references, a cartographer's tribute to the theatre of the fiercest fighting in the D-Day landings. The still desolate coastline frequently recalls the stormy conditions that prevented the Americans from setting up their own Mulberry harbour to land their equipment. More eloquent than any museum are the 9,386 white marble crosses of the **American military cemetery** on a cliff overlooking Omaha Beach at Colleville-Saint-Laurent.

The Utah Beach museum and

monument are 5 kilometres (3 miles) inland from La Madeleine, near Sainte-Marie-du-Mont. Caen, Bayeux and local tourist offices can direct you to the 27 Allied and German military cemeteries in the region.

Surrounded by the perilous seas, Mont-Saint-Michel symbolizes the Archangel's stand against Satan.

Mont-Saint-Michel

No way of getting round the claim of its most fervent admirers, the island sanctuary at the border between Normandy and Brittany is indeed a *Merveille de l'Occident*—a "Wonder of the Western World". That first glimpse of the steepled abbey rising on its rock from the sea is a moment invested with ineffable mystery. Whatever your faith or

lack of it, sooner or later a visit to this formidable and exquisite fortress of the Christian Church is imperative.

Sooner or later, because you must choose your moment carefully. If you want to recapture something of the atmosphere of the medieval pilgrimages, when thousands of the faithful swarmed across the island, loading up with souvenirs and fake relics and fighting their brethren for a meal or a bed, join the new secular pilgrims in the summer months, arriving by the busload rather than mule. But if your mood is more contemplative, go in the early spring, autumn or even winter, when you can wander around the abbey and its village like a monk.

The bay around the mount's granite outcrop has been steadily silting up in recent years, so that it's an island only during the spring tides. These are most dramatic during the spring and autumn equinox, when the sea comes in at a rate of nearly 50 metres (164 feet) a minute over a distance of 15 kilometres (9 miles). This proved highly dangerous to the pilgrims who approached the abbey across the sands (the causeway joining the island to the mainland was not built until 1874).

On what was once a Celtic burial ground (originally named Mont-Tombe), the bishop of

> *First Look*
> *A detailed visit of the Mont-Saint-Michel is certainly worthwhile, but it's that perspective from a distance that's the most moving. For those coming from Caen, stop in Avranches for a panorama of the bay from the Jardin des Plantes or drive out to the coast road (D911) between Saint-Jean-Le-Thomas and Carolles. Best of all, if you're prepared to splash out and get high above the madding crowd, fly over the abbey on the special excursions organized from Avranches airport. But if you have no time for any of these, do at least get off the main highway, N176, when approaching the mount to take the D43 coast road via Courtils for that all-important first view.*

nearby Avranches began by building an oratory in the 8th century, at the prompting, he said, of the Archangel Michael. In 1017, Benedictine monks started on the flat-roofed abbey that you can see in the Bayeux Tapestry, propped up on a platform with blocks of brown granite brought from the Channel islands of Chausey, 40 kilometres (25 miles) away.

By the 14th century, the abbey was surrounded by a fortified village. The pilgrims flocked there throughout the Hundred Years' War, paying tolls to the English who controlled the surrounding territory but could never break through the mount's defences. After a steady decline, the monastery was dismantled even before the Revolution, but was saved from total destruction only to end ignominiously as a state prison.

Beginning on the upper terrace with a splendid **view** of the bay, the hour's guided tour (English, French and German) takes you through three levels of abbey buildings: the church, cloister and refectory at the top; the Salle des Chevaliers (Knights' Hall) and Salle des Hôtes (Guests' Hall) in the middle; and the store room and almonry underneath.

The **abbey church** combines a sturdy Romanesque nave with a lighter, more airy Flamboyant Gothic chancel. The choir and chancel stand not on the island's granite core but on a platform formed by three crypts, with the massive columns of the **Crypte des Gros Piliers** doing most of the work. In a magic space looking out to sea, the beautifully sculpted columns of the **cloister** create a perfect framework of grace and delicacy for a moment's meditation.

With the cloister, the ethereally lit **refectory,** grand **Knights' Hall** and elegant **Guests' Hall** together make up the masterpiece of 13th-century Gothic architecture which earned the abbey its name of *la Merveille.*

BRITTANY

This province, as its natives never tire of telling you, is a country apart, proud of its regional culture, its robust seclusion. The people are remote on their Armorican peninsula, the Far West of Europe, suspicious of the vacationing Parisian but unostentatiously hospitable to the foreign visitor.

Only a separate holiday can do the region complete justice, but for a first visit as part of a larger French tour, you get at least a sense of Brittany's craggy coasts on the Côte d'Emeraude (Emerald Coast) from Cancale to Cap Fréhel. Relax a while at the gentler seaside resorts of Dinard on the north coast or La Baule on the south, and explore the prehistoric menhir country around Carnac. In the interior, capture the essence of Breton piety in the calvaries of the Parish Closes *(enclos paroissiaux)* at Saint-Thégonnec and Guimiliau, and perhaps hike around the forests and rocky landscapes between Huelgoat and Roc Trévezel.

Côte d'Emeraude

After Mont-Saint-Michel, the Emerald Coast's 70 kilometres (43 miles) of rugged cliffs and caves alternating with quiet beach resorts offer a delightful confrontation with nature and sunny self-indulgence.

Start out at the little port town

of **Cancale**, a major centre of oyster-breeding since earliest Celtic times. Modern techniques now make the oysters good to eat all year round and not, as of old, just in the months with an "r". Look out over the oyster beds from the port's jetty, **Jetée de la Fenêtre**.

Take the coast road D 201 to **Pointe du Grouin**, a cliff 40 metres (130 feet) high, with a spectacular view of the Chausey Islands to the north and itself a good example of Brittany's coastal wilderness.

Look east across the Bay of Mont-Saint-Michel for a last glimpse of the abbey before heading west to **Saint-Malo.** This town is steeped in seafaring history; its sailors left their name on the Malouines, claimed by the British as the Falklands. It remains an important fishing port for cod and, more romantically, an attractive yacht harbour.

In World War II Saint-Malo was badly bombed as a last bastion of the Germans, but the old town, surrounded on three sides by the sea, has been tastefully restored. Its **ramparts**, built and rebuilt from the 12th to the 18th century, make a bracing walk, with the stretch between Saint-Philippe bastion and the Tour Bidouane opening up a vista along the whole Emerald Coast. At low tide you can walk or wade out to the little island of Grand Bé, with its simple, unadorned tomb of the locally born Romantic writer Chateaubriand.

In the **Musée d'Histoire de la ville**, just across the lively Place Chateaubriand, the town's naval history is told through the lives of its great navigators and pirates and all the colourful paraphernalia of sailing.

Like many French seaside resorts, **Dinard** is a "discovery" of the British in the 19th century, long before French city slickers even dreamed of dipping a toe in the sea or lying on that gritty stuff called sand. The British, soon followed by Americans, appreciated the broad, sheltered beach, the particularly mild microclimate—palms, fig trees, tamarisk and camellias all flourish here—and easy access across the Channel.

In a still faintly Victorian atmosphere, Dinard has preserved all the assets of a good resort: luxury villas, long paved promenades, plush hotels, elegant boutiques, discothèques, casino, parks and gardens and a public Olympic-size swimming pool.

The spectacle at **Cap Fréhel** is one of the most thrilling in Brittany. From cliffs 70 metres (230 feet) above the tumultuous

The art of Brittany gossip: bend an ear without bending the bonnet.

sea, you look out across a wild defenceless promontory, a chaos of ruddy sandstone and slabs of black schist, huge waves breaking across the rocks of the Grande and Petite Fauconnière bird sanctuaries, scattered with colonies of cormorants and black and white guillemots. On a clear day, the new **lighthouse** (145 stairs), gives you a view of more than 100 kilometres (70 miles).

Parish Close Road

The *enclos paroissial* epitomizes the pious life of rural Brittany. This architectural ensemble encompasses church, cemetery, charnel house and calvary, grouped in a square and entered via a triumphal arch. In a morning's tour from Morlaix, 160 kilometres (100 miles) west of Dinard, you can take in three of the most important on a route

signposted as the "Circuit des Trois Enclos".

Saint-Thégonnec represents the ultimate flowering of the art, its triumphal arch setting the tone for the majestic **calvary** of 1610. Among the 40-odd expressively sculpted figures dressed in the costume of Henri IV's time, notice the roped hands of the blindfolded Jesus and the angels collecting his blood; his tormentor, in breeches, is thought to be Henri IV himself. The **ossuary**, now a chapel, is late Renaissance in the very elaborate Breton manner—Corinthian columns, lanterns, niches and caryatids. The **church** has an even more elaborate Baroque pulpit.

At **Guimiliau**, over 200 Old and New Testament figures are sculpted on its **calvary**. The elegant Renaissance style lends an unusual sophistication to the nightmarish superstitions of medieval Brittany also incorporated in the sculpture. Look for the servant girl hurtled into hell for flirting with the devil. The **church** has fine granite statues of Jesus and the Apostles on its porch. Inside, eight spiral columns support the mighty canopy of the 17th-century carved oak **baptistry.**

A lightning bolt toppled the church tower of **Lampaul-Guimiliau** in 1809, but the interior of the **church** remains impressive. The 16th-century polychrome rood beam spanning the nave is decorated with 12 prophetesses (chancel side) and scenes from the Passion. In the Flagellation, the artist seems quite carried away with the sadistic brutes wielding whip and cudgel on Jesus, tied to a tree.

At nightfall, the parish calvary's gesticulating world comes to life.

131

Huelgoat

This pretty little town is mainly attractive as a base for excursions into the nature reserve of forests, rivers and pools in the **Parc régional d'Armorique**.

You can fish for perch and carp in the lake or trout in the Rivière d'Argent (Silver River); or just glide around the lake among the swans. At the top end of the lake, you wander into dense forest through a fantastic chaos of rocks and grottos variously inhabited by the Devil, some more or less innocent virgin, and King Arthur himself.

Carnac

Like the wild countryside of the interior, the megalithic monuments of Brittany's **menhir country** on the south coast take you back into the legends and mists of time.

Carnac is surrounded by fields with thousands of gigantic stones (menhirs) in mysterious alignments and circles (cromlechs) set up some time between 5500 and 3500 B.C., at the rate of one stone a year. Scholars timidly suggest the alignments are associated with cults of the sun or moon, and the cromlechs may be astronomical arrangements for predicting such phenomena as eclipses.

The alignments occupy three main fields a short walk north of town along the D 196. **Le Ménec,**

the biggest, has 1,099 menhirs in 12 rows (plus 70 menhirs in a cromlech around part of the hamlet of Le Ménec). The field of **Kermario** has a dolmen (chamber built of flat slabs on pillars) and 1,029 menhirs in 10 rows. Among them is the Giant of Manio, a menhir over 6 metres (20 feet) high, shaped like a clenched fist. Most impressive is the **Kerlescan** alignment, 594 menhirs that form what local legend calls a frozen army. Once a year, the stones rise up in the middle of the night and march around.

The best time to see them all is early morning, looming out of the mist, or at sunset, throwing dramatic shadows.

La Baule

Best beach in Europe, say its regulars. Five kilometres (three miles) of fine sand from Pornichet to Le Pouliguen stretch in a perfect half-moon, past chic sailing and beach clubs, along an **esplanade** of luxury hotels with a casino at the centre. If you tire of the easy life on the beach front, take an excursion west around the wilder coast of the peninsula past Batz-sur-Mer (pronounced *Bah*) to the pretty little fishing port and resort of Le Croisic.

Brittany's megalithic menhirs remain a 5,000-year-old mystery.

LOIRE VALLEY

The Loire is the longest river in France—1,012 kilometres (628 miles) from its source in the Vivarais mountains south of Saint-Etienne to the estuary west of Nantes—but the region of the most interesting châteaux, from Chambord to Angers, covers barely a fifth of that.

The itinerary we propose for visitors coming down from Paris bypasses Orléans on the *autoroute* to exit at Blois and, after a side trip to Chambord, heads west on the N 152 to Angers. Just reverse the route if you're coming in from Brittany.

For centuries, the Loire river was a vital highway between the Atlantic and the heart of France, making Orléans a major distribution centre for exotic goods from the Orient. The gentry put their carriages on rafts and sailed to Brittany—six days from Orléans to Nantes. Commercial traffic declined in the 17th and 18th centuries, reviving briefly with the advent of the steamship in 1832, but finally succumbed to silting up and the onslaught of the railways.

Today, the Loire is a sleepy waterway, running deep only with the autumn rains or post-winter thaw, and turning its sandbanks and mud flats into veritable islands during the summer.

Son et Lumière

It was the Loire Valley châteaux that started the craze for sound and light shows back in the 1950s. With their rich historical background of romance and murder most foul, they are still the ideal places for these English- and French-language dramatizations in a spectacular setting that at night takes on the quality of a fairy tale. Most of them run continuously throughout the summer months. The syndicat d'initiative at Blois (phone: 54.74.06.49) can give you details of the programmes. The best are at Chambord (the pioneer), Blois, Chenonceau and Azay-le-Rideau.

Blois

Built on a hill overlooking the Loire river, the town itself invites the visitor to linger a while in the narrow winding streets leading from the cathedral to the château, with handsome old houses situated on Place Saint-Louis and Rue Porte-Chartraine.

The entrance to the **château** is through the brick and stone gateway of the late Gothic Louis XII wing, completed in 1503. Across the courtyard on the right-hand side is the château's most distinc-

The staircase at Blois provided the château with the grandest of grandstands for royal ceremonies.

tive feature, the splendid **François I wing**. It was built only a dozen years after the Louis XII wing but, reflecting the contrast between the debonair Renaissance prince and his dour predecessor, is a world apart in elegance and panache.

The open loggias of its magnificently sculpted octagonal stone **staircase** dominate the façade. They served as a kind of grand-stand for courtiers watching important guests arriving on state occasions. The little beasts carved on the balconies and elsewhere around the château are the royal family's personal emblems, including Louis XII's porcupine,

Flirting at Chambord has shifted from the rooftop terrace to the castle grounds.

François I's salamander, Anne de Bretagne's ermine.

On the first floor of the François I wing, look out for the wood-panelled **cabinet** (study) of Catherine de Médicis, conniving queen mother and regent to three kings of France. Many of the 237 carved panels, each different, were believed to conceal poisons as well as jewels and state papers. On the second floor, in 1588, as guides never tire of telling, her son Henri III used not poison but a dozen men armed with swords and daggers to do away with his archrival Duke Henri de Guise.

Chambord

Upriver east of Blois in a huge densely wooded park surrounded by 32 kilometres (20 miles) of high walls, the brilliant white **Château de Chambord** is the most extravagant of all the royal residences in the Loire Valley. To have easy access to the wild boar and deer (still to be seen from observation platforms on D 112 and D 33), François I built himself this glorified 440-room hunting lodge. Later kings abandoned it as too big and unheatable—despite 365 fireplaces.

There is an astounding fantasy if not harmony in the arcaded towers and terraces, alternating storeys of arched and rectangular windows, and maze of turrets, stone lanterns and chimneys.

It's believed the central four-towered **donjon** that makes a dream palace out of a classically feudal castle keep may have been designed by Leonardo da Vinci, whom François brought to the Loire Valley in 1516. He's certainly the kind of fellow to have created the celebrated **double-ramped spiral staircase** in the donjon's centre, which enables people to go up and down it without crossing each other.

Such aids to clandestinity were vitally important for the jolly shenanigans that went on among François' suite of 2,000 courtiers, as you can imagine for yourself up on the balustraded **rooftop terrace** (which affords a nice **view** of the forest). The nooks and crannies among the chimneys and turrets served as trysting alcoves for those who couldn't get one of the 440 rooms to themselves.

From Blois, take the N 152 along the picturesque right bank of the Loire before crossing over to **Amboise** for a brief look at the remains of the château, largely dismantled under Napoleon. Leonardo da Vinci spent his last days in a small manor house nearby, the **Clos-Lucé**, now a museum illustrating his inventive talents. A bust in the château gardens marks the site of his grave. Chenonceaux (unlike the château, the town is spelt with an *x*) is on the south side of Amboise forest.

Chenonceau

Raised on arches to span the Cher river, the château and its pretty gardens still evoke the romantic ghost of its beautiful chatelaine, Diane de Poitiers, mistress to Henri II. She owed her legendary health and complexion to regular washing and sensible eating—she swam nude in the river and grew her own artichokes in the gardens.

In the **apartments,** along with some fine 16th-century Flemish tapestries, French, Italian and Spanish furniture, you'll see Diane's neatly kept household accounts. It's not clear that Primaticcio's contemporary portrait of her as Diana goddess of hunting does full justice to her beauty.

After his death, Henri II's widow Catherine de Médicis took Chenonceau for herself and added the galleried floors of ballrooms and reception halls that complete the bridge across the river.

If the short walk from the main gate is too much for you, you can take an **electric train** in summer, and there are **boat rides** on the river when the water is deep enough.

Loches

South of Chenonceaux on the Indre river, the delightful medieval village of Loches is as much an attraction as the château itself.

The **church of Saint-Ours** is a fascinating piece of Romanesque architecture with two steeples at either end of the nave, which itself has two bizarre octagonal pyramids in place of a roof. In the interior, the **narthex,** or entrance hall, has some fine, if partially mutilated, sculpture. Over the nave, the hollow pyramids appear to be designed in the style of chimneys for a castle kitchen.

Wander along Rue Saint-Ours and Rue du Château and take a walk around the **ramparts.** Particularly interesting is the 11th-century **donjon** (keep) which formed part of the town's southern defences. Two 15th-century additions served as prisons for royal enemies—most notoriously for the Duke of Milan, who was kept there in total darkness for eight years, only to drop dead on the day of his release, overcome by the blinding sunlight.

At the other end of the fortifications, the terrace of the **Logis royal** (Royal Lodge) affords a lovely view over the village and the Indre valley. Architecturally, the lodge offers an interesting transition from sober Gothic to more decorative Renaissance. Inside is a little gem of Gothic art: Anne de Bretagne's private oratory, the niches of its stone walls finely carved with her ermine emblem and the symbolic cords of the Franciscan order.

Azay-le-Rideau

If French life can still evoke an image of grace and elegance, the **château** at Azay is its epitome. This late Gothic treasure of dazzling white stone beneath grey slate roofs casts a serene reflection into the waters of the Indre river, 30 kilometres (19 miles) south-west of Tours.

It was erected in the early 16th century by François I's treasurer, Gilles Berthelot, partly on a Venetian-style foundation of wood piles close-driven into the river bed. Berthelot's wife Philippe supervised the design and the feminine delicacy of its forms, especially the slender conical turrets at each corner and the double-arched loggias of the **main staircase.** Notice inside how, with the château no longer serving the function of a fortress, the staircase innovated with straight flights and landings rather than the old spiral form that was designed to fend off invaders.

Madame Berthelot built the large vaulted **kitchen** almost on a level with the river, so that an indoor well provided the closest thing to running water, and an unusually hygienic stone drain sent back the slops. You can see the kind of utensils and cake tins her cooks would have used. At least, until the king confiscated the castle because her husband was cooking the royal books.

Angers

The perfect base for exploring the Loire Valley from its western end, this bustling university town offers some first-class modern shopping in the pedestrian zone around the **Place du Ralliement**.

The ruins of the 13th-century Eglise Toussaint have been beautifully restored and incorporated into the town's **Musée des Beaux-Arts** (37, rue Toussaint) to house a unique collection of sculptures by David d'Angers. This Who's Who of the heroes revered in 19th-century France includes not only Balzac and Hugo, but also Gutenberg, Paganini and a plaster bust of George Washington, the bronze of which stands in the United States Congress. In the imposing 12th- and 13th-century Gothic **Cathédrale Saint-Maurice**, look out for the excellent **stained-glass windows** covering 800 years of the noble art.

If not the most beautiful, the **château** is certainly the most formidable in the Loire Valley, a real defensive fortress, its black ramparts still forbidding despite having had their towers decapitated at the order of Henri III. The château's proudest possession is the magnificent 14th-century **Apocalypse Tapestry** narrating the gospel of Saint John in moving detail. Seventy pieces of this remarkable work survive, out of an original hundred.

139

SOUTH-EAST

Travelling through the south-east of France from the Alps, or down the Rhône Valley from Lyon through Provence to the Côte d'Azur (French Riviera) is like strolling out of your hotel on a crisp sunny morning and walking slowly down to the beach for a dip in the sea or a lazy sunbathe. It's one long exercise in self-indulgence.

In the Savoie Alps, the resorts around the Mont Blanc, Western Europe's highest mountain, can be as exhilarating for the outdoor life in summer as they are for their superb winter sports facilities (see pp. 194–5), and unrivalled *après-ski* attractions. Life is less energetic but equally refreshing down on the lovely lakes of Annecy and le Bourget.

The Rhône Valley region around Lyon is the epicentre of French gastronomy, so loosen your belt—and your purse-strings. But first work up a healthy appetite wandering around Lyon's charming back streets and alleyways and checking out the meat and vegetables in the early-morning street markets.

In Provence, you take your jacket off and undo a few buttons and do some serious basking among the olive trees and vineyards. On energetic days, there are Roman theatres and amphitheatres to explore, the papal palace at Avignon and a feudal fortress at Les Baux. By which time you'll be ready to do nothing, in great style, in the fleshpots of the Côte d'Azur, or some desultory shopping and museum-seeing in the back country.

We also suggest a couple of resorts and excursions on Napoleon's wild and beautiful island of Corsica.

SAVOIE

Like many mountain regions, the province of Savoie remained, despite occasional invasions, proudly independent of its more powerful neighbours, cannily playing off Italy and France against each other over the centuries until finally voting by plebiscite to throw in its lot with France in 1860.

Except for a few smugglers, geologists and botanists, the

The sun packs the sweetest of smells in the herbs of Provence.

French steered clear of the Alps until the mountain-climbing craze was launched by the conquest of Mont Blanc in 1786. It wasn't until 1924, with the first Winter Olympic Games at Chamonix, that skiing—at the time only cross-country—attracted international attention and a demand for ski resorts. As a result, most French resorts are 20th-century creations with first-class winter sports facilities, but lacking the quaintness and old traditions that people associate with their longer-established counterparts in Austria and Switzerland. Chamonix and Megève are among the best resorts, with a real town life other than modern hotels and ski lifts, and serve as good bases for summer hikes or excursions into the mountains.

Annecy and Aix-les-Bains are both towns with considerable history and character to make them worth exploring in their own right before embarking on tours of their lakes.

Chamonix

The neighbourhood around the church has enough old-fashioned charm to retain something of the town's 19th-century pioneering atmosphere. For a fuller sense of what it was like when mountain-climbing and skiing were in their infancy, spend an hour in the **Musée alpin**, tracing the history of the region, its heroes and their exploits, in photos and displays of equipment.

For your summer excursions by cable car and rack railway, don't forget to take a sweater, sunglasses and binoculars for the sudden change in altitude, brilliant sunlight and fabulous panoramas. And go carefully until you're used to the rarefied atmosphere.

The cable car (téléphérique) ride up to the **Aiguille du Midi** (3,800 metres/12,470 feet) is the most spectacular in the French Alps, for its view of the **Mont Blanc**'s snow-covered peak, altitude 4,807 metres (15,770 feet), and the surrounding landscape. For some easy hiking, stop off at the lower station of Plan de l'Aiguille (2,310 metres/7,580 feet).

The cable car to **Le Brévent** (2,525 metres/8,284 feet), northwest of Chamonix, lets you take in the whole north face of the Mont Blanc and the Aiguille du Midi, too. For a close-up view of a glacier and formidable ice caves, take the cable car and rack railway up the Montenvers to the dazzling **Mer de Glace** (Sea of Ice). There's also a little **zoo** of mouflon mountain sheep, chamois goats, marmots, minks and other creatures. You're unlikely to see them in any other natural setting here, since they were frightened off the mountains by helicopters taking spoiled skiers to remote pistes.

Megève

This perennially fashionable resort is particularly popular for families. The slopes provide sufficient challenge without being breakneck, so that instructors can pay special attention to children. For summer visitors, in addition to superb facilities for tennis and swimming, the town's verdant setting of grassy alpine meadows and pine, spruce and larch forest is ideal for hikes.

A cable car takes you to **Mont d'Arbois** (1,833 metres/6,014 feet) for a great view of the Aravis peaks and the Mont Blanc. Hikers continue to **Mont Joly** (about 5 hours to and from Mont d'Arbois cable-car station) for an even more spectacular view.

Annecy

This is one of those gracious towns that are still the quiet joy of provincial France. Cross the **Parc du Pâquier** to a waterfront observation platform for a first view of the lake and its backdrop of mountains. The lakeside promenade back towards town takes you over the self-explanatory Pont des Amours and west to the

That pretty little Palais de l'Isle was once Annecy's prison.

15th-century Dominican **Eglise Saint-Maurice.**

In the middle of the Thiou river (whose source is the lake itself) stands the 12th-century prison, **Palais de l'Isle.** Explore the **old town** and its handsome 15th- and 16th-century houses along Rue Perrière and Rue Sainte-Claire.

The imposing **château**, former home of the Counts of Geneva, contains an interesting museum devoted to local archaeology and folklore and the natural history of the Alps. The castle terrace is the best vantage point for pictures of the old town.

The cruises around **Lake Annecy** start out from the Thiou river. Some of them include a cable-car ride to the top of **Mont Veyrier** (1,291 metres/4,230 feet) and its spectacular panorama of the Alps, but all give you a marvellous swan's-eye view of the jagged snowcapped peaks of the Dents de Lanfon and the rugged La Tournette to the east, and gentler Entrevernes and Taillefer mountains to the west. If you decide to drive, take the D 909 east to the Mont Veyrier cable car, continuing on to the pretty town of **Menthon-Saint-Bernard** and its medieval castle high above the lake. The D 42 takes you up to the **Col de la Forclaz** (1,157 metres/3,800 feet), while the lakefront road leads to a gastronomic temple at Talloires.

Aix-les-Bains

This spa town on the edge of the Lac du Bourget has for centuries offered cures for rheumatism and broken hearts. Ever since 4th-century Roman Emperor Gratianus took his natural hot bath here, people have been plunging into what they call the *bouillon* or "hot broth" at 42°C (107.6°F). In the 19th century, Romantic poet Alphonse de Lamartine stopped off to fix his liver and a bout of melancholy with a lyric tribute, *Le Lac*, that had his fans weeping enough tears to flood the lovely chestnut trees and poplars on its banks.

The **Musée du Docteur-Faure** (Villa des Chimères, Boulevard des Côtes) exhibits some excellent Rodin bronzes and watercolours, and works by Degas, Sisley, Corot and Cézanne. But by and large, the great pleasure here is to do nothing at all, siesta, take the waters, siesta, stroll along the **Boulevard du Lac** and siesta.

The major attraction is the **lake cruise**, starting out from the Grand Port. With its "harmonious waves...moan of the wind, sigh of the reeds, light perfume of the balmy air", the lake is truly as romantic and dreamy as Lamartine claimed. One of the destinations of the cruise is the neo-Gothic **Abbaye de Hautecombe**, well worth a visit if you can attend a mass performed with the Gregorian chant.

RHÔNE VALLEY

From its source high in the Swiss Alps, the Rhône courses down to the Mediterranean, bending southwards at Lyon. It has always been France's vital central artery for river, road and rail traffic between the north and south. Its valley was the main path of the Roman conquest of Gaul, the key to Lyon's medieval commercial wealth. Today it is the most direct route from Paris to the Mediterranean.

Located at the crossroads between north and south, Lyon was the ideal choice as the Roman capital of Gaul. It has become the natural capital of French gastronomy: at the conjunction of Atlantic and Continental climates, the farmers get the best out of a subtle mixture of the cooler and damper north with the first hints of Mediterranean warmth and light. The regions around Lyon produce some of the best food in the country: poultry from Bresse; freshwater fish from the Savoie lakes; Charolais beef; and pears, apples and cherries from orchards north of town and peaches and apricots from those south.

The fruit industry started in earnest in the 1880s as a reaction to the dreaded phylloxera disease that struck the local vineyards. Today, the **Beaujolais country** thrives as never before, and wine-lovers on the way down to Lyon detour through such sweet-sounding places as Juliénas, Chénas, Morgon and Brouilly. Continuing south, opposite Tournon, they may like to sample a celebrated *Côtes du Rhône* at Tain-l'Hermitage.

Lyon

Prosperous since the Middle Ages for its trade fairs, banking and silk manufacture, Lyon still has a bouncy pride and taste for the good life.

Besides the great shrines of *haute cuisine* in and around the city, appropriately sumptuous in décor and price, you should also seek out the little bars and cafés and the old-fashioned bistrots that the Lyonnais call *bouchons* (after the bunches of straw or foliage that served as a sign for the restaurant). But it's not easy to make your way around town to find them. The city is built across the looping confluence of the Saône and Rhône rivers, with hills on either side and a peninsula in the middle. A street map is a must.

So head first for the tourist office on the huge **Place Bellecour**, in the middle of the peninsula between the two rivers. The square has a pretty flower market, and you know you're approaching the south of France when you see your first serious games of *boules* there.

145

Eating sometimes needs explanation in the gourmet mecca of Lyon.

Cross over the Pont Bonaparte to stroll around the fine Renaissance houses of Lyon's **old town** between the Saône river and the Fourvière hill. Some of the best are along the Rue Saint-Georges, Rue Saint-Jean and Rue Juiverie.

In the handsome **Hôtel de Gadagne** (Rue de Gadagne) you can see a museum of the history of Lyon and the marionettes of the town's celebrated Guignol theatre. If your French is up to it, you may enjoy the plays of traditional folklore, parodies of opera or contemporary satire performed at the Palais du Conservatoire—details at the tourist office.

To take in the full sweep of the city, ride the funicular railway from Gare Saint-Jean up the hill to the **observatory** at the Church of Notre-Dame-de-Fourvière.

The town's **Musée des Beaux-Arts**, housed in a 17th-century Benedictine abbey (20, place des Terreaux), has a rich collection of European paintings and sculpture. Most notable are three Rodin bronzes in its cloister, and works by Perugino, Veronese, El Greco and Rubens, Courbet, Manet and Matisse.

PROVENCE

Though much of France is cool and green and rational, it likes to think of itself as a Mediterranean country, warm, golden and passionate. Blame it on the seductive charm of Provence. On those rare occasions when the Frenchman seeks to be loved, he seems to be trying to pass as a Provençal, a jovial, generous fellow with a colourful, pleasant-sounding, but not necessarily profound gift of the gab.

Understandable in a region where the sun is the most benevolent of dictators. The monuments of the Roman Empire still stand proudly in Orange, Arles and Nîmes, like the medieval strongholds in Les Baux and Avignon, but the most important pleasure of Provence remains the sensuality of its landscape. Squat little vineyards stretch to the foot of the rugged Alpilles, cypresses loom like signposts to the sea above the twisted olive trees and almond groves, while the aromatic umbrella pines provide a natural shelter for your siesta.

Sweet-smelling Provence. . . . As you drive through the scrubland they call *garrigue*, keep your window rolled well down to let in the fragrance of lavender and the wild rosemary, thyme and savory to which local market gardeners add sage, tarragon and marjoram for the famous *herbes de*

147

Provence. Even the garlic and onions are sweet in Provence.

The accent is on unabashed indolence, but Provence bristles with cultural activity in the summer months, each town using its ancient amphitheatre, cathedral or palace as a mag-nificent setting for festivals of music, theatre and the other arts (see p. 200).

(see p. 200).

The itinerary we propose deals in turn with different layers of Provençal life: the "Roman" towns of Orange, Vaison, Nîmes and Arles; the medieval bastions of Les Baux and Avignon; the ancient villages of the Lubéron mountains; and finally the cheer-ful streets of Aix-en-Provence.

Salade niçoise is all the better for a first pressing of oil from Castillon's olive groves.

Orange

The grandiose ancient monuments of this once prosperous Roman trading centre on the road from Arles to Lyon strike a delightfully incongruous note in the peaceful Provençal backwater of today.

Since this is the gateway to Provence, make an appropriate entrance into town from the north, at the great three-arched **arc de triomphe**. Built in A.D. 21, it stands on a traffic island across the old N 7, which here traces the route of the ancient Via Agrippa. The friezes of battling soldiers, weaponry and naval equipment sculpted on the north side celebrate Julius Caesar's victories over Gallic tribes of the region and the merchant fleet of the Greek colony in Marseille.

The town's other great Roman monument, the **théâtre antique**, is on the south side of town. Historians regard this as the finest and best preserved of all the surviving theatres in the Roman Empire, unique for its towering scenic wall still standing, with a statue of Emperor Augustus to greet you. Originally, 7,000 spectators came from all over Provence to watch a circus, Greek tragedy, Latin comedy or lottery draw. It still provides a wonderful stage for the July festival's opera and symphony concerts. Out of season, test— even with a whisper—its exceptional acoustics.

From the top of Colline Saint-Eutrope, you get a good bird's-eye **view** of the theatre in relation to the triumphal arch and the Rhône valley beyond.

Vaison-la-Romaine

A pretty excursion 30 kilometres (19 miles) north-east of Orange along the D 975 takes you to the

site of one of the most important towns of Roman Provence, excavated north of Vaison's modern and medieval quarters. To understand better the layout of the ancient town, its streets, houses, shops, fountains and theatre, visit the **museum** on the Puymin hill. It displays some superb marble sculpture of the 2nd century A.D., most notably a Venus, the Emperor Hadrian and his wife Sabina.

Visit too the medieval houses of the **haute ville** (upper town), overlooking the Ouvèze river.

Pont du Gard

Take the A9 *autoroute* southwest from Orange to the Fournès-Remoulins exit and follow the D981 to the parking lot in front of the "bridge".

In the Gardon valley's wonderful natural setting of forest and river, this gigantic 2,000-year-old **aqueduct** is without doubt the most impressive of all Roman monuments preserved from ancient Gaul. It carried spring water from near Uzès to the town of Nîmes, over a distance of 35 kilometres (22 miles).

Quite apart from its historic impact, it's worth the visit for what is likely to be one of the more memorable picnics of your French tour, well away from the crowds (avoid the dreadful local restaurants). But first, hold the hand of your little ones (vertigo victims abstain) and take the easy marked path up to the roof of the aqueduct, 49 metres (160 feet) above the river.

Built of huge granite blocks joined without mortar in three tiers of arches, 6 at the base, 11 at the middle level and 35 at the top, this highly functional construction is also remarkably beautiful, in total harmony with its landscape. The roof walkway is 275 metres (300 yards) long, not too difficult to negotiate with a minimum of care. The best **view** of the ensemble is from the river bank near the Château Saint-Privat, beyond the aqueduct.

Nîmes

Emperor Augustus made a gift of this town to the veterans of his victorious battle against Antony and Cleopatra in Egypt, commemorated to this day in the Nîmes coat of arms with the chained crocodile of the Nile. The grand **amphitheatre** *(arènes)* was built for gladiator battles; later it was used for the less equal combats between lions and Christians. Having served as a fortress for the invading Visigoths in the 5th century and as a communal residence for the poor in the Middle Ages, it has now resumed the ancient bloody tradition with summer bullfights.

The more pacific Greek-style temple known as the **Maison**

carrée is an elegant monument of the same period (1st century B.C.), noted for the finely sculpted Corinthian capitals on its columns. After a varied history as town hall, residence, stable and church, it was saved from a project of Louis XIV's minister Colbert to move it stone by stone to Versailles. Today it houses a small **museum** of Roman sculpture and mosaics.

The **Jardin de la Fontaine,** a pretty tree-shaded 18th-century park on the slopes of the Mont Cavalier at the north-west edge of town, offers a refreshing respite from the summer heat—and a good **view** of the surround-

The Romans' Pont du Gard is a great feat of engineering but also strikingly beautiful.

151

ing mountains. The park is built around the spring of Nemausus that gave the town its name; it includes a ruined temple attributed to the hunting goddess Diana and a Roman tower of no known significance at all.

The sculpture in the cloister of Saint-Trophime deserves detailed examination.

Arles

An important town in Roman Gaul, replacing Lyon as capital towards the end of the Empire, it boasts a powerful **amphitheatre** *(arènes)*, seating over 20,000 in the days of the gladiators. For the most spectacular view, climb up to the broad path that runs along the roof of the arches on its perimeter. Less fortunate than the one at Orange,

the **theatre** *(théâtre antique)* has been reduced to ruins over the centuries as builders carted away masonry for their houses, churches and town walls, but the remains in a pleasant park are quietly eloquent of its noble past.

In the **Eglise Saint-Trophime** (on Place de la République), you can see the Roman influence recurring in the triumphal-arch design of its splendid porch. This masterpiece of Provençal Romanesque sculpture depicts the Last Judgment in the tympanum above the doors, surrounded by statues of the saints. Nearby, the church cloister, **Cloître Saint-Trophime**, with its beautiful sculpted capitals on the pillars, is a haven of peace.

South-east of town, cut off by a railway track, you'll find the melancholy remains of the

> ### Looking for the Ghost of Van Gogh
> *Van Gogh wrote in a letter from Arles: "Oh, the beautiful sun of midsummer! It beats upon my head, and I do not doubt that it makes one a little queer." It inspired his most fertile period, but also triggered the frenzy in which he cut off an ear and had himself committed to an asylum in nearby Saint-Rémy. He died a year later back in the outskirts of Paris. Today, the tourist office in the Boulevard des Lices provides a map tracing 30 of the sites he painted while in Arles. His house and favourite café have both gone, bombed in 1944, but, beside the last stones of the Alyscamps and the Jardin public, the sun is as strong as ever. You can find surrounding fields filled with the sunflowers and olive trees he loved to paint, and still imagine the painter tramping the road to Tarascon in the inadequate shade of the plane trees.*

153

Alyscamps, famous Roman and medieval burial grounds that were a favourite subject of Van Gogh when he came to live in Arles in 1888. Today, just a few sarcophagi remain in an avenue leading to the ruins of the Eglise Saint-Honorat.

La Camargue

At the delta of the Rhône, where its two arms spill into the Mediterranean, the Camargue has been reclaimed from the sea to form a national **nature reserve,** with modern resorts along the coast. The region is famous for its white horses, which you can hire to ride along the sandflats, and for the black bulls that race through the streets of Provençal towns to the bullfight.

With permission from the Directeur de la réserve, La Capelière, Arles, you can visit the nature reserve, popular with birdwatchers for its wild duck, herons and pink flamingos.

Les Baux-de-Provence

The astounding natural location of this medieval citadel, a single massive outcrop of rock cut adrift from the Alpilles mountains like a ship of war separated from its fleet, exerts a unique grip on the popular imagination.

The invasion of the tourist buses in high season has made the little village surrounding the old fortress unbearably crowded.

But a visit in early spring, autumn or, best of all, on a brilliant crisp winter's day can be a rare moment invested with all the magic of the Middle Ages.

The barons of Les Baux put the star of the Nativity on their coat of arms, claiming to be descendants of Balthazar, lord of the treasury among the Three Wise Men. It was with that brazen pride that they ruled 79 towns of medieval Provence, and their impregnable redoubt became a centre of courtly love much prized by travelling troubadours. For centuries they defied the papal authority in Avignon and the kings of France, offering refuge to rebellious Protestants during the Wars of Religion until Louis XIII ordered the destruction of the fortress in 1632—and made the residents pay the costs.

The demolition of the citadel was clearly a halfhearted job, as you can see when you stroll through the **Ville morte** (Dead City), entrance at the Musée lapidaire, Hôtel de la Tour-du-Brau. The ramparts, castle walls and ruined chapels all reveal their own startling views over the sheer ravines to the surrounding mountains.

The jagged peaks of the Alpilles are the last gasp of the great Alpine chain that sweeps in a 1,200-kilometre (750-mile) arc from Vienna. If you're tempted by a hike or bike ride around the valleys, drive on into **Saint-Rémy-de-Provence**, where the *syndicat d'initiative* provides detailed itineraries and advice on renting a bicycle.

🏛 Avignon

The City of the Popes is today a proud cultural centre, home of one of Europe's greatest arts festivals and all year round a lively and cheerful town of good cafés, art galleries and fashionable shops. They no longer dance on the Pont d'Avignon, but there's plenty going on in the discothèques.

The opulence and luxury have disappeared from the **Palais des Papes**, but your visit will still give you an idea of the grandeur and above all the embattled situation of these maverick popes entrenched behind the ramparts of a feudal fortress. The entrance is on the west side, through the Porte des Champeaux, and the guided tour takes you across the Grande Cour (transformed into an open-air theatre for the summer festival) to the **Palais vieux**. Its forbidding design reflects the pious austerity of its builder, Benedict XII, quite out of keeping with his high-living successors.

East of Benedict's cloister is the **consistory**, where the pope met with his cardinals, today decorated with the superb **frescoes** of Simone Martini transferred from the porch of Notre-Dame des Doms cathedral. The process of raising the frescoes from the porch walls revealed Martini's original drawings, which are now

---

Popes, Pro and Anti

Imagine the secretary-general of the Soviet Communist Party deciding to leave Moscow and build a new Kremlin in Krakow. That's what it was like in 1309 when Pope Clement V moved his Holy See from the turmoils of Italy to Avignon. Seven popes, all French, made their home beside the Rhône. Like Rome, Avignon became a city of pomp and intrigue. It attracted great Italian artists, such as the poet Petrarch and Sienese painter Simone Martini, but was soon decried as "an unholy Babylon" of gaudy luxury and vicious riffraff. Not at all to the liking of the pious mystic, Catherine of Siena, who brought Pope Gregory XI back to Rome in 1377.

But a year later, more power struggles caused the Great Schism —doctrinal problems were not uppermost in papal deliberations in those days. Rival popes, known as anti-popes, set up shop back in Avignon for another 40 years. The Schism ended, the infighting returned once and for all to Rome, but Avignon remained part of the papal lands in Provence until the French Revolution.

---

displayed beside the finished paintings.

In Clément VI's more decorative **Palais nouveau,** Martini's disciple Giovannetti has painted frescoes of the Old Testament prophets on the ceiling of the Grand Audience Hall.

Beyond the much-remodelled cathedral, north of the palace, is the pleasant garden of the **Rocher des Doms,** extending to the outer ramparts and giving you your best view of the **Pont d'Avignon,** more properly named the Pont Saint-Bénézet, broken off halfway across the Rhône river. In fact, they used to dance *under* the bridge, on a little island.

The newly restored **Petit Palais,** at the northern end of the Place du Palais, displays, together with Gothic sculpture and frescoes of the Avignon school, a collection of Italian painting from the 13th to 16th century, including major works by Taddeo Gaddi, Veneziano, Botticelli and, the museum's masterpiece, Carpaccio's *Holy Conversation.*

Centre of the bustling life of the modern town is the airy **Place de l'Horloge,** surrounded by cafés and a pedestrian zone of smart shops along the Rue des Marchands. At the far end is the Place Jérusalem and an old synagogue.

For a walk through the **old town,** start at the 14th-century **Eglise Saint-Didier,** with its excruciatingly painful altar sculpture of *Jesus Carrying the Cross* by the Dalmatian artist, Francesco Laurana. The Rue du Roi-René takes you past some handsome 17th- and 18th-century houses. On the pretty cobblestoned **Rue des Teinturiers,** you can see where the dyers used to work the paddlewheels for their Indian-style cloth in the little Sorgue river emerging here from its underground course.

Lubéron and Vaucluse

Starting out from Cavaillon, home of France's, nay, the world's, most succulent cantaloupe melons, head east to the Lubéron mountains, the heart of the Provençal countryside and now a protected regional park. Whole valleys are carpeted with lavender, and the *garrigue* scrubland is ashimmer with every colour and fragrance of the sunny Mediterranean. The villages have been lovingly restored, a few of them so recently that they need a little time for the stone of the houses to recapture its subtle patina, but the Provençal sun and wind weather things fast.

Avignon's July festival centres on the medieval Palais des Papes.

Perched on a spur of rock, the village of **Oppède-le-Vieux** has been rescued from its ruins by writers and artists seeking a residence off the beaten track. The best-intentioned visitor respects the peace of the writer and buys a canvas or two from the painter. **Ménerbes** is also up on a hill, with a medieval fortress that served as the Protestants' last redoubt in the 16th-century Wars of Religion. Behind the church on the outskirts of town, you have a fine **view** over the mountains to the Vaucluse plateau and the distant peak of Mont Ventoux.

Bonnieux juts out over the Coulon valley. From its terrace up on the hill behind the town hall, look north-west to the rust-coloured ravines surrounding **Roussillon**. To set off that startling red, the villagers of Roussillon paint their houses with every imaginable variation of ochre from the nearby quarries.

Its dramatic location looking across to the Lubéron from the southern edge of the Vaucluse plateau has made **Gordes** one of the most prosperous villages in the region, popular for its boutiques and little galleries. Its houses hug the hillside on steep, winding streets, leading to a 16th-century castle at the top. A couple of kilometres south-west of Gordes is the strange little

Village Noir, consisting of *bories*, old dry-stone cabins grouped around a baker's oven and serving as a museum of rural life in Provence.

Aix-en-Provence

It was the first Roman town in Gaul, a citadel and spa founded in 125 B.C. as Aquae Sextiae, but there's nothing left of that. Aix is one of those blessed towns that win the affection of their visitors without the aid of spectacular monuments, grand cathedrals or richly endowed museums. Elegant, charming and cheerful, it forces a grateful smile out of the most world-weary traveller.

The town's great treasure is a street. There are few more refreshing experiences than to arrive in Aix at the end of a hot afternoon and walk along the majestic green arbour formed by the plane trees arching across the **Cours Mirabeau** and its fountains. One side of the street is a quiet row of gracious buff-coloured 17th-century mansions, abandoned by their aristocratic owners to banks or genteel pastry shops dispensing *calissons*, the celebrated local delicacy made from ground almonds, orange and candied melon. The other side is a bustle of cinemas, boutiques and cafés. A rendezvous on the terrace of the Café des Deux Garçons is one of the rare obligations that Provençal life imposes.

People still come to take the waters—the moss-covered fountain in the middle of the Cours Mirabeau spurts water with a natural heat of 34°C (93.2°F). But the university keeps the spirit of the town young, and cosmopolitan—Aix being one of the few provincial towns where non-French films are shown in original versions. You'll find fountains and little squares scattered all over the old town north of the Cours Mirabeau; one of the most attractive squares is the tranquil **Place d'Albertas.**

The cathedral is less worthy of your attention than its exquisite little Romanesque **Cloître Saint-Sauveur,** a peaceful refuge for a quiet read. Chamber music and choral recitals are held there during the summer music festival. The operas are performed behind the cloister, in the Palais de l'Ancien Archevêché.

Paul Cézanne spent most of his life in Aix, and his studio (Atelier de Cézanne, 9, avenue Paul-Cézanne) has been preserved as a little **museum** including his palette and other personal belongings. But the best way to evoke his memory is to make the pretty drive out to the subject of his most famous landscapes, the **Montagne Sainte-Victoire,** 14 kilometres (9 miles) east of Aix on the D 10.

CÔTE D'AZUR

When the British invented this playground in the 19th century, they called it the French Riviera, distinguishing it from the Italian one that begins round the corner at Ventimiglia. Nowadays, it's considered more chic to use its French name, the Côte d'Azur.

In summer, it's overcrowded, but that's the fun of it. You can always head back into the hills for a moment's peace. It's the country's safest bet for good weather, hot days and balmy nights. Apart from an occasional unsightly modern apartment block, the coastline outside the resorts still has considerable charm. The native umbrella pines share the landscape with acacia, eucalyptus and palm trees, imported by the British for the inevitable gardens they built around their villas. For years they came only for the mild winter to cure their chilblains, going home for the summer when, in those days, the coast was infested by mosquitos.

Most of the beaches are great, the boys and girls gorgeous, and the older set have a Fellini-esque charm that makes for very entertaining people-watching.

Nobody knows any more where the Côte d'Azur begins and ends. Purists restrict it to the stretch of coast from Cannes to Menton. That takes in only the original, more expensive resort towns: Juan-les-Pins, Antibes, Nice and Monte Carlo, with Menton dismissed as a pretty but too sleepy retirement community. In recent years, the tourist industry has extended the "Côte" westwards to include popular family-style resorts like Saint-Raphaël and Sainte-Maxime, and the special glamorous phenomenon of Saint-Tropez.

You have to really stretch your imagination to include Marseille, too, but this tough and gritty metropolis is hard to overlook, particularly for the *bouillabaisse*. The Marseillais insist it's the best, and it's not wise to argue with the Marseillais. In fact, to keep them happy, we'll start with Marseille and work our way east.

Marseille

This noisiest and most boisterous of ports is not exactly a tourist attraction. But as France's oldest city, founded by Greek colonists 2,500 years ago, it's not to be ignored.

Its pushy, gabby citizens have more personality in their little finger than most provincials in their whole body. They play the meanest game of *boules*. The politicians make their Boston, Chicago or Liverpool counterparts look like choirboys, and endless police raids have still not broken the French Connection.

Soak up the atmosphere along the main thoroughfare of the **Canebière**, where sailors the world over have broken their hearts and noses.

The **Vieux Port** marks the spot where the Phocaean-Greek merchants of Asia Minor docked to create their Western Mediterranean trading post. Today, it's a colourful harbour for yachts and motor launches. On the Quai des Belges, you can take a cruise out to the **Château d'If**, the island prison that was the scene of Alexandre Dumas's *Count of Monte Cristo*. It also offers a great view of the harbour and town.

Saint-Tropez

The town made famous by the film and rock stars of the 1960s, and whose popularity has been perpetuated by fashion photographers, their models and sundry groupies of the good life, is still going strong. People have always complained that this colourful little fishing port was being "ruined" by its celebrity. Saint-Tropez deserted in wintertime has an undeniably enchanting melancholy, but only for habitués who have known the summer madness.

The essence of Saint-Tropez has always been the crazy parade of people along the **Vieux Port**, nipping in and out of boutiques with their ever more audacious fashions, on and off the flashy yachts and table-hopping through the cafés. Like the Deux Magots in Paris or the Deux Garçons in Aix, the **Sénéquier** might almost be consecrated by the Ministry of Culture as a national people-watching monument where, lounging in their scarlet canvas chairs, the pretty watch the beautiful, and others.

It's unlikely you'll find any masterpieces among the paintings of the harbourside artists, but the **Musée de l'Annonciade** (Place Charles-Grammont) has a quite outstanding collection of works from 1890 to 1940—many of them studies of Saint-Tropez itself. In a handsomely renovated 16th-century chapel, blessed with

Not so easy to get a new perspective on Saint-Tropez's old port.

161

that wonderful natural Mediterranean lighting, they include important canvases by Bonnard, Van Dongen, Matisse and Braque.

Away from the harbour, the town keeps its Provençal character intact on the **Place des Lices**, shaded by plane trees for the morning market, a late afternoon game of *boules* or sunset apéritif at the Café des Arts. For a view over the port, climb up to the 16th-century **citadel**, from which a community of families from Genoa used to defend the town on a coast under constant attack from pirates.

Drive out of town south along the D 93, signposted *Route des Plages*, to Tahiti or Pampelonne for the best **beaches**—fine sand shaded by lovely umbrella pines, but beware of the occasional stinging jellyfish.

Cannes

Pure piece of hedonism, this luxury resort offers a magnificent beach front, the most elegant of boutiques and jewellery shops, the ultimate in grand hotels. Exquisite destiny for a sleepy little fishing village that was "made" by a nearby cholera epidemic in 1834. That's what stopped British law reformer Lord Brougham on his way to Italy. He fell in love with Cannes's climate, built himself a villa, and his aristocratic pals soon followed.

Overlooking the fine white-sand beaches, the **Croisette** is the resort's grand palmtree-lined promenade, from the Palm Beach casino past the great hotels to the old port and the gigantic new **Palais des Festivals**. This is the venue of the international film festival in May and recorded music festival (MIDEM) in January. If you like a mob scene, these are good opportunities to gawk at the stars of show busi-

ness, but don't expect to get in to any of the galas unless you have professional accreditation.

Up on the hill above the port, **Le Suquet** preserves something of the old fishing village, and gives you a fine **view** of the coast. This may whet your appetite for a boat cruise (from the port's Gare maritime) to the **Iles de Lérins** where you can stroll through groves of pines and eucalyptus and beautiful flower gardens.

Boules *is not the kind of sport that gets your weight down.*

A few kilometres east of Cannes are two towns renowned for their craftwork. At **Vallauris**, the ceramics and pottery industry was revived almost single-handedly by Picasso, who worked there after World War II. He also decorated its Romanesque chapel with murals entitled *La Guerre et la Paix* and left a bronze statue on Place Paul-Isnard. **Biot**, worth visiting for its nicely preserved 16th-century centre, is popular for heavy tinted glassware with tiny champagne-like bubbles.

Refreshing fountain for hot days in Saint-Paul-de-Vence.

Saint-Paul-de-Vence

This feudal fortified village is situated amid colourful terraces of vines, bougainvillea and mimosa, with cypresses as their sentinels. For the **view** over the valley, take a drink on the terrace of the Colombe d'Or restaurant. If you stop for dinner, you can see the restaurant's famous collection of paintings by Matisse, Derain and Utrillo.

An even more impressive collection of modern art awaits you at the splendid **Fondation Maeght**, on a grassy hill just outside the town. Here, sculpture takes pride of place, with an imposing black stabile by Alexander Calder at the entrance, some monumental pieces by Miró in the gardens and a matchless array of Giacometti statues in their own courtyard.

Nice

An ancient Greek trading post, the town manages to combine the atmosphere of a bracing resort with a gutsy, bustling city life. The people are by nature highly independent—Nice was not incorporated into France until 1860—and tend to look down on the indolence of neighbouring Cannes. The good shopping and first-class restaurants more than make up for the pebble beach.

Instead of sprawling on sand, natives and visitors alike take the air on the grand **Promenade des Anglais**, financed by the town's English colony in 1822 to replace a wretched little footpath. Its most remarkable landmark is the pink-domed **Hôtel Negresco**, a masterpiece of *Belle Epoque* wedding-cake architecture. The promenade ends with a spectacular display of flowers and fountains in the **Jardin Albert-Ier**.

The **vieille ville** is at its best at the early morning **fish market** on Place Saint-François. Find out what's good that day for your evening meal. The **port** is worth a visit for a genteel waterside dinner or, more amusing, a drink at the rough-and-ready sailors' taverns.

For a good view over the port and the Baie des Anges, climb up to the little park on top of the hill still known as **Le Château**, even though its castle was destroyed nearly 300 years ago. The ruins you can see are the remains of the 11th-century cathedral.

Les Corniches

The route from Nice to Monaco, along the precipices of the Maritime Alps' southern slopes, offers one of the most spectacular drives in the country. There are actually three winding roads or Corniches, all safe but exciting —*Grande*, the high road, starting out from the Avenue des Diables-Bleus in Nice, *Moyenne*, in the middle, beginning at Place Max-Barel) and *Inférieure*, along the coast from Boulevard Carnot, but nearly always traffic-jammed.

The **Grande Corniche**, built by Napoleon, follows the route of the ancient Roman road, Via Aurelia. Stop off at **Belvédère d'Eze** and **La Turbie** for great views of the coast, especially at night for the lights of Monaco. In La Turbie, climb up to the remains of a curious 2,000-year-old Roman monument, the towering **Trophée des Alpes** built by Emperor Augustus to celebrate victories over 44 Gallic tribes, named in the inscription on the base.

Highlight of the **Moyenne Corniche**, the best road of the three, is the hilltop village of **Eze** hanging at a dizzying angle above the sea, once the fortress of Ligurian brigands. In summer, it's a bit of a tourist trap, but take a look at the cacti, tropical flowers (and ruins of a 14th-century castle) in the **Jardin exotique**. Its terrace affords the best view of the coast.

Monaco

The cliché is the truth, a phenomenon deserving close examination. It really is a millionaire's paradise. Ever since the roulette wheel and baccarat tables began earning enough money to do away with taxes in the 19th century, the minute principality has attracted the cream of dethroned Eastern European monarchs, tired American moguls and Nordic striplings resting their tennis elbow and athlete's foot.

Surrounded by **exotic gardens** to provide a little sweet-scented breathing space, gleaming skyscrapers have sprung up to pack all that wealth into the tiny area between mountain and Mediterranean. North of the square-shaped port, **Monte-Carlo** is the centre of the principality's luxury. The world's most celebrated **casino** was designed by Charles Garnier, architect of the Paris Opera House, and has the same grandiose nonsense all over the façade, foyer and gambling-rooms. Don't miss the lovely nude nymphs smoking cigarillos on the ceiling of the Salon Rose.

Across the square, the **Hôtel de Paris** is another monument of unabashed ostentation. In the lobby, gamblers in search of luck have stroked Louis XIV's bronze equestrian statue until the horse's fetlock shines like the gold they lose next door. The outrageous Second Empire décor of the dining-room provided the perfect setting for famed chef Auguste Escoffier to create his outrageously elaborate sauces.

The **Palais du Prince** up on Monaco Rock is a fairy-tale affair, Neo-renaissance and Neo-baroque, with a quaint **changing of the guard**, fife, drums and all, at 11.55 a.m. every day.

Table For One
One evening back in the 1920s, James Gordon Bennett didn't like being kept waiting for his usual table at Monte-Carlo's Café Riche. So the multimillionaire American newspaper publisher bought the café, fired the manager and gave it to Ciro, his favourite waiter.

CORSICA

In every sense a region apart from the rest of France, this rugged island offers dramatic coastlines and a wild interior of densely forested hills. Still largely unspoiled, it is the ideal place to escape the Riviera crowd. The population of less than quarter of a million is concentrated mainly in the two major towns of Bastia (industrial and noisy) and the more attractive Ajaccio. The people are less fierce than they look and give you a simple, unaffected welcome.

Alternate indolent days on the beach with some of the Mediterranean's best deep-sea diving, boat excursions around pirate coves, canoeing and fishing on inland rivers or hikes and picnics in the mountains. For the holidaymaker, the best resorts are along the indented shorelines of the western and southern coasts, for which Ajaccio's airport or harbour (for the car ferry from Nice, Toulon or Marseille) provides the ideal gateway. Give yourself plenty of driving time, as the roads are narrow and tortuous. To be on the safe side, calculate an average of 40 to 50 kph.

Ajaccio

At the head of the Gulf of Ajaccio, Napoleon's birthplace is the liveliest of Corsican towns, but tourists impatient to get out to the seaside resorts are usually content with a stroll around the **port** and a pilgrimage to the **Maison Bonaparte** (Rue Saint-Charles). A guided tour will tell you how, on Assumption Day (August 15), 1769, pious mother Letizia was rushed out of church with her first birth pains. She made it no further than a first-floor sofa to bring little Nabulio kicking and screaming into the world he was soon to conquer. The sofa you see there now is a replica, the original having been stolen during the Revolution. You can also see paintings of Napoleon's parents and officers, the sword he wore as lieutenant-colonel and other memorabilia.

South of Ajaccio, the major seaside resorts are **Porticcio** and **Propriano**, both with sandy beaches and good opportunities for sailing and deep-sea diving.

Sartène

Constant prey in olden days to the pirates of North Africa, this heavily fortified town has preserved its medieval appearance around the massive granite **hôtel de ville**, once the palace of the Genoese governors. There are strange perspectives to be discovered from the narrow streets, staircases and archways suddenly opening out to a view of the sea down below on one side or the Rizzanese valley on the other.

Bonifacio

This proud port city occupies a narrow peninsula surrounded by towering white chalk cliffs, in striking contrast to the red granite predominant in the rest of the island.

The best way to appreciate the spectacular location of the old town perched high on the cliffs is to take a **boat cruise** from the marina at the entrance to Bonifacio. The cruise takes you deep into the limpid blue waters of the **Sdragonato cave**. The "skylight" in its roof is shaped exactly like a map of Corsica. As the boat passes along the southern side of town, notice the **Escalier du roi d'Aragon**, a staircase cut diagonally into the cliff face, used by the soldiers of the Spanish king in an abortive siege of the town in the 15th century. When visiting the old town on foot, take an exhilarating walk down the staircase to the base of the cliffs and along the water's edge, climbing gradually back up to the southern end of town.

Some Hero

You wouldn't believe, from all the statues and souvenirs, and the streets named after them, that Corsica once heartily hated the whole Bonaparte clan.

In the 1760s, when nearly 500 years of rule under the republic of Genoa was coming to an end, Carlo Maria Buonaparte fervently supported Corsican independence. But the island was ceded to France in 1768, and Carlo Maria promptly became an equally fervent supporter of Louis XV. His son Napoleon, born a year later, became a Corsican nationalist but went on with brother Lucien to champion the French Revolution's opposition to the island's separatism. The family house in Ajaccio was plundered to cries of "Death to the traitors of the fatherland!" Things didn't improve when Napoleon became Emperor. The city celebrated his abdication by tossing his statue into the Mediterranean.

Porto-Vecchio

Surrounded by a pretty forest of cork oaks and sweet-smelling eucalyptus, the gulf surrounding Porto-Vecchio has an ever-expanding series of luxury resorts, the best being out on the fine sandy beaches of **Cala Rossa**.

Inland, there are some beautiful excursions to be made into the forests of **l'Ospedale** and **Zonza**. The cork oaks are stripped of their valuable bark every ten years or so, baring a russet-brown trunk until the cork grows back again.

For a picnic up on the wild, lovely mountain pass of **Bavella**, take some of the great local tomatoes, smoked liver sausage *(figatelli)* and ewe's or goat's milk cheese *(broccio)*. Be careful with the heady Corsican wines before sundown; the most enjoyable are the *rosés*.

Golfe de Porto

Some of France's most grandiose panoramas of sea and landscape are clustered around this gulf 70 kilometres (43 miles) north of Ajaccio.

Piana is the most delightful of its sleepy village resorts, unspoiled by commercialization and blessed with the nearby natural wonders of **Capo Rosso** and the **Calanche.** These rugged red granite cliffs and boulders have been hurled down to the sea

Craggy backdrop to the beaches on Corsica's Golfe de Porto.

by volcanic eruptions and eroded there by wind and water into the most bizarre and fanciful shapes. Some of the Calanche boulders are hidden in a forest of sea pines, lying there like sleeping monsters. Over the centuries, they have been nicknamed Dog, Eagle or Turtle, but you'll recognize your own big-nosed geography teacher or even, along the well-marked walk of the **Chemin du Château-fort,** an unmistakably bouffant-hairstyled prime minister. Thick-soled shoes are recommended for your walks over the rocks.

Be sure to take a **boat cruise** from the little resort town of Porto. The best one goes out to the cliff caves on the northern edge of the gulf, to the isolated fishing village of **Girolata,** and the marvellous nature reserve of **Scandola,** a coastal haven for eagles, bald buzzards and other rare species nesting on the peaks of the jagged volcanic rocks.

In the interior, drive along the winding mountain road to Evisa and the cool, quiet **Forest of Aitone**. Off the D 84 road just 3 kilometres (2 miles) north-east of Evisa is a sign reading *Piscine*. Follow the path: it's not a municipal chlorine-saturated swimming pool, but a series of clear, clean, natural pools formed in smooth slabs of rock by the **Cascades d'Aïtone** (waterfalls). A sheer delight.

SOUTH-WEST

From the southern edge of the Loire Valley to the Pyrenees, the area encompasses what vote-hungry politicians call *la France profonde*, the French heartland distant in geography and spirit alike from the vanities and preoccupations of Paris.

Apart from a comparatively recent *autoroute* skirting the region from Tours down to Bordeaux, and another from Bordeaux to Toulouse and Montpellier, road access from Paris has been slow and complicated. This has been tough on the local economy of the central regions but has kept the landscape blessedly unspoiled.

In and around the lovely valley of the Dordogne, the Périgord beckons with its rich cuisine, fortified towns, fascinating cave paintings and other prehistoric remains. From the Basque country to the Mediterranean, you can explore the sunny mountains of the Pyrenees, country of France's most popular king, happy-go-lucky Henri IV. And in between, the historic towns of Montpellier, Albi and Toulouse.

The Atlantic coast remains the preserve of the country's most independent-minded ports, the Protestant stronghold of La Rochelle and proud, prosperous Bordeaux, with its hinterland of great vineyards.

PÉRIGORD

This rich and fertile country is densely forested and crisscrossed by rivers flowing from the plateau of the Massif Central out to the Atlantic. Of these, the Dordogne has carved out through the centre a beautiful winding valley of gentle greenery.

In the village markets, the fruit and vegetables, mushrooms and nuts of every description bear witness to the region's self-sufficiency in food. Gourmets lament the dwindling supply of truffles snuffled out by the pigs under a special kind of oak tree, but the *pâté de foie gras* and slowly roasted *confit* of goose and duck are as succulent as ever. Even the salads of the Quercy region are all the more subtle for their dressing in walnut oil.

If so many relics of Stone Age men have been found here rather than elsewhere in France, it's because they favoured the unique combination of abundant fish supplies in the rivers and dwell-ings safe from wild animals in the caves and grottos riddling the valley cliffs.

With a similar concern for self-protection, the proliferation of ramparts and fortresses throughout the Périgord is a vestige of the many wars against the English, between Protestant and Catholic, and resistance to marauding bands of brigands left behind at the end of each battle.

Bourges

Capital of the flat region of Berry on the northern "frontier" of the Périgord, the town is worth a brief detour, if you're taking the N 20 highway down from Orléans.

The intricate harmony of the five portals of its façade, and the peculiar grace of its silhouette make **Cathédrale Saint-Etienne** one of the country's half-dozen Gothic masterpieces. The church is dominated by the massive nave and graceful flying buttresses linking the five chapels to the chancel (best view from the arch-bishop's gardens behind the cathedral). The Last Judgment portrayed on the centre portal is an example of 13th-century sculpture at its best. Inside, note the magnificent vaulting and the 13th-century **stained-glass win-dows**, around the choir and apsi-dal chapels.

The **Palais Jacques-Cœur**, a rare jewel of Gothic secular

171

architecture, was the residence of a wealthy merchant, treasurer to Charles VII. The elegance of the palace becomes apparent only in the inner courtyard, with its seven turreted staircases and handsome balconies. The mottos engraved around the windows proclaim the self-made man: *A vaillans (cœurs) riens impossible* (To valiant hearts, nothing is impossible) and *Dire, faire, taire* (Say, do and shut up). Note the pigeon loft from which, 400 years before Reuters and Associated Press, Jacques Cœur organized a private news service with carrier pigeons.

As fast as traffic on the N 20 highway allows, hurry via the porcelain-capital of Limoges and market town of Brive-la-Gaillarde into the heart of the Périgord Noir, so-called because of the dominant dark green of its oak forests. South-west of Brive is the beginning of France's beginnings—the Stone Age caves along the Vézère river.

Vallée de la Vézère

Exploring the valley that shelters the earliest signs of European civilization and man's artistic awakening is by no means a dry and dusty archaeological tour of fossils and bones. The region in any case would be idyllic for hikes and picnics. Around the caves that pockmark the cliffs overhanging the Vézère river is a green and pleasant countryside of meadows, vineyards and orchards and a profusion of graceful willows and poplars at the water's edge.

Montignac is the departure point for your visit to the world-famous cave paintings of **Lascaux**. Concealed and protected against atmospheric changes for 17,000 years, these awe-inspiring frescoes and engravings of bulls, horses, ibex, bison and deer were discovered in 1940—by four boys chasing their dog down a hole. Within a few years, the humidity of human bodies and the exhaust fumes wafted in from passing traffic caused a rapid deterioration, and the caves had to be closed to the general public.

Now, the original caves (four galleries of 200 paintings and 1,500 engravings) can be seen only by special appointment. An authoritative guided tour in French or English is available for a maximum of *five* people each day. Write to: Directeur des Antiquités préhistoriques d'Aquitaine, 26–28, place Gambetta, 33000 Bordeaux.

Although the thrill of seeing the original work of these prehistoric artists is undeniable, the astonishingly realistic replica created at **Lascaux II** makes a very satisfying alternative. Anthropologists and artists have reproduced the *Salle des Taureaux* (Hall of Bulls) with 100 pictures of the animals that shared the environment of Stone Age man.

Complete your visit with a side trip to **Le Thot**, where the museum has some excellent audio-visual exhibits and models of cave life; the nearby park has been turned into a zoo devoted to descendants of the animals portrayed at Lascaux.

Back on the river, you pass the 16th-century **Château de Losse** (visitors can admire its Italian Renaissance furniture and tapestries) on your way to **Saint-Léon-sur-Vézère**. Surrounded by poplars and willows, the town's buff-stoned 11th-century church, with its stone-slabbed roof and graceful windowed steeple, is a characteristic example of Périgord Romanesque. For a wonderful view of the valley, climb to the top of **La Roque Saint-Christophe**, a spectacular long cliff 80 metres (262 feet) high and honeycombed with caves inhabited 20,000 years ago.

The French taste in grandiloquent epithets for its cultural centres is fully indulged, and not totally unjustified, at **Les Eyzies-de-Tayac**, *"capitale de la préhistoire"*. Besides its important **museum** in the remains of a medieval castle, the village is at the centre of literally dozens of major palaeolithic excavation sites, explored only since the 19th century by the French pioneers of studies in prehistory.

The Cro-Magnon shelter *(Abri de Cro-Magnon)* on the north side of town is the spot where railway workers uncovered in 1868 three 30,000-year-old human skeletons beside their flint and bone tools. The forefathers of the painters of Lascaux were the most advanced of our direct prehistoric ancestors. Anthropologists say that these tall, large-brained men with high forehead *(homo sapiens sapiens)* were of a

---

Stone Age Art
Because no household tools or weapons were found near the paintings of the deep galleries, scholars have deduced that most of the French caves were not dwellings, but sanctuaries where Stone Age man depicted the beasts he hunted and probably worshipped. For his home, he preferred cave entrances or the shelter of a cliff overhang. Some of the frescoes show animals pierced with arrows or spears, perhaps a form of sympathetic magic to promote success in the hunt.

The artists depicted their potential game with red and yellow oxidized iron, powdered ochre, black charcoal and animal fats. They blew powdered colour on to the walls of the caves through hollow bones or vegetable stalks, basically the same technique as aerosol-graffiti artists in the latter-day caves of a modern subway.

---

physical type still to be seen in parts of south-western France.

For cave paintings, all accessible by guided tour only, the most attractive site is the **Grotte de Font-de-Gaume**, reached by an easy walk up on a cliff above the eastern edge of town. The pictures of mammoths, bison, horses and reindeer are between 15,000 and 40,000 years old. The **Combarelles** cave, further east, is a long winding gallery where the pictures are engraved rather than painted, and very often superimposed.

The caves of the **Grotte du Grand Roc** north-west of Les Eyzies are a natural rather than historical phenomenon, but well worth a visit for the weirdly shaped stalagmites and stalactites and the panorama of the Vézère valley.

Dordogne

This valley is so beloved by British and Dutch holidaymakers that cunning travel agents quite happily extend its name to the whole Périgord region. For the British in particular, its rolling green countryside of river, meadow, copse and hedgerow, fertilized with the blood of their ancestors in the Hundred Years' War, is a "home from home", with the bonus of a ruined castle or two, roast goose and walnut liqueur.

The river is good for fishing

and canoeing, and if you haven't brought your own bike to explore the back country, you can rent one at Sarlat.

Start at the confluence of the Vézère and Dordogne rivers, where the hilltop village of **Limeuil** affords a fine view of both valleys and their bridges meeting at right angles down below. Drive south away from the river to **Cadouin**, with its impressive 12th-century Cistercian **abbey**, a major Périgord Romanesque church with wooden belfry on a remarkable split pyramidal cupola. The soberly designed church contrasts with the more decorative Gothic and Renaissance sculpture of the cloister.

Back on the river, perched above a 150-metre (490-foot) ravine, the redoubt of **Beynac-et-Cazenac** is a splendid fairy-tale castle, much frequented by English troublemakers in the Middle Ages. The barons of Beynac lost it in turn to Richard the Lion-Heart and Simon de Montfort, Earl of Leicester, before turning it into a handsome Renaissance palace. Across the river stands Beynac's rival, **Castelnaud,** in ruins, and the 15th-century castle of **Fayrac**, with drawbridge, battlements and pepperpot towers nicely restored.

The mysterious Dordogne valley is a place for romantic dreamers.

You get a magnificent view of all three castles from **La Roque-Gageac**. It has won a prize as one of the most beautiful villages in the country, especially true when the late afternoon sun catches the houses' stone-tiled roofs. It's also an antique-collectors' paradise (amateurs beware).

Sarlat, capital of the Périgord Noir, is a lovely old town, bustling in high season but of unrecognizable quiet charm in spring and autumn. The **Saturday market** on the Place du Marché-aux-Oies is a joy, as are the narrow streets of the old town east of the busy Rue de la République. Look out for the Gothic and Renaissance houses on Rue Fénélon, Rue des Consuls, especially **Hôtel Plamon**, and Place du Peyrou's grand **Maison de La Boétie**, across from the cathedral. An open-air summer festival is held on Place de la Liberté. And don't leave without trying that humblest and most delectable delicacy: *pommes sarladaises*, thin-sliced potatoes sautéed in goose fat with garlic and parsley, the sweetest death known to Western man.

Porcelain geese invite you to try some Périgord foie gras. Padirac's stalactites are more forbidding.

Rocamadour

Since the 12th century, sightseers and religious pilgrims alike have been flocking to this spectacularly situated fortified town up on its cliff top above the Alzou river (best appreciated from the eastern vantage point of L'Hospitalet on D 673). Founded on the tomb of a hermit, Saint Amadour, believed to have mystic curative powers, Rocamadour attracted Henry II of England and many French kings after him.

The modern mob scene buzzing around the souvenir shops and the **Chapelle miraculeuse de Notre-Dame** captures something of the medieval frenzy. The secular visitor may prefer to get there by the elevator rather than the 216 steps of the Via Sancta, which reformed heretics and other penitents were obliged to negotiate on their knees with heavy chains around their neck and arms.

The great chasm *(gouffre)* of **Padirac**, 16 kilometres (10 miles) north-east of Rocamadour, is one of the Périgord's most exhilarating natural wonders. Elevators take you 100 metres (328 feet) down to a subterranean river for a delightfully spooky boat ride past huge stalactites and stalagmites formed by the calcite residue and deposits of thousands of years of dripping water.

ATLANTIC COAST

Decidedly more businesslike than those of the Mediterranean, the major Atlantic coastal towns are notable for their civic pride, and the resorts appeal more to the sailor than the beach-lover. What the vineyards around Bordeaux lack in attractive landscape and villages (apart from Saint-Emilion) they make up for in the quality of their wines, with good possibilities for tasting.

La Rochelle

One of the most handsome of France's ports, this historic bastion of Protestantism seduces the visitor with its quiet charm and dignity.

Surrounded by lively cafés, with an avenue of trees along one quay, the old harbour still serves the fishing fleet and small sailboats. Its entrance is guarded by two 14th-century towers remaining from the town's fortifications. To the left, the **Tour Saint-Nicolas** served as fortress and prison. At the foot of the **Tour de la Chaîne**, a gunpowder storehouse, lies the huge chain slung across to Saint-Nicolas to bar passage at night. The grand old lighthouse (and second prison), **Tour de la Lanterne**, now stands inland at the end of the ramparts of the Rue Sur-les-Murs. You'll find prisoners' graffiti on the walls of the graceful octagonal steeple, as you climb up to the balcony for its view over the city and the bay.

The Gothic tower gate and belfry, **Porte de la Grosse-Horloge,** leads into the prosperous old merchant quarters. Note the gracefully vaulted shopping arcades and galleries of the 16th- and 17th-century houses. On the Rue des Merciers, don't miss the handsome Renaissance **hôtel de ville**, with its Italian-style courtyard, staircase and belfry. Another elegant house is the double-gabled **Hôtel de Pontard** hidden away at the rear of a garden at the savings bank (Caisse d'Epargne, 11, rue des Augustins).

The **Musée des Beaux-Arts** (28, rue Gargoulleau) includes an important portrait of Martin Luther by Lucas Cranach and notable canvases by Giordano and Ribera.

Ile de Ré

Gleaming white villas and smart little hotels, a sunny microclimate, pine-shaded beaches, good oysters and mussels—this cheerful island is much appreciated as a holiday resort, especially for the sailing possibilities from the harbour of its "capital", **Saint-Martin-de-Ré**. Visit the **Phare des Baleines**, a light-

A great meal to be had from the oyster beds of Arcachon.

house at the west end of the island (257 steps to the view at the top).

Excursions depart from La Rochelle's Vieux Port. Advance booking is necessary for the car ferry that leaves the commercial harbour of La Pallice.

Bordeaux

Useful as an obvious base of operations for wine-enthusiasts, this commercial metropolis may be too busy for other holiday-makers.

Ship folk will head for the great **port** to see the freighters

Built to protect the town during bitter conflict between Protestants and Catholics, La Rochelle's fortifications now make a picturesque car park.

and tankers from Asia, Australia, Africa and the Americas. Guided tours by launch depart from the landing stage *(embarcadère Vedettes)* of the vast Esplanade des Quinconces.

Landlubbers prefer the cafés, shops and galleries around the **Place de la Comédie**, a main centre of city life. The square is dominated by the **Grand Théâtre**, the jewel of Bordeaux's many 18th-century buildings. It is a temple-like structure of 12 Corinthian columns, its entablature adorned with the statues of the Greek muses and the goddesses Juno, Venus and Minerva. The majestic double staircase inside inspired Charles Garnier for his design of the Paris Opera House.

South of the imposing Place de la Bourse, the old **Quartier Saint-Pierre** around the church of the same name is a masterpiece of urban renewal. The once ill-famed slum has grown into a lively neighbourhood of art galleries and quaint little shops, with an open-air market on Place Saint-Pierre. On the beautifully renovated houses along Rue Philippart and Rue Bahutiers, notice the grotesque masks and winged angels sculpted over the doorways.

The dimensions of the Flamboyant Gothic **Cathédrale Saint-André** rival those of Notre-Dame de Paris, which is only 6 metres (20 feet) longer and 4 metres (13 feet) wider. It has some remarkable sculpture over the porches. Inside, the unusual, almost blasphemous Renaissance **bas-reliefs** on the organ loft show Jesus ascending to heaven on an eagle like a Greek god, and descending to Limbo among diabolical figures of the Underworld.

The **Musée des Beaux-Arts** (cours d'Albret) includes works of Veronese, Perugino, Rubens and Van Dyck and major paintings by Delacroix and Matisse.

For a guided **wine tour**, contact the Maison du Vin, 1, cours du 30-juillet, 33075 Bordeaux. This wine-growers' association also organizes tastings.

Saint-Emilion

At the western end of the Dordogne valley, this is undoubtedly the most attractive of the Bordeaux wine villages, enhanced by the golden-tinted stone of the medieval houses around its sleepy Place du Marché. Unique in Europe, the 1,000-year-old church known as the **Eglise Monolithe** was carved out of the solid rock on which the village was built. After wandering around the old ramparts and narrow streets, take a rest in the ivy-covered ruins of the 14th-century **Cloître des Cordeliers**. The local Maison du Vin can give advice for your tour of the surrounding vineyards.

181

PYRENEES

The mountains that form France's natural barrier with Spain present for the most part a landscape of gentle rolling greenery, in marked contrast to the more formidable Alps. Snowcapped peaks are few and distant, and rugged "moon-scapes" an exception. Even the mountain streams tend more to the babbling brook than the turbulent torrent.

This is the land of tough-and-tumbling rugby. But after the match, camaraderie knows no bounds, much enhanced by a bottle or two of full-bodied Madiran or robust Roussillon.

Tourism is a little-developed industry. Cross-country skiing is greatly favoured, with the result that the mountain scenery is unspoiled by pylons and chair lifts. The Pyrenees are ideal for hiking and camping, one of the rare regions still open to "discovery".

Biarritz

Nostalgia-fans will appreciate the patina of faded grandeur of this resort, where Queen Victoria once promenaded along the front, Bismarck fell madly in love with the wife of a Russian ambassador, and the Prince of Wales took care of all the others.

Today, hortensias and tamarisks still ornament the seafront gardens. But the **Grande Plage** is no longer considered a hazard,

Sun-worshippers on the Biarritz promenade will be here any minute.

unlike in 1900 when it was known as the *Plage des Fous* (Madmen's Beach). And fewer suicidal shots ring out from the casinos. The Villa Eugénie, from which the wife of Napoleon III made Biarritz fashionable, has become the **Hôtel du Palais**, an extravagant monument of idle

luxury where the barmen tell you stories of the heiresses who seduced their grandfathers. Dare all and take tea beside the fantastic swimming pool.

The easy beach walk is from the lighthouse of **Cap Saint-Martin** out to the rugged **Rocher de la Vierge**. Beyond, the big waves of the Plage de la Côte des Basques are more suitable for expert surfers and windsurfers than for desultory bathers.

When you're a little sun-silly, cool off at the aquarium of the **Musée de la Mer**. Or take a pleasant day trip to nearby **Bayonne** where the **Musée Basque**, in a 16th-century mansion, offers a valuable introduction to the folklore of the region.

Saint-Jean-de-Luz

Less famous than Biarritz, this charming little fishing village has converted from whale to tuna

*Basque country invites both
the energetic hiker and siesta-fans.*

(tunny) and anchovy, and similarly has small-scale but delightful attractions around its sheltered **harbour.** The cafés, galleries and boutiques are lively, the artist's colony not at all phony and the timbered houses of the shipbuilders' old **Quartier de la Barre** tastefully preserved.

The town's great claim to fame is the wedding of Louis XIV to the Spanish Infanta Maria Theresa in 1660; the houses that lodged them, **Maison de Louis XIV** and **Maison de l'Infante**, still stand by the port. The austere exterior of the 15th-century **Eglise Saint-Jean-Baptiste**, where the wedding was celebrated, doesn't prepare you for the characteristic Basque ornament inside: carved oak galleries to separate the classes of worshippers on three sides of a single nave, with polychrome wooden vaulting and a grandiose three-tiered gilded and crimson Baroque altar.

Pays Basque

The fierce regional pride of the Basques is nourished in the most serene and restful landscape imaginable. Amid sunny valleys and rolling green hills, their gabled houses are immaculately maintained, gleaming white, set off by russet brown timbering. The Basques are as pious as the Bretons, and decorate the interiors of their churches with meticulous carpentry.

From Saint-Jean-de-Luz, take the D918 south to **Ascain**. Its village square is surrounded by handsome 17th-century houses, and there's a typical wooden-galleried church. A rack railway at Col de Saint-Ignace carries you 900 metres (2,950 feet) up to the top of **La Rhune** for an exhilarating view of the Atlantic Ocean and the western Pyrenees.

Sare is a favourite stop for gourmets and hikers—or a healthy combination of the two. You can measure the villagers' religious fervour by the grand Baroque altar in the church. And there's no more attractive demonstration of the Basques' independent-minded nature than the main street of **Aïnhoa**, where each sturdy-beamed whitewashed house is of a different height, jutting out at a different angle. The church, too, is worth visiting for the gilded timbers of its choir.

Saint-Jean-Pied-de-Port was the last stage before crossing into Spain on one of the main routes of pilgrimage to Santiago de Compostela. Follow the pilgrims' path around the **ramparts**, up a stairway through Porte Saint-Jacques to the **ville haute**.

Don't Put All Your Basques In One Exit

The origins of this people settled on the Spanish and French sides of the Pyrenees, in the old kingdom of Navarre, remain a mystery. Their language is known to be older than the invasion of the Indo-Europeans and is still spoken in the mountains.

The 80,000 French Basques are less militant than their 600,000 Spanish cousins, but they lovingly cultivate the traditional arts, particularly their songs and dances, imbued with a strange melancholy passion. In times of hardship, to avoid the scattering of the family wealth, one child was designated heir to the house and land, not necessarily the eldest, while the others emigrated, most often to the Americas. The Basque ball-game of pelota turns up around Miami, for instance, as jai alai.

185

Note the charming red sandstone houses along the **Rue de la Citadelle** leading to an old bridge across the Nive river, with a pretty view of the town's Gothic church. For the panorama across the Nive valley, climb up to the **citadel** which Louis XIV had built to defend against a potential Spanish invasion.

Leave the D933 at Larceveau to cut east across the **Col d'Osquich**, delightful walking and picnic country with a constant view of the Pyrenees peaks to the south. End your tour of the Pays Basque at **Oloron-Sainte-Marie**, with a visit to its 12th-century **Eglise Sainte-Marie**, notable for the remarkable sculpture of medieval life on its Romanesque portal in white Pyrenees marble.

Pau

The town holds a special place in French hearts as the birthplace of their beloved Henri IV in 1553. More recently, after their victorious campaigns against the French in the Pyrenees, the Duke of Wellington's veterans appreciated its balmy climate and retired there to make it something of a British colony. The British provided two mayors—Taylor and O'Quinn—and left their mark with the country's first golf club, horse racing and fox hunting, all still going strong.

Today, the **Château de Pau**, more Renaissance palace than

> *King Pong*
> It has often been told that his grandfather, determined to make a man of the future Henri IV as fast as possible, rubbed the new-born babe's lips with a clove of garlic and a few drops of the local Jurançon wine. The garlic habit stuck, and Henri, indefatigable horseman and infrequent bather, made a point of honour of cultivating a pungent body odour as a badge of virility. On the rare occasions when he slept with his own wife, who did care for personal hygiene, she complained she had to change the sheets two or three times a night.

fortress, heavily restored in the 19th century, remains an interesting museum of Gobelins tapestries and paraphernalia from the early life of the country's most popular king. Difficult to distinguish legend from fact in the life of this lusty womanizer. But it's doubtful whether Henri IV actually did sleep in the great tortoiseshell said to be his cradle.

Stroll along the terrace at the foot of the Château, known as the **Boulevard des Pyrénées**, for the region's most spectacular view of the snowcapped peaks lining the southern horizon like a white crystal necklace. The chief treasure of the **Musée des Beaux-Arts** is a fascinating Degas, *The New Orleans Cotton Exchange*.

Saint-Bertrand-de-Comminges

Pleasant detour off the Pau–Toulouse road, this fortified hilltop town has a fine Romanesque-Gothic **cathedral** that merits an extended visit. Inside, the superb 16th-century wooden sculptures of the **choir stalls** make up a cheerful compendium of Pyrenees characters, high and low. Look out, too, for the Renaissance pulpit and organ (recitals throughout the summer). The open Romanesque arcades allow the peaceful little **cloister** to take full advantage of the mountain backdrop—notice the four Apostles carved in the middle of the western arcade.

Toulouse

Centre of the national aerospace industry, with a vigorous local culture and bright and breezy street life, the city has an infectious enthusiasm to it. The charm works quickly if you hang out at the cafés on **Place Wilson** or shop in the boutiques in the nicely refurbished old houses of the **Rue des Changes** and **Rue Saint-Rome**, and the second-hand book shops around the church of Saint-Sernin.

The red brick of its major monuments and old houses, the dominant building material of the region, has won Toulouse the name *la ville rose*. The structural prowess of its architects in this medium can be seen in the magnificent 11th-century **Basilique Saint-Sernin**, a true masterpiece among France's Romanesque churches. On the south side of the church, note the 12th-century **Porte Miègeville** and the vigorous sculpture of the Apostles gazing up at the Ascension of Jesus on the tympanum.

Dedicated to the first bishop of Toulouse, the church served as a major gathering place for the pilgrimage to Santiago de Compostela, which explains the need for such a vast nave and the eight doors to let the masses in and out. Be sure to see the seven beautiful 11th-century marble **bas-reliefs** on the wall of the ambulatory beyond the choir. They portray Jesus triumphant, flanked by angels and two Apostles.

The church of **les Jacobins**, burial place of philosopher and theologian Thomas Aquinas, is a Gothic fortress church comparable to Albi's cathedral, with a noble tower and elegant twin-columned **cloister.** For years it suffered many indignities, even serving as a stable for Napoleon's artillery corps. Modern restoration has retrieved the polychrome beauty of its interior—subtle dark reds, pink and buff—illuminated by the 20th-century stained glass.

The town's civic pride is given concrete expression in the grand

Gothic and Renaissance houses of merchants who made their fortune in woad for the textile industry. They proclaimed their success with the highest tower they could build. The **Hôtel de Bernuy** (1, rue Gambetta), now a high school, reveals its splendours once you are inside the gates. The first courtyard has a monumental Renaissance stone loggia and arcade, while a second courtyard is in traditional red brick and boasts an octagonal tower for its staircase. At the equally splendid **Hôtel d'Assézat**, set back from the Rue de Metz and home of various scholarly academies, you can climb the lanterned tower for a panoramic **view** of the city.

At the corner of Rue de Metz and Rue d'Alsace-Lorraine, the **Musée des Augustins** houses in a converted medieval monastery one of the richest collections of religious sculpture in France—treasures recovered from the cloister of Saint-Sernin and the monastery of Notre-Dame de la Daurade, both destroyed in the 19th century, and from the cathedral of Saint-Etienne, reduced today to an ungainly hodgepodge. Among the Romanesque sculptures, look out for King David tuning his harp and the death of John the Baptist. Most important of the Gothic pieces is a Madonna and Child known as *Notre-Dame-de-Grâce*.

Carcassonne

This is the town for all who like fairy-tale castles. It has served as a fortress for the Gallo-Romans, Visigoths, Franks and medieval French; you can see layers of their masonry in the ramparts.

You'll get your best overall view of the town from the *autoroute*—most dramatic with the night-time illuminations. Try to slow down without causing a traffic jam. Most people park on the east side of the old town *(la Cité)* and walk over the drawbridge of the **Porte Narbonnaise,** convenient for the *syndicat d'initiative* and the souvenir shops of Rue Cros-Mayrevieille.

But you'll get a better feel for the medieval atmosphere of a fortified town, its ramparts and lookout towers, if you park on the west side, by the church of Saint-Gimer, and walk up around the old **Château Comtal**. After a look at the ancient sarcophagi and medieval sculpture in the castle's little museum, take the guided tour around the parapets.

If the battlements and pepperpot towers, the dungeons, moats and drawbridges strike you as a bit too much, put some of it down to the romantic imagination of Viollet-le-Duc. Much

Saint-Sernin basilica towers over a Toulouse bric-à-brac market.

188

is authentic, but the great 19th-century architect who performed the restoration work had a somewhat fanciful idea of feudal architecture and stuck on all kinds of frills and furbelows if he lacked the original plans. The most blatant example of this is the Romanesque-Gothic **Basilique Saint-Nazaire**, which Viollet-le-Duc thought was originally part of the fortifications, so he added battlements to the west façade. Inside the church are some fine 13th- and 14th-century **stained-glass windows** and sculptures in the choir. Summer concerts are held in the amphitheatre beside the church.

Albi

This serene and cheerful town, built like Toulouse with red brick and so known as *Albi la Rouge*, was once the scene of brutal religious persecution.

The grandiose Gothic **Cathédrale Sainte-Cécile** bears witness to that turmoil. In the Middle Ages, Albi provided a controversial refuge for the Cathar "heretics", also called Albigeois or Albigenses, whose austere doctrines of simple opposition of good and evil were an implicit reproach to the luxurious life of the Church in Rome. In 1208, Pope Innocent III sent a military crusade to wipe out the movement that had spread to Toulouse, Carcassonne and Béziers.

Twenty-five years later, the first Inquisition was established to take care of the remnants. To impress the citizens of Albi with the reasserted power of the Roman church, the cathedral was built in 1282 as a red brick "fortress of the faith", massive enough to resist any heresy.

While the square tower reinforces the cathedral's castle-like character, the stone canopied **porch** makes a more decorative contrast. Inside, the ornamental effect is carried further with the Flamboyant Gothic stone tracery and statuary of the choir's magnificent **rood screen**.

In the bishop's 13th-century residence, Palais de la Berbie, the **Musée Toulouse-Lautrec** honours the painter (who was born in Albi in 1864) with the country's largest collection of his works and sketchbooks. You can follow the artist's tragic life from the first paintings of his aristocratic youth—a self-portrait, his mother, a ride in a dogcart—to his brothel days in Montmartre with *Au salon de la rue des Moulins*, *A la toilette*, and the Paris music hall stars Jane Avril and Yvette Guilbert.

Montpellier

This is a lively university town at the Mediterranean end of the South-West, with a good TGV link back to Paris.

The centre of city life—

theatre, cafés and cinemas—is around the airy, bustling **Place de la Comédie.** For a quieter coffee, try the pretty **Place du Marché-aux-Fleurs,** shaded by plane trees around a Henry Moore sculpture. You'll discover handsome 17th- and 18th-century **mansions** on the Rue des Trésoriers de France and Rue des Trésoriers de la Bourse, with imposing stairways in the inner courtyards.

The **Musée Fabre** (13, rue Montpellieret) is admired for its important works by Courbet and Delacroix, as well as Veronese and Zurbarán.

For many, the most attractive spot in town is the classical late 17th-century **Promenade du Peyrou,** spacious gardens with triumphal arch, equestrian statue of Louis XIV and, on a mound at the far end, a hexagonal *château d'eau* (water tower) that looks more like a love temple, providing a fine view south to the Mediterranean and north to the Cévennes mountains.

Finish off your trip with a dip in the sea at the pleasant, unpretentious resort of **Sète,** famed for its nautical jousts in the harbour. Then, although it's quite hard going, walk up to the terrace of the little **Mont Saint-Clair** for one last view of the Pyrenees to the west and, out over the Mediterranean, to the Alpilles of Provence to the east.

WHAT TO DO

With such a weight of culture, of monuments and natural sights, it would be easy to forget that France is also a country where the good life is still to be enjoyed far from the châteaux and cathedrals. Sports are popular, the self-indulgent shopper is pampered, and night life is cultivated with a special care. Sightseeing is only the beginning of a visit to France.

Sports

After years of excessive attention to intellectual pursuits, the French have turned increasingly to outdoor sports. Everybody and his grandmother are out running, jumping, hiking and biking. For skiing and spectator sports, the most modern facilities have been installed, greatly enhanced by France's selection as host for the 1992 Winter Olympic Games, in the Haute-Savoie. The enormous diversity of climate and geography means that every imaginable kind of sport is available.

Jogging seems to have turned from fad to daily habit, and there's always a park or river bank where you can get away from the car fumes. Large hotels increasingly have saunas and gyms to complete your work-out. Paris organizes a spring marathon along the Seine and around the Bois de Boulogne.

No better sport than **hiking** to get the most out of the French countryside. Every little *syndicat d'initiative* can provide you with itineraries, many of them marked in red or blue on trees or lampposts along the trail. Good exercise without being exhausting, some of them are guided tours for botany or geology enthusiasts. More ambitious hikers can try the challenging routes known as *grandes randonnées* marked out through the Alps, the Pyrenees and the Lubéron mountains in Provence (details from the Fédération française de randonnées pédestres, 8, avenue Marceau, 75008 Paris). Even for the most modest hike, be sure to equip yourself with proper footwear, not just skimpy tennis shoes. French manufacturers have specialized in lightweight boots for summer hiking to replace the heavy clodhoppers of old.

Mountaineering novices can get training through the Club alpin français, 7, rue La Boétie, 75008 Paris, while the club's local branches in resort towns of the Alps and Pyrenees dispense advice and information to experts and novices alike.

Whether your main means of transport is car, train or even boat, **cycling** is ideal for excursions. Take off into the hills on a

bike rentable at some 250 railway stations throughout the country. It's an especially pleasant way to visit the vineyards of Champagne, Alsace or Burgundy.

Horse riding is a delight in the forests of the Ile-de-France and Brittany or around Pau in the Pyrenees, among many other possibilities. The *loisir-accueil* (leisure and hospitality) department of major regional tourist offices can tell you where to

hire a horse for the day. For a prolonged riding holiday with accommodation and meals included, write to the Association nationale pour le tourisme équestre, 15, rue de Bruxelles, 75009 Paris.

For ecological reasons, **hunting** is declining in popularity these days, but the best "shoots" for experienced hunters (with a 48-hour licence from the local prefecture) are still available in

Solitary challenge for a kayak over rapids on the Dordogne river.

Sologne, the Vosges and the Périgord. The season is generally from mid-September to the end of January.

Fishing is going as strong as ever: freshwater for trout and pike in the Annecy and le Bour-

193

get lakes, trout, carp, shad and bream in the Burgundy rivers, the Dordogne, and tributaries of the Loire. Get your licence through the local *société de pêche* (fishing association). Sea fishing is better in the Atlantic than the Mediterranean. Good deep-sea expeditions are usually advertised down at the port, most notably along the Brittany coast and La Rochelle.

Water sports are amply catered for. The Côte d'Azur has cleaned up most of its polluted beaches so that **swimming** is much safer there these days, but you'll find the Brittany and smaller Normandy resorts much less crowded. The pollution count is tested regularly, and the percentage is displayed at local town halls. Watch out for the occasional stinging jellyfish *(méduse)* in the Mediterranean. Be careful at some of the more secluded Atlantic beaches where there are no lifeguards on regular duty. Municipalities have excellent Olympic-size pools, and more and more hotels are installing them, too.

The **wind-surfing** craze has calmed down a little, but enthusiasts can still rent a board *(planche à voile)* in all the major resorts. Straight **surfing** is a strictly Atlantic sport, best at Biarritz.

Sailing continues to grow in popularity. If price is no object, you can hire a 30-metre vessel with ten-man crew down at Cannes or Antibes, and, on the Atlantic coast, at the equally well-equipped Saint-Malo, La Baule or La Rochelle. For those with their own boat, berths may be easier to find in Atlantic ports than on the Côte d'Azur. Inland, the great boating adventure is **canoeing**, particularly in the Périgord. For details of nationwide facilities and the list of navigable rivers, write to the Fédération française de canoë-kayak, 17, route de Vienne, 69007 Lyon.

Back on dry land, possibilities to play **tennis** are endless, so pack a racket. Tennis courts are hard surface, in municipal parks or attached to hotels. The latter can often help you with temporary membership to private clubs.

For **golf**, bring your own home club membership card for easier access to the best courses in the major seaside resorts—Le Touquet, Cabourg, Deauville, La Baule, Biarritz and Mandelieu (Cannes). Around Paris, there are international-class courses at Saint-Nom-la-Bretèche, Saint-Cloud, Chantilly and Fontainebleau.

Winter sports fans don't usually need a guidebook to tell them where to go. Generally speaking, the Alps are best for downhill **skiing** and the Pyrenees

Sweaty tryout for the scrummage down in Carcassonne.

for cross-country *(ski de fond)*. For the latter, you might also consider Corsica.

In France, only a few long-established ski resorts such as Megève and Val-d'Isère have some tradition and a village life to supplement the activity on the slopes. These are best for families who want first-class ski schools for kids and other beginners. Write, too, to the Association des maires des stations de sports d'hiver, 6, boulevard Haussmann, 75008 Paris, for a list of other mountain villages in the Alps, and also the Pyrenees, where hotel and skiing facilities are more modest but where village life is not completely submerged by ski and *après-ski*.

Inveterate skiers will head for the modern, highly specialized *stations*, with excellent facilities, hi-tech equipment, the most challenging *pistes* and frenetic discos but little character—Les Arcs, Tignes, La Plagne and Avoriaz. Wherever you go for your skiing, if you're not travelling with children, try to go outside the school holidays.

Of the spectator sports, **bicycle racing** remains very popular. The Tour de France in

Piglets and Pétanque

Perched on a borderline between sport and folklore, the grand Provençal game of boules or pétanque is the perfect expression of regional character. At a distance, all seems tranquil in the sandy village square, where half a dozen or more somewhat portly, gently perspiring fellows lob heavy metal balls along a shady avenue of plane trees. But draw nearer and you'll discover a ferocious combat, in which the ambient good humour barely conceals the high passions fuelled by mutual scorn, recrimination and pastis.

The object of the game is quite simply to get the maximum number of balls as close as possible to a little wooden jack, the co-chonnet (literally piglet). Good boules acquire the patina of medieval cannonballs. Players form teams of two (doublettes), three (triplettes), or four (quadrettes). They may be meticulous pointeurs, aiming close to the jack, or debonair tireurs, bombing the opponent's ball out of the way. Pétanque is properly the short-distance game in which the player stands feet together at a mark in the gravel. In la longue, the players can take a couple of strides to build up momentum.

The most important piece of equipment is a piece of string, to determine the distance between the boules and the cochonnet and who pays the next round of pastis.

July, with its grand finale along the Champs-Elysées in Paris, is as important as a Cup Final for English football or a World Series for American baseball. Each stage of the race, most strenuous and exciting in the Alps or Pyrenees, resembles a local festival with each village considering it a privilege to be blessed with the cavalcade of grimacing, groaning stars.

If **football** (soccer) is a national sport, with Bordeaux, Nantes and Paris regularly providing championship teams, **rugby** is at its best in the southwest—Béziers, Narbonne, Toulouse and Agen being among the most famous teams. For once, the rough and tumble are all on the field rather than among the vociferous but good-natured spectators.

Pelote is a Basque speciality, along the lines of squash, but played with a leather-bound ball hurled at the wall with an elongated basket-glove known as a *chistera*.

The Roman amphitheatres of Arles and Nîmes make dramatic settings for the annual summer **bullfights**.

Monte-Carlo has a major **tennis** tournament in May, important warm-up for Paris's French Open at Roland-Garros in June, just before Wimbledon. See if your hotel concierge can get you tickets.

In **motor racing**, the most spectacular events, in late May or early June, are the Grand Prix at Monaco and the 24-hour race at Le Mans (a day trip from the Loire Valley or Normandy).

Horse-racing enthusiasts in Paris go to Auteuil for the steeplechase and Longchamp for flat racing, June and early October being the months for the great classics. Chantilly (in June) and Deauville (in August) claim equally prestigious events.

Entertainment
After something of a lull in the seventies, the performing arts are booming again in France. The cultural decentralization has worked faster than the political. While Paris is still the undisputed major focus for theatre and music, you'll find plenty going on in the provinces, particularly in summer when even the tiniest Provençal or Périgord village stages some kind of arts festival.

There's something for every kind of brow, from the highest to the unashamed low.

Paris After Dark
The Paris night scene has lost none of the glitter and bounce that Toulouse-Lautrec made famous at the turn of the century. The Moulin Rouge (Place Blanche) still puts on one of the great boisterous floor shows of Europe. The rest of Pigalle is indeed sleazy, but it always was. Exceptions to the rule, Chez Michou (Rue des Martyrs) remains a witty cabaret of talented transvestite impersonators, and the Folies-Bergère (Rue Richer), the music hall that launched the careers of Joséphine Baker, Maurice Chevalier and Mistinguett, is still going strong.

Over on the Champs-Elysées, the Lido continues the grand tradition of girls wearing nothing but feathers and balloons, while the Crazy Horse Saloon (Avenue George-V) relies just on cunning patterns of light to clothe the most beautiful naked ladies in Paris (very few of them actually French).

On the Left Bank there are two floor shows that combine pretty girls and pretty transvestites in a nonstop riot of pastiche and satire: the Alcazar (Rue Mazarine) and Paradis Latin (Rue du Cardinal-Lemoine).

Music
For lovers of **classical music**, the Paris Opéra once more attracts international stars, and the Orchestre de Paris is thriving under musical director Daniel Barenboim. If you haven't booked ahead, it's worth going directly to the Opéra and the Pleyel or Gaveau concert halls for tickets, since agencies add at least 20 per cent to the price, and cancella-

tions are returned directly to the hall.

In the provinces, Lyon, Strasbourg and Lille all have first-class orchestras, and the festivals (see p. 200) bring top performers from all over the world.

The French seem to take their **jazz** much more seriously these days than Americans do. Paris has some 15 clubs; in summer the action moves down to the Côte d'Azur. Of the Paris clubs, the New Morning (Rue des Petites-Ecuries) attracts all the major American and European musicians, while Le Dunois (Rue Dunois) is a modest, intimate place cultivating the avant-garde.

Republican Guards turn out for a grand gala at the Paris Opéra.

You can hear good mainstream jazz at the Bilboquet (Rue Saint-Benoît), Le Furstemberg (Rue de Buci) and the bars of the Méridien hotel (Boulevard Gouvion-Saint-Cyr) and Concorde-Lafayette (Place du Général-Koenig).

Rock music concerts are held at the spectacular new Zénith (La Villette, *métro* Porte de Pantin).

Discothèques go in and out of fashion as fast as the music that's played in them. The expensive and exclusive Paris discos hide out around the Champs-Elysées, notably on the Rue de Ponthieu and Avenue Matignon, while the younger crowd haunts exhilarating eardrum-busters around les Halles. At the coastal resorts, the expensive discos are often attached to the casino and the big hotels, with a more relaxed atmosphere in the smaller back-street places.

Theatre

The Comédie-Française (Rue de Richelieu) is the high temple of French classical drama—Molière, Racine and Corneille—while slowly expanding its repertory. On the Left Bank, the Odéon (Place de l'Odéon), in keeping with its new title as the Théâtre de l'Europe, puts on international works, with prestigious guest companies performing in English, German and Italian. Even with a minimum of French, playgoers can enjoy the innovative contemporary theatre under the direction of Peter Brook at the Bouffes du Nord (Boulevard de la Chapelle), Patrice Chéreau at the suburban Théâtre des Amandiers (Nanterre) and Ariane Mnouchkine at the Cartoucherie de Vincennes (Avenue de la Pyramide).

Some of the major centres of provincial theatre are Nancy, Strasbourg, Toulouse, Lyon, Avignon and Montpellier.

Cinema

For serious movie-fans, Paris is an unrivalled treasure island, a film-crazy town where directors and screenplay writers achieve a celebrity equal to that of star actors and actresses. Not even Los Angeles or New York can match the French capital's average of 300 different films showing each week. Practically all of them are available in at least one cinema in *VO*, an original, undubbed version with French subtitles. Study the weekly entertainment guides, *Pariscope* or *L'Officiel du Spectacle*, especially for the obscure little jewels offered by the town's two *cinémathèques* (Palais de Chaillot and Centre Pompidou).

Don't be intimidated by the queues; you nearly always get in. The usherettes *(ouvreuses)* expect to be tipped, it's their only income. Give them at least one franc.

199

Festivals

Folklore and tradition have dwindled since World War II. In their place, there has been a veritable explosion of arts festivals, drawing on local, national and international talent, performed in the wonderful historic settings of palaces, châteaux, cathedrals, monasteries and Roman amphitheatres.

We offer here a far from exhaustive list of both the traditional and new cultural festivals.

January: *Avoriaz* (Savoie) science-fiction film festival; *Champagne* and *Burgundy* village processions for wine-growers' patron Saint Vincent.

February (or early March): *Nice* Mardi Gras carnival.

March: *Cluny* chamber music.

April: *Bourges* rock music; *Strasbourg* choral music; *Arles* Easter bullfights in Roman amphitheatre.

May: *Cannes* International Film Festival; *Saint-Tropez* "Bravade" religious procession; *Amiens* jazz.

June: *Versailles* chamber music at the château; *Strasbourg* music; *Honfleur* Whitsuntide Fête des Marins (sailors, at harbour); *Nîmes* Whitsuntide bullfights in Roman amphitheatre; *Paris* Festival du Marais (music and theatre); *Paris* air show at Le Bourget airport (biennial); *Dijon* (until August) music and theatre, especially street theatre.

July: *Avignon* international theatre (in Palais des Papes), music, opera, dance and cinema; *Aix-en-Provence* opera; *Arles* international photography seminars, exhibitions and audiovisual shows in amphitheatre; *Montpellier* music, opera and dance (starts last week in June); *Orange* opera in the amphitheatre; *Nice* jazz; *Bayonne* folklore; *Albi* (music in cathedral and palace); *Paris* Festival Estival, music and theatre (till September).

August: *Annecy* fireworks by the lake; *Chartres* organ recitals in cathedral; (August 15) Assumption Day procession and Mass; *Aix-en-Provence* jazz; *Colmar* wine fair; *Le Touquet* chamber music.

September: *Lyon* Dance Biennale; *Deauville* American film festival; *Paris* Festival d'Automne, music and theatre, till December; *Dijon* wine festival; music; *Mont-Saint-Michel* procession and Mass for Saint Michael.

October: *Angers* avant-garde music; *Nancy* jazz.

November: *Burgundy* (Beaune, Nuits-Saint-Georges, Meursault and Chablis) wine festivals; *Dijon* gastronomy fair; *Cannes* dance.

December: *Les Baux-de-Provence* Christmas Eve Fête des Bergers (shepherds) and Midnight Mass.

Shopping

To shop seriously in France, you need a clear plan of attack. Unless you're buying things you want to use during your vacation, such as clothes or sports equipment, it doesn't make sense to shop right at the beginning of the trip and have to lug the stuff around the country.

Paris is still a shopper's paradise, not only for the fashions, perfumes and other luxury goods for which it has always been famous, but also for a comprehensive selection of handicrafts and gourmet delicacies that at one time could be found only in the provinces. If possible, divide

"You're joking! I saw the same thing in Lyon for half the price."

your Paris stay in two, the major part at the beginning, to see the town, with a couple more days at the end of the tour to do your shopping. Try to compare price and quality—you can't always be sure it will be cheaper "on the spot" than in Paris.

Paris: The Big Stores

The department stores best equipped for dealing with foreigners are **Galeries Lafayette** and **Printemps**, next door to each other on the Boulevard Haussmann. Both have hostesses to help non-French-speaking customers, as well as the convenience of grouping selections from the major designers in their clothes departments. The Galeries probably has the edge in the fashion and perfume departments, china and household goods, while Printemps leads in its lingerie and vast toys and adult gift departments.

For those who like dressing up in baker's overalls, waiter's jackets, butcher's aprons and plumber's pants, the **Samaritaine** at the Pont-Neuf has an enormous selection of professional uniforms—52 trades represented.

FNAC is a chain of breezy, new-style department stores (Rue de Rennes, Forum des Halles and Avenue Wagram) specializing in books, discount records, cameras, hi-fi, electronics and sports goods.

Fashion

These days, the fashion pendulum occasionally swings to New York, Rome or Tokyo, but the capital for all of them, the showplace for their talent, remains Paris. From the Right Bank, around the Rue du Faubourg-Saint-Honoré, avenues Montaigne and George-V and over to Place des Victoires and les Halles, the *haute couture* houses and their *prêt-à-porter* (ready-to-wear) boutiques have spilled over to the Left Bank, around Saint-Germain-des-Prés.

Look out not only for the "old school" of Dior, Givenchy, Lanvin, Saint-Laurent, Ungaro and Louis Féraud, but the new generation of Gaultier, Mugler, Montana and their foreign competitors, Yamamoto, Issey Miyake, Valentino and Missoni —as well as the scores of cheaper satellite boutiques that turn out clever variations on the innovators' designs. For the designers' perfumes, you'll probably get a better deal in the duty-free shop at the airport.

For leatherware, in addition to its fabled silk scarves, **Hermès** (Rue du Faubourg-Saint-Honoré) is an institution all on its own, catering for the well-heeled horseman, globetrotter or man-and-woman-about-town, with high-quality luggage, stirrups, saddles and boots, and the ultimate diary and address book.

It isn't fruit juice, but perfume down in Provence.

While Paris fills practically every clothes need you can imagine, you might find good old-fashioned stuff out in the provinces—oilskins *(ciré)* or the sturdy dufflecoat *(kabig)* in Brittany or a heavy woollen sweater *(chandail breton)*. And Saint-Tropez is still famous for sexy, imaginative casual wear.

Antiques

Astronomic prices for the genuine article should not frighten you away from antique-hunting in the exquisite shops of Paris's 6th and 7th *arrondissements*. The *Carré des Antiquaires*, a little rectangle bounded by the Quai Voltaire and the Boulevard Saint-Germain, the Rue du Bac and the Rue des Saints-Pères, constitutes a veritable museum of ancient Egyptian and Chinese art, pre-Columbian, African and Polynesian, as well as Louis XV, Second Empire, Art Nouveau and Art Deco. It has the advantage that here, you're allowed to touch the objects—and pay for breakages.

The prices are more manageable at the weekend **flea markets**, although many of their stalls are manned by professional antique dealers. The *marché aux* *puces de Saint-Ouen* at Porte de Clignancourt (tough to park, but an easy walk from the *métro* station) groups half a dozen markets. Vernaison specializes in musical instruments, lead soldiers, old toys, buttons, brass and tinware; Biron has mostly antique furniture; Malik is a great favourite with the young for its *Belle Epoque* dresses, First World War military uniforms, 1920s hats and an amazing assortment of Americana. Paul Bert might have that undiscovered masterpiece that every flea-market addict dreams of—but get there early, practically at dawn, before the professionals rummage among the unloading trucks. Jules Vallès is the smallest and cosiest, especially good for Art Nouveau lamps, military souvenirs, theatre costumes and old dolls.

The **bouquinistes** (secondhand book sellers) along the Seine, most of them between the Pont Saint-Michel and the Pont des Arts, still turn up the odd rarity in periodicals as well as old books.

In the provinces, apart from what you come across by chance in little out-of-the-way villages, your best bets for antiques are in historic cities like Strasbourg, Colmar, Dijon, Rouen, Lyon or Avignon. The Loire Valley has good flea markets, especially at Angers on Saturdays.

Household Goods

In a country where cooking is so highly prized, kitchenware is particularly good. The old Paris food-market district of les Halles has held on to its restaurant-supply shops, offering an astonishing array of pots and pans, kitchen knives and other utensils at the venerable Dehillerin (18, rue Coquillière) and MORA (13, rue Montmartre).

Normandy and Brittany are both known for their rustic pottery, while Gien, in the Loire Valley, and Limoges (the only reason for stopping there) produce excellent chinaware. In the back country behind the Côte d'Azur, Vallauris is a major centre for ceramics and nearby Biot for glassware (see p. 164). If you don't want to risk breakables, consider the superb Provençal olive-wood salad bowls and fruit plates that you'll find in the Lubéron.

Gourmet Delicacies

While you can probably get almost everything in Paris, food and wine are things which it's more fun and more often (but not always) cheaper to get where they're produced. Every region has a wealth of specialities, well displayed and easy to find.

But if you do prefer to do your food shopping in Paris, the most famous luxury grocery shop is Fauchon (26, place de la Made-

205

leine). Despite its aristocratic reputation, the service is friendly, courteous and multilingual. Salespeople become (mildly) annoyed only if you suggest they might not have what you're looking for. You'll also find groceries specializing in regional delicacies, with self-explanatory names like *Aux produits de Bretagne* or *Aux produits de Bourgogne*. There are street markets all over town, particularly good if you want to take some cheese or sausage back on the last day. The most colourful are on the Rue Mouffetard, Place Maubert and Rue de Seine on the Left Bank and Rue des Martyrs and Avenue du Président-Wilson on the Right Bank.

For wine, the best bargains in Paris are at the Nicolas chain. One of the largest selections is at Lucien Legrand (1, rue de la Banque—bankers and stockbrokers being notorious connoisseurs). The more adventurous will want to stalk the vineyards of Alsace, Burgundy, the Loire Valley and Bordeaux. You'll get a better price on Champagne in Reims or Epernay than back in Paris.

The strong alcohols may be better bargains at the duty-free shop, but the choice will be limited. Cognac and Armagnac, and other local *liqueurs* and *eaux-de-vie* are best bought in their region.

EATING OUT

There are some tourists who come to France without visiting a single museum or church and who would not dream of "wasting" their time shopping. And yet they come away with tales of adventure, excitement, poetry and romance—and the feeling they know the country inside out. They have spent their time wining and dining and sleeping between meals. The onslaught of fast food and *autoroute* cafeterias has not staled the infinite variety of France's regional cuisines, and you can enjoy anything from a gorgeous feast to a simple selection of piquant sausage and pâté in the knowledge that eating and drinking are not just a means of satisfying hunger and thirst.

Not all budgets or waistlines would permit such single-minded dedication to eating your way across France. But reserve at least a few evenings to that unique institution, a great French meal. And go all the way: hors d'œuvre, fish course, meat course, cheese, dessert, brandy and coffee. As playwright Jean Anouilh once said, "Everything ends this way in France—everything. Weddings, christenings, duels, burials, swindlings, diplomatic affairs—everything is a pretext for a good dinner."

Where to Eat

In the big cities, you have a wide choice: gourmet restaurants, relatively expensive; large, family-style *brasseries* or intimate *bistrots*, more moderately priced; cafés or wine bars for a cheaper snack. Fast-food chains are very successful and need no introduction.

The fixed-price *menu* (appetizer, main course and dessert) is often the best deal, particularly in the major gourmet establishments, where you get a first-class introduction to the restaurant's specialities without paying the much higher *à la carte* prices. Look, too, for the house wine (*réserve de la maison*) usually served in carafes by the *quart* (quarter) or *demi* (half) litre.

In that lovely insular phrase which even the American continent seems to have adopted, the typical "continental" **breakfast** (*petit déjeuner*) is still croissant, brioche or bread and butter with coffee, tea or chocolate. Increasingly, orange juice is offered as an extra, but you must insist on *orange pressée* if you want it freshly squeezed. Big hotels offer English- and American-style breakfasts. But we recommend you go out as often as possible to the corner café—it's great to watch a town getting up in the morning when you don't have to go off to work.

Traditionally, a French **lunch** (*déjeuner*) is as important as dinner, but you may not want to handle two big meals a day when you're travelling. A good alternative is a café salad, or a cheese, ham or pâté sandwich made in a long *baguette*. Or a picnic. *Charcuteries* and *traiteurs* (caterers) pack complete meals, hot or cold. A corkscrew is more important than a credit card—don't leave home without it.

The **evening meal** (*dîner*) in the provinces is served early—8.00 or 8.30 p.m., compared with 8.30 or 9 p.m. in Paris and such favourite Parisian resorts as Deauville, Saint-Tropez or Cannes. The French are much more relaxed than you might have expected about how you dress for dinner, and if the smart places expect a jacket, only a very few insist on a tie.

What to Eat

There are some general notions to French eating habits that you'll find all over the country. First things first. Forgoing the **starter** (*entrée*) does not necessarily mean that the main course will be served more quickly. Besides, it's worth trying some of the simplest dishes that do work genuinely as appetizers: *crudités*—a plate of raw vegetables, green pepper, tomatoes, carrots, celery, cucumber; or just radishes by themselves, served with salt and butter; *charcuterie*

—various kinds of sausage and other cold meats, notably the *rosette* sausage from Lyon, *rillettes* (a soft pâté of pork or goose) from Le Mans and ham *(jambon)* from Bayonne or Auvergne; vegetable soups *(potage)* or fish soups served with *croûtons* and a Provençal sauce of garlic and chilli pepper *(rouille)*.

Most big cities get their **fish** fresh every day except Monday. Trout *(truite)* is delicious *au bleu* (poached absolutely fresh), *meunière* (sautéed in butter) or *aux amandes* (sautéed with almonds). At their best, *quenelles de brochet* (pike dumplings) are much lighter and airier than their English translation. Sole and turbot take on a new meaning when served with *sauce hollandaise*, that miraculous blend of egg yolks, butter and lemon juice with which the Dutch have only the most nominal connection.

For your **main dish**, expect the meat to be less well done than in most countries—extra-rare is *bleu*, rare *saignant*, medium *à point*, and well done *bien cuit* and frowned upon. Steaks *(entrecôte* or *tournedos)* are often served with a wine sauce *(marchand de vin)*, with shallots *(échalotes)*, or—rich sin—with bone marrow *(à la moelle)*. Roast leg of lamb *(gigot d'agneau)* is also served pink *(rose)* unless you specify otherwise.

While each region favours its specialities, the most famous **cheeses** are available everywhere: the blue *Roquefort*, soft white-crusted *Camembert* or *Brie* (the crust of which you can safely remove without offending true connoisseurs), and countless goat cheeses *(fromage de chèvre)*.

Desserts are the most personal choice of the meal, the moment you plunge back into childhood.

Planning the day's entertainment over a quiet lunch en tête-à-tête.

Try a heavenly *mousse au chocolat* or diabolical *profiteroles*, little ball-shaped éclairs filled with vanilla ice cream and covered with hot chocolate sauce. Or a *sorbet* (sherbet)—blackcurrant *(cassis)*, raspberry *(framboise)* or pear *(poire)*. And fruit tarts—apricot *(tarte aux abricots)*, strawberry *(aux fraises)*, and most magical of all, *tarte Tatin*, hot caramelized apples baked under a pastry crust, attributed to the Tatin sisters of Sologne after one of them accidentally dropped the tart upside down on the hotplate when taking it out of the oven.

Regional Cuisine

Once acquainted with these basics, you're ready to start your tour of the regional specialities. There's no specifically "Parisian" cuisine; but the capital can offer a sample of almost everything you'll find around the country.

Picardy, for those coming in from the north, offers its speciality, *flamique à porions*, a leek pie best served piping hot. This, with one of the region's great vegetable soups, will keep you going all the way into Paris and beyond. In Amiens, try the traditional *pâté de canard* (duck pâté).

Alsace is rich in freshwater fish and game, and makes a subtle mixture of French, German and even Jewish cooking— *carpe à la juive* will be recognized as gefilte fish. Wonders are performed with cabbage. *Choucroute* cooked in Riesling with juniper berries, a cup of kirsch tossed in at the end, makes poetry out of sauerkraut. *Civet de lièvre* is jugged hare fit for a king, and braised goose with apples *(oie braisée aux pommes)* warms the cockles of the coldest heart. The prince of Alsatian cheeses is the pungent *Munster*.

Burgundy, inspired by the high life led by its grand old dukes, is ideal for those with solid appetites. This wine-growing region produces the world's greatest beef stew, *bœuf bourguignon*: beef simmered in red wine for at least four hours with mushrooms, small white onions and chunks of bacon. The corn-fed poultry of Bresse is the aristocrat of French fowl—enjoy it at its simplest, roast or steamed. Charolais beef, from the lovingly tended white cattle of southern Burgundy, produces the tenderest steaks. *A la dijonnaise* will usually mean a sauce of Dijon's mustard, distinctively flavoured

The art of nouvelle cuisine *is to make a dessert a feast for the eye as well as for the palate.*

by the sour juice of Burgundy grapes. *Jambon persillé* (parsleyed ham) is another Dijon speciality. *Escargots* (snails) are mostly imported from Eastern Europe these days to meet the heavy demand, but Burgundians still make the best butter, garlic and parsley sauce, also used with *cuisses de grenouilles* (frogs' legs) from the Dombes region. Among the great Burgundy cheeses are the moist orange-crusted *Epoisses* and *Soumaintrain*.

Normandy makes full use of its prolific dairy farms. Cream and butter are staples of the cuisine, the secret behind the sumptuous *omelette de la mère Poulard* that you'll find at Mont-Saint-Michel. The rich, slightly sour-tasting *crème fraîche* also makes the perfect accompaniment to a hot apple pie. The local apples turn up with flambéed partridge *(perdreau flambé aux reinettes)* and in chicken with apple-brandy sauce *(poulet au Calvados)*. The Normandy capital is famous for its *caneton à la rouennaise*, a duckling of unusually deep red meat with a spicy red wine sauce thickened with minced duck livers. Tough guys and dolls who tackle *tripes à la mode de Caen* should know it contains all the various compartments of a cow's stomach, plus the trotters, stewed in a bouillon. Besides the *Camembert* cheese,

be sure to sample the stronger *Livarot* and square, tangy *Pont-l'Evêque*.

Brittany is best for its magnificent seafood, served fresh and unadorned on a bed of crushed ice and seaweed, a *plateau de fruits de mer*. It will include oysters *(huîtres)*, various kinds of clam *(palourdes, praires)*, mussels *(moules)*, scallops *(coquilles Saint-Jacques)*, large prawns *(langoustines)*, periwinkles *(bigorneaux)* that you winkle out with a pin, large whelks *(bulots)* and chewy abalones *(ormeaux)*. Purists prefer their lobster *(homard)* steamed or grilled to retain the full, undisguised flavour. Lobster *à l'américaine* (or *à l'armoricaine,* in fact a Parisian invention) swims in a shellfish stock enriched with tomato, cognac, cream and herbs.

The Loire Valley has some excellent freshwater fish (eel, perch, trout and pike) in a light *beurre blanc* (white butter sauce). A major delicacy is *matelote d'anguille* (eel stewed in red wine). Angers and Tours both claim to make the best *andouillette* (tripe sausage), while *rillettes* of duck, goose or pork meat make another fine starter.

The only thing better than a dozen oysters is two dozen oysters.

For a lusty main dish, try *noisette de porc aux pruneaux* (pork tenderloin with prunes). One of the best goat cheeses in the country is the *Valençay*, shaped like an Aztec pyramid.

Lyon, the gastronomic capital of France, is renowned for the quality of its pork, wild game, vegetables and fruit, while giving the common or garden onion its letters of nobility. Onion soup *(soupe à l'oignon)* is a local invention; *à la lyonnaise* most often means sautéed in onions. If you have a robust stomach, try *gras-double* (tripe) or *andouille*, a sausage made of chitterlings. More "genteel" dishes include, for starters, artichoke hearts *(cœurs d'artichaut)* with foie gras, or *gratin de queues d'écrevisses* (baked crayfish tails); as main dishes, 7-hour braised leg of lamb and *poularde demi-deuil* —chicken in semi-mourning, because of the white meat and black truffles.

Bordeaux cooking naturally enough also exploits its wines, the *bordelaise* sauce being made with white or red wine, shallots and beef marrow, served variously with *entrecôte* steaks, boletus mushrooms *(cèpes)* or lamprey eels *(lamproies)*. A surfeit of them may have killed a few medieval kings but the right amount never hurt anyone. Oysters and mussels from nearby Arcachon are excellent. Try the region's Pauillac lamb *à la persillade* (with parsley).

Provence, embracing the **Côte d'Azur**, marries Mediterranean seafood with garlic, olives, tomatoes and the country's most fragrant herbs. But for a starter, have the local fresh sardines, just grilled and sprinkled with lemon. More spicy is *tapenade*, a mousse of capers, anchovies, black olives, garlic and lemon— delicious on toast. From the coast between Marseille and Toulon comes the celebrated *bouillabaisse*, a fish stew that might contain *rascasse*, John Dory, eel, red mullet, whiting, perch, spiny lobster, crabs and other shellfish, seasoned with garlic, olive oil, tomatoes, bay leaf, parsley, pepper and (not authentic without it) saffron. Provençal cooks also do a fine *daube de bœuf* (beef stew with tomatoes and olives).

Périgord is famous for its *pâté de foie gras*, truffles, in ever dwindling supply, and for all the richness of goose and duck, most notably *confit d'oie* or *confit de canard*. The bird is cooked slowly in its own fat and kept for days, weeks and even months in earthenware jars. The *confit* is the base of the hearty Toulouse or Castelnaudary *cassoulet*, with beans, pork, mutton, and sausage. And don't forget *pommes sarladaises*, potatoes sautéed in goose fat, garlic and parsley; dandelion salad *(salade de pissenlit)* dressed with walnut oil and bits of bacon, and chestnuts, roasted and served with partridge or made into rich desserts.

Wine

Ordering French wine is not as intimidating as you may think. If you happen to like red wine more than white, you can safely and acceptably order red with fish; a chilled Brouilly, Morgon or Chiroubles of the Beaujolais family goes well with both fish and meat. Dry Burgundy or Loire Valley whites are indeed exquisite with fish, and you can drink Alsatian whites with everything, with impunity. Remember, in a French restaurant, *you* are king. You prefer beer? Go ahead, it goes especially well with Toulouse sausage and Alsatian *choucroute*.

But if you want a few basic pointers about the classic wines, the **Burgundy** reds divide easily into two categories, those that can be drunk relatively young—the supple *Côte de Beaune* wines of Aloxe-Corton, Pommard and Volnay—and those that need to age a little, the full-bodied *Côte de Nuits* wines of Vougeot, Gevrey-Chambertin, and Chambolle-Musigny. The great Burgundy whites include Meursault and Puligny-Montrachet.

Bordeaux wines have four main regional divisions: Médoc, aromatic, mellow red with a slight edge to it; Graves, an easy-to-drink red, dry and vigorous like the Burgundies; Saint-Emilion, dark, strong and full-bodied; and the pale, golden Sauternes, sweet and fragrant, perfect with foie gras. The lesser Bordeaux can all be drunk a couple of years old, but good ones need at least five years.

The **Loire Valley** produces fine dry white wines, such as Vouvray and Sancerre, and robust reds such as Bourgueil and Chinon.

Of the **Côtes du Rhône**, the best known red is the fragrant, deep purple Châteauneuf-du-Pape, but look out, too, for the Gigondas and Hermitage and, for lunchtime drinking, the Tavel rosé.

The great white wines of **Alsace** are known after their grapes—Gewürztraminer, Riesling and Sylvaner.

For your after-dinner drink, besides *Cognac* or the mellower *Armagnac*, there's a wide range of fruit brandies *(eaux-de-vie)* made from pear, raspberry, plum or cherry, as well as the famous apple *Calvados*. Or, for a sparkling finish, the nation's pride and joy: Champagne, described by the connoisseurs as *aimable, fin et élégant*, "friendly, refined and elegant".

A votre santé!

BERLITZ-INFO

CONTENTS

A ACCOMMODATION (See also CAMPING, YOUTH HOSTELS.)

Hotels. Hotels throughout France are officially classified from one-to four-star luxury establishments. Room prices, fixed according to amenities, size and the hotel's star rating, must be posted at reception desks and on the inside of each room door.

For advance reservations, especially during holiday periods, you can obtain lists of officially approved hotels throughout the country from the French national tourist office (see p. 240).

On the spot, tourist offices and *syndicats d'initiative* can supply local hotel lists. Note that a hotel labelled simply *Hôtel* may not have a restaurant, especially in big towns. The *Accueil de France* offices located in tourist offices in the cities will make room reservations for a small fee. Major airports and railway stations have hotel reservation desks. From the arrivals hall of Paris's Roissy–Charles-de-Gaulle airport, a push-button system gives you free access to a broad selection of hotels for reservations throughout Paris.

Châteaux-Hôtels de France. These converted châteaux, covering the whole of France, are an expensive but worthwhile romantic alternative, notably in the Loire Valley. They are listed together with **Relais de Campagne,** a similar chain offering a wider variety of hotels in country settings, rating from two to four stars. Some are genuine, old-time stagecoach inns. The book is available from tourist offices.

Logis de France and **Auberges de France** are government-sponsored hotels, often outside towns, many with character and charm. A free book can be obtained from the national tourist office before leaving (on the spot you have to pay for it). *Logis* are in the one-and two-star bracket; *auberges* are three- or four-star establishments.

Pensions can be small hotels or guest houses. They are usually family-owned and provide meals.

Gîtes de France; gîtes ruraux. Officially sponsored, (sparsely) furnished holiday cottages or flats (apartments). Rental costs include all charges. Sleeping arrangements may be in dormitories.

House rental. Local tourist offices, *syndicats d'initiative*, can recommend agencies with complete lists of houses and apartments to let. You should reserve well ahead.

Note: *Hôtel de ville* is not a hotel but the town hall.

a double/single room	**une chambre pour deux personnes/une personne**
with/without bath/shower	**avec/sans bains/douche**
with a double bed	**avec un grand lit**
What's the rate per night?	**Quel est le prix pour une nuit?**
I'm looking for a flat (apartment) to rent for a month.	**Je cherche un appartement à louer pour un mois.**

AIRPORTS *(aéroport)*

Paris is the major gateway to France, but many international flights operate to other big cities. All French airports have duty-free shops and efficient transport to the town centre.

Paris is served by two airports, Roissy–Charles-de-Gaulle, about 25 km. (15 mi.) north-east of the city, and Orly, 16 km. (10 mi.) to the south. Most intercontinental flights use the ultra-modern Roissy.

Roissy and Orly are linked by coach. In normal traffic conditions, the journey between airports takes about an hour and a quarter. You can also get a coach from Roissy to the Porte Maillot terminal in Paris, and one from Orly to the Invalides terminal. Both journeys take at least 40 minutes. The coaches leave every 20 minutes, between 6 a.m. and 11 p.m.

Trains from the Gare du Nord to Roissy (R.E.R. line B) leave every 15 minutes and take 35 minutes. From the Quai d'Orsay, Saint-Michel or Gare d'Austerlitz (R.E.R. line C) to Orly the trip takes 40–60 minutes. Trains run frequently from early morning to late at night.

Taxis from the airport to the centre of Paris are expensive for single passengers but worthwhile for three.

Where's the bus for ...?	**D'où part le bus pour ...?**
Can you help me with my luggage?	**Pouvez-vous m'aider à porter mes bagages?**
How much is that?	**Combien est-ce que ça coûte?**

BICYCLE AND MOPED HIRE *(location de bicyclettes/vélomoteurs)* **B**

Cycling is a highly popular sport in France, so it's possible to hire bikes (*bicyclette* or *vélo*) in most towns. You can hire a bicycle at

219

railway stations; it isn't necessary to return it to the same station. You will need your passport or identity card, and you'll have to pay a deposit, unless you hold a major credit card.

Mopeds (*vélomoteur*, *cyclomoteur* or *mobylette*) are also available for hire (same conditions as for bikes). Minimum age to ride a moped is 14; for scooters from 50 to 125 cc 16 years; over 125 cc 18 years. Crash helmets are compulsory. Enquire about rentals at your hotel or the local tourist office.

I'd like to hire a bicycle.	**Je voudrais louer une bicyclette.**
for one day/a week	**pour une journée/une semaine**

C CAMPING

Campsites are officially graded from one to four stars. There are about 9,000 sites in France, including more than 100 in the Paris area. During peak season you should make reservations well in advance; in the Midi it is essential.

For certain campsites you will require an official up-to-date camping card, or *carnet*, that gives you third-party insurance and sometimes a discount.

Free camping *(camping sauvage)* is not allowed. If you want to camp on private property, you must first get permission from the owner.

For further information about camping consult the special leaflet issued by the French national tourist office, and get your camping card, renewable annually, from:

Fédération française de camping et de caravaning, 78, rue de Rivoli, 75004 Paris; tel. 42.72.84.08 or
Camping Club de France, 218, bd. Saint-Germain, 75007 Paris; tel. 45.48.30.03.

Have you room for a tent/ a caravan?	**Avez-vous de la place pour une tente/une caravane?**
May we camp on your land?	**Pouvons-nous camper sur votre terrain?**

CAR HIRE *(location de voitures)* (See also DRIVING.)
All major car-hire firms in France handle French-made cars and occasionally foreign makes. Locally based firms generally charge less than the international companies, but you may have to turn

the car in where you took it out. There are some good deals to be had if you book your car together with your plane or train ticket.

To hire a car you must produce a valid driving licence (held for at least one year) and your passport. Depending on the model and the hiring firm, minimum age for renting a car varies from 21 to 25. Holders of major credit cards are normally exempted from the advance deposit payment. Third-party insurance is usually automatically included; with an extra fee per day you can obtain full insurance coverage.

I'd like to hire a car tomorrow.	**Je voudrais louer une voiture demain.**
for one day/a week	**pour une journée/une semaine**
unlimited mileage	**kilométrage illimité**
Please include full insurance.	**Avec assurance tous risques, s'il vous plaît.**

CIGARETTES, CIGARS, TOBACCO *(cigarette; cigare; tabac)*
Tobacco is a state monopoly in France. French cigarettes include brands with dark or light tobacco (respectively *cigarettes brunes* or *blondes*), with or without filter. Dozens of foreign brands are available at higher prices. Pipe tobacco comes in a variety of cuts, from sweet to strong. There are plenty of licensed tobacconists *(débit de tabac)* bearing the conspicuous sign "Bar-Tabac" or "Tabac-Journaux" and a double red cone; they are often at café cash desks.

A packet of .../A box of matches, please.	**Un paquet de .../Une boîte d'allumettes, s'il vous plaît.**
filter-tipped/without filter	**avec/sans filtre**

CLIMATE AND CLOTHING
Broadly, the further south you go the warmer. The northern and western areas of France (including Paris) enjoy a temperate climate. The region to the east and in the interior Massif Central has warmer summers and colder winters. The Mediterranean coastal area is marked by hot, dry summers and mild, showery winters. With the exception of this coast, rainfall is sporadic all year round with most precipitation between January and April and least in August and September. Snow can be a problem in winter, but mostly in mountain areas.

Paris weather is usually good. Once it gets started, much later in

April than Cole Porter told us, the spring is unbeatable. Summer is often hot but not scorching, autumn gloriously romantic and gently warm, winter quite supportable. Paris under snow, a rare event, is spectacular.

Except in winter, medium-weight attire is usually adequate. However, even in the southern summer, when light cotton clothes are all you need during the day, a sweater or a jacket comes in handy for an occasional chilly evening. You are likely to need rainwear at any time of the year.

Clothes for restaurants are much less formal than you might have imagined. The French like to look *good*, whether casual or formal. Ties for men and dresses for women are rarely compulsory. Avoid shorts in cathedrals and keep your beach wear for the beach.

COMMUNICATIONS

Post office *(poste)*. You can identify French post offices by a sign with a stylized blue bird and/or the words *Postes et télécommunications*, *P & T* or *PTT*. In cities, the main post office is open from 8 a.m. to 5 p.m., Monday to Friday, and 8 a.m. to noon on Saturdays.

Letter boxes are painted yellow, often set into a wall. Stamps can be bought in post offices, in *débits de tabac* (tobacconists), or from vending machines, also yellow.

Poste restante (general delivery). If you don't know ahead of time where you'll be staying, you can have your mail addressed to you c/o *poste restante* in any town. Towns with more than one post office keep mail at the main post office *(poste principale)*. You'll have to show your passport to retrieve mail.

Telegrams *(télégramme)*. All local post offices accept telegrams, domestic or overseas. You may also dictate a telegram over the telephone (special English-language service from Paris, tel. 42.33.21.11).

Telephone *(téléphone)*. Long-distance and international calls can be made from any phone box, but if you need assistance in placing the call, go to the post office or ask at your hotel. If you make a call from your hotel, a café or a restaurant, you are likely to be charged a little extra.

There are two types of pay phones. One takes a range of coins, the other is card operated. Cards are sold at post offices, railway ticket counters and shops recognizable by a "Télécarte" sign, and are available for 40 or 120 charge units.

For long-distance calls within France, there are no area codes (just dial the 8-digit number of the person you want to call), *except* when telephoning from Paris or the Paris region to the provinces (dial 16 and wait for the dialling tone, then dial the 8-digit number of the subscriber) and from the provinces to Paris or the Paris region (dial 16, wait for the dialling tone, then dial 1 followed by the 8-digit number). If you need the assistance of an operator, dial 36.10.

To ring abroad from France, dial 19 followed, after the change of tone, by the country's number (listed in all boxes), the area code and the subscriber's number. If direct dialling is not available to that country, or if you don't know the telephone number of the subscriber, dial 19 and wait for the tone, then dial 33 followed by the code number of the country in question to reach the operator (UK 44, U.S.A. and Canada 11). If you do not know the number of the country, call the international information, 19.33.33.

It's cheaper to make long-distance calls after 6 p.m.

express (special delivery)	**exprès**
airmail	**par avion**
registered	**recommandé**
A stamp for this letter/ postcard, please.	**Un timbre pour cette lettre/ carte, s'il vous plaît.**
I want to send a telegram to ...	**J'aimerais envoyer un télégramme à ...**
Have you any mail for ...?	**Avez-vous du courrier pour ...?**
Can you get me this number in ...?	**Pouvez-vous me donner ce numéro à ...?**

COMPLAINTS

Hotels and restaurants. To avoid unpleasant scenes with waiters or hotel employees, ask immediately to see the manager (*maître d'hôtel* or *directeur*). If you fail to obtain on-the-spot satisfaction, you can refer the matter to the nearest police station *(commissariat de police)*. If the police cannot help, apply to the regional administration offices (*préfecture* or *sous-préfecture*), asking for the *service du tourisme*. Stay cool: in France, smiles work miracles.

Bad merchandise. Within about ten days of purchase a store will usually exchange faulty merchandise (if you have the receipt), but you will hardly ever get your money back.

I'd like to make a complaint.	**J'aimerais faire une réclamation.**

CRIME AND THEFT *(délit; vol)*

The entertainment districts of Paris, Nice, Marseille and Lyon are places to be wary in. Don't panic, but keep to well-lit streets at night and watch your wallet, especially in crowded buses or trains.

If you have items of real value, keep them in the hotel safe and obtain a receipt for them; it's a good idea to leave large amounts of money and even your passport there as well.

Don't leave valuables visible in your parked car. Any loss or theft should be reported at once to the nearest *commissariat de police* or *gendarmerie* (see POLICE).

Keep a photocopy of your plane tickets and other personal documents, with a note of the phone and telex numbers of your travel agent: it could come in useful in case of loss or theft.

My ticket/wallet/passport has been stolen.	**On a volé mon billet/porte-feuille/passeport.**

CUSTOMS AND ENTRY REGULATIONS

Visitors from E.E.C. countries need only a valid passport to enter France. Visitors from other parts of the world should check with the French consulate to see if they need a visa. Though Europeans and North American residents are not subject to any specific health requirements, visitors from further afield may require a smallpox vaccination. Check with your travel agent before departure.

The following chart shows what main items you may take into France duty-free:

Into:	Cigarettes	Cigars	Tobacco	Spirits	Wine
[1]	400	100	500 g.	1 l.	2 l.
[2]	300 or	75 or	400 g.	1½ l. and	5 l.
[3]	200	50	250 g.	1 l.	2 l.

[1] Visitors arriving from outside Europe.
[2] Visitors arriving from E.E.C. countries with non-duty-free items.
[3] Visitors arriving from E.E.C. countries with duty-free items, or from other European countries.

For what you can bring back home, ask before your departure for the customs notice setting out allowances.

Currency restrictions. There's no limit on the importation of local or foreign currencies or traveller's cheques. Unless a declaration was made on entry, non-residents are only allowed to reconvert up to 12,000 French francs into foreign currencies when leaving the country.

I've nothing to declare.	**Je n'ai rien à déclarer.**
It's for my own use.	**C'est pour mon usage personnel.**

DRIVING

To take your car into France you will need:

- International Driving Permit or your national driving licence
- Car registration papers
- Insurance coverage (the green card is no longer obligatory but comprehensive coverage is advisable)
- Nationality plate or sticker
- Red warning triangle
- A set of spare bulbs

Drivers and passengers of cars fitted with seat belts are required by law to wear them. Children under 10 must stay in the back seat.

Driving regulations. As elsewhere on the Continent, drive on the right, overtake (pass) on the left, yield right-of-way to all vehicles coming from the right (except on the roundabouts/traffic circles) unless otherwise indicated.

Speed limits. On dry roads, 130 kph (around 80 mph) on toll motorways (expressways), 110 kph (68 mph) on dual carriageways (divided highways), 90 kph (56 mph) on all other roads, and 45 or 60 kph (28 or 37 mph) in built-up areas. *Note:* when roads are wet, all limits are reduced by 10 kph (6 mph). The word *rappel* means a restriction is continued. Don't exceed the speed limits; all roads are patrolled.

Road conditions. French roads, all of them with greatly improved surfaces, are designated by an A, standing for *autoroute* (motorway); an N for *nationale,* national highway; a D for *départementale,* or regional road; and a V for a local road *(chemin vicinal).* The *nationales* sometimes prove too narrow during peak holiday periods: around the 1st and 15th of July, the 1st and 15th of August and the 1st of September.

The motorways are privately owned, with sizeable tolls *(péage)* according to vehicle size and distance travelled. All amenities (restaurants, toilets, service stations, etc.) are available, plus orange S.O.S. telephones every 2 kilometres.

For a more leisurely drive, take the alternative routes *(itinéraire bis)* signposted by arrows: a green arrow on a white background indicates north–south, while the opposite direction is shown by a white arrow on green background.

Parking. In town centres, most street parking is metered. The blue zones require a parking clock, *disque de stationnement* (obtainable from petrol stations or stationers), which you set to show when you arrived and when you must leave. Some streets have alternate parking on either side of the street according to which half of the month it is (the dates are marked on the signs). Fines for parking violations are heavy; in serious cases your car may be towed away or have a wheel clamp attached.

Breakdowns. Switch on the flashing warning lights, and place a warning triangle 50 m. behind your car. Call the *gendarmerie* who will send a breakdown service. It's wise to have internationally valid breakdown insurance, and to ask for an estimate *before* undertaking repairs (that have VAT or sales tax added).

Fuel and oil. Fuel, increasingly self-service, is available in super (98 octane) and normal (90 octane). Lead-free fuel is difficult to find. All grades of motor oils are on sale. Service-station attendants expect to be tipped.

Fluid measures

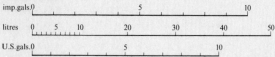

Kilometres to miles

km	0	1	2	3	4	5	6	8	10	12	14	16
miles	0	½	1	1½	2	3	4	5	6	7	8	9	10

Road signs. Most road signs are the standard pictographs used throughout Europe, but you may encounter these written signs as well:

Accotements non stabilisés	*Soft shoulders*
Chaussée déformée	*Bad road surface*
Déviation	*Diversion (detour)*
Gravillons	*Loose gravel*
Impasse	*Cul-de-sac (dead end)*
Nids-de-poule	*Pot-holes*
Priorité à droite	*Yield to traffic from right*
Ralentir	*Slow down*
Sauf riverains	*Entry prohibited except for residents*
Sens unique	*One-way street*
Serrez à droite/gauche	*Keep right/left*
Sortie de camions	*Lorry (truck) exit*
Stationnement interdit	*No parking*
Véhicules lents	*Slow vehicles*
driving licence	**permis de conduire**
car registration papers	**carte grise**
Full tank, please.	**Le plein, s'il vous plaît.**
regular/super/diesel/ lead-free	**normale/super/gas-oil/ sans plomb**
Check the oil/tyres/battery, please	**Veuillez contrôler l'huile/ les pneus/la batterie.**
I've had a breakdown.	**Ma voiture est en panne.**

ELECTRIC CURRENT   E

The 220-volt, 50-cycle AC is now almost universal, though 110 volts may still be encountered. If you bring your own electrical appliances, remember to buy a Continental adaptor plug before leaving home (round pins, not square).

What's the voltage—110 or 220?	**Quel est le voltage—cent dix ou deux cent vingt?**
an adaptor plug	**une prise de raccordement**
a battery	**une pile**

EMBASSIES AND CONSULATES *(ambassade; consulat)*

Contact your embassy or consulate when in trouble (loss of passport, problems with the police, serious accident). Opening times are variable, so it's best to phone in advance. All embassies are in Paris. There are consulates in other major cities: you'll find them in the phone book *(bottin* or *annuaire)* under "Consulats".

Australia (embassy/consulate)	4, rue Jean-Rey, Paris 15e; tel. 45.75.62.00
Canada (consulate)	35, av. Montaigne, Paris 8e; tel. 47.23.01.01
Eire (consulate)	12, av. Foch (enter from 4, rue Rude), Paris 16e; tel. 45.00.20.87
New Zealand (embassy/chancellery)	9, rue Léonard-de-Vinci, Paris 16e; tel. 45.00.24.11
South Africa (chancellery/consulate)	59, quai d'Orsay, Paris 7e; tel. 45.55.92.37
United Kingdom (consulate)	35, rue du Faubourg Saint-Honoré, Paris 8e; tel. 42.66.91.42
U.S.A. (consulate)	2, rue Saint-Florentin, Paris 8e; tel. 42.96.12.02

Where's the embassy/consulate?	**Où se trouve l'ambassade/le consulat?**
I'd like to phone the ... embassy.	**Je voudrais téléphoner à l'ambassade ...**
American/British/Canadian/Irish	**américaine/britannique/canadienne/irlandaise**

EMERGENCIES *(urgence)*

For real emergencies you can get assistance anywhere in France by dialling number 17 for the police *(police secours)*; call number 18 for the fire brigade *(pompiers)*, which also comes for such emergencies as drowning. See also separate entries in this section such as EMBASSIES AND CONSULATES, HEALTH AND MEDICAL CARE, POLICE, etc.

Though we hope you'll never need them, here are a few key words you might like to learn in advance:

Careful!	**Attention!**
Fire!	**Au feu!**
Help!	**Au secours!**
Stop thief!	**Au voleur!**
Can you help me?	**Pouvez-vous m'aider?**

GETTING TO FRANCE G

See a good travel agent well before your departure for help with
your timetable, budget and personal requirements.

By Air

Scheduled flights

Paris is the major gateway to France, though a number of international flights operate to Lyon, Nice and many other cities,
including Ajaccio, Bastia and Calvi in Corsica. Therefore, to avoid
having to do miles from point of departure to point of arrival,
look into regional possibilities.

Paris is served by two intercontinental airports, Roissy–Charles-
de-Gaulle and Orly (see also p. 219). Average journey time between Paris and Johannesburg is 14 hours, London 1 hour, New
York 7 hours (less than 4 hours by Concorde), Toronto 9 hours.

Charter flights and package tours

From the U.K. and Eire. Most tour operators charter seats on
scheduled flights at a reduced price as part of a package deal which
could include a weekend or a couple of weeks' stay, a simple bed
and breakfast arrangement or a combined "wine tour" and visit to
Paris. Among the inclusive holiday packages are special tours for
visitors with a common interest such as cookery courses, school
trips or art.

From North America. Paris is the starting point for many tours of
France. Wine-tasting, gourmet and cooking tours, as well as tours
of the château country are included in package deals leaving from
over a dozen major American and Canadian cities. You can also
choose from fly/drive and fly/rail schemes.

From Australia and New Zealand. Package deals for Paris are
offered by certain airlines. You can also travel by independent
arrangement (the usual direct economy flight with unrestricted
stopovers) or go on an air-and-car-hire arrangement.

From South Africa. There are excursion fares and numerous package deals that include Paris and other European sights.

By Car

Cross-channel operators offer plenty of special deals at competitive prices; a good travel agent will help you to find the suitable ferry for your destination.

By Bus

Regular services operate from London to Paris (via Calais). Numerous lines join Paris and regional cities such as Bordeaux, Lyon or Nice.

By Rail

All the main lines converge on Paris. There is an excellent network of ultra-rapid express trains, TGVs (1st and 2nd class, advance booking compulsory, certain trains with supplement). Paris–Lyon takes 2 hours, Paris–Besançon 2½ hours, Lille–Lyon 5 hours. Auto-train services *(Trains Autos Couchettes)* are also available from all major towns.

The journey from London to Paris takes from 6 to 11 hours by train. British and French railways offer London-to-Paris services with the possibility of overnight carriages from London. From Boulogne hoverport, there's a 2-hour, 20-minute turbo-train service to Paris (Gare du Nord).

Tickets. Visitors from abroad can buy a *France-Vacances Spécial* pass, valid for specified periods of unlimited travel on first or second class, with reductions on the Paris transport network and one or two days free car rental (with first class only), depending on type of card.

The *Rail Europ S* (senior) card, obtainable before departure only, entitles senior citizens to purchase train tickets for European destinations at reduced prices.

Any family of at least 3 people can buy a *Rail-Europe F* (family) card: the holder pays full price, the rest of the family obtain a 50% reduction in France, Switzerland and 13 other European countries; the whole family is also entitled to a 30% reduction on Sealink and Hoverspeed Channel crossings.

Anyone under 26 years of age can purchase an *Inter-Rail* card which allows one month's unlimited second-class travel.

People living outside Europe and North Africa can purchase a *Eurailpass* for unlimited rail travel in 16 European countries including France. This pass must be obtained before leaving home.

GUIDES AND INTERPRETERS *(guide; interprète)*
Syndicats d'initiative (see TOURIST INFORMATION OFFICES) can help
you find qualified official guides and interpreters. Guides engaged
all day should be offered lunch.

Bus companies offer many guided tours, and reputable travel
agencies furnish guides and cars. It's customary to tip the guide.

We'd like an English-speaking guide.	**Nous aimerions un guide parlant anglais.**
I need an English interpreter.	**J'ai besoin d'un interprète anglais.**

HAIRDRESSERS, BARBERS *(coiffeur)*   **H**
Prices vary widely according to the class of establishment, but
rates are usually displayed in the window. Most hairdressers are
closed on Monday.

I'd like ...	**Je voudrais ...**
a haircut	**une coupe**
a shampoo and set	**un shampooing et une mise en plis**
a blow-dry	**un brushing**
Don't cut it too short (here).	**Pas trop court (ici).**
A little more off (here).	**Un peu plus court (ici).**

HEALTH AND MEDICAL CARE (See also EMERGENCIES.)
Make sure your health insurance covers illness or accident on holiday. Your insurance representative, automobile association or
travel agent can give you details of special travel insurance.

Visitors from E.E.C. countries with corresponding health insurance facilities are entitled to medical and hospital treatment
under the French social security system. Before leaving home,
make sure you find out about the appropriate form(s) required to
obtain this benefit. Doctors who belong to the French social security system *(médecin conventionné)* charge the minimum.

The stomach trouble that hits many travellers is generally not
due to drinking tap water, which is safe in towns all over France.
Fatigue, too much sun, change of diet and too much food and
drink are the causes of most minor complaints. Serious gastro-

intestinal problems lasting more than a day or two should be looked after by a doctor. Don't be surprised if a doctor prescribes suppositories; in France, they're considered the best and fastest way of getting drugs into the bloodstream.

Chemists or **drugstores** are easily recognized by a green cross. The personnel is helpful in dealing with minor ailments.

Where's the nearest (all-night) chemist?	**Où se trouve la pharmacie (de garde) la plus proche?**
I need a doctor/dentist.	**Il me faut un médecin/dentiste.**
I feel sick.	**J'ai mal au cœur.**
I've a headache.	**J'ai mal à la tête.**
stomach ache	**mal à l'estomac**
fever	**de la fièvre**

HITCH-HIKING *(auto-stop)*
This is permitted everywhere except on motorways (expressways). If you do hitch-hike, it's always wiser to go in pairs. It's easier to get a lift if you hold up a big piece of card with your destination marked on it.

Can you give us a lift to ...?	**Pouvez-vous nous emmener à ...?**

L LANGUAGE
Although a certain number of Frenchmen speak some English, the French frankly much prefer a tourist making an effort to speak French, even if it's only the odd word.

The Berlitz phrase book FRENCH FOR TRAVELLERS covers almost all the situations you're likely to encounter in your travels in France. The Berlitz French–English/English–French pocket dictionary contains a 12,500-word glossary of each language, plus a menu-reader supplement.

Good morning/ Good afternoon.	**Bonjour.**
Good afternoon/ Good evening.	**Bonsoir.**
Goodbye.	**Au revoir.**
Speak slowly, please.	**Doucement, s'il vous plaît.**

LAUNDRY AND DRY-CLEANING *(blanchisserie; teinturerie/ nettoyage à sec/pressing)*

If your hotel will not take laundry, you can have clothes cleaned reasonably quickly in chain dry-cleaners (not recommended, however, for fragile fabrics or difficult spots).

When will it be ready?	**Quand est-ce que ce sera prêt?**
I must have it tomorrow morning.	**Il me le faut pour demain matin.**

LOST PROPERTY

Restaurants and café personnel are quite honest about keeping forgotten or lost objects until the owner reclaims them. In the case of wallets, they will probably turn them over to the nearest *commissariat de police*.

I've lost my wallet/handbag/ passport	**J'ai perdu mon portefeuille/ sac/passeport.**

MAPS M

Small street maps *(plan)* are given away at tourist offices, banks and hotels. Detailed country or regional maps *(carte)* are sold in bookshops and at newsstands.

The maps in this book were prepared by Falk-Verlag, Hamburg.

MONEY MATTERS

Currency *(monnaie)*. For currency restrictions, see CUSTOMS AND ENTRY REGULATIONS. The *franc*, France's monetary unit (abbreviated F or FF) is divided into 100 *centimes*. Coins come in denominations of 5, 10, 20 and 50 centimes and 1, 2, 5 and 10 francs. Banknotes: 20, 50, 100, 200 and 500 francs.

Banks and currency-exchange offices *(banque; bureau de change)*. Hours may vary, but most banks are open Monday to Friday from 8.30 or 9.30 a.m. to noon and 1.30 to 4.30 p.m. Some currency-exchange offices operate on Saturdays as well. Your hotel will usually change currency or traveller's cheques into francs, but the rate is not favourable—nor is it in shops where traveller's cheques are often accepted. Always take your passport along when you go to change money. Note that small towns do not always have banks.

Credit cards *(carte de crédit)* can be used in an increasing number of hotels, restaurants, shops, etc.

Traveller's cheques *(chèque de voyage,* sometimes referred to as *"travelair")* are accepted throughout France, but always have some ready cash with you, too. **Eurocheques** are also accepted; some places add a small percentage to cover bank charges.

Sales tax *(TVA,* pronounced *tay-vay-ah).* The sales (value-added) tax is imposed on almost all goods and services. In hotels and restaurants, this is accompanied by a service charge (see TIPPING).

Visitors returning home to a non-E.E.C. country can have the TVA refunded on larger purchases. Fill out a form and give a copy to the customs when leaving France for the refund to be sent to your home.

Could you give me some change?	**Pouvez-vous me donner de la monnaie?**
I want to change some pounds/dollars.	**Je voudrais changer des livres sterling/des dollars.**
Do you accept traveller's cheques?	**Acceptez-vous les chèques de voyage?**
Can I pay with this credit card?	**Puis-je payer avec cette carte de crédit?**

N NEWSPAPERS AND MAGAZINES

In addition to French national and local newspapers, you'll find the Paris-based *International Herald Tribune, Wall Street Journal,* and many English daily papers in major cities all over France, usually on publication day. For the best information on what's on in Paris, buy the weekly magazine *Pariscope.* In the provinces, the *syndicat d'initiative* often publishes a similar, smaller periodical. Magazines in many languages are available at larger newsstands.

Have you any English-language newspapers?	**Avez-vous des journaux en anglais?**

P POLICE

Despite what the French say about their police, most outsiders find them friendly, intelligent and helpful to tourists. In case of need, dial 17 anywhere in France for police help.

In cities and large towns you'll see the blue-uniformed *police municipale*, the local police force who keep order, investigate crime and direct traffic. In the country, *gendarmes* are responsible for traffic control and crime investigation.

Where's the nearest police station?	Où est le poste de police le plus proche?

PRICES

To give you an idea of what to expect, here are some average prices in French francs (F). However, inflation makes them unavoidably *approximate*, and there are considerable regional and seasonal differences.

Airport transfers. Bus to Orly 27 F, to Roissy 34 F. Train (2nd class) to Orly 20 F, to Roissy 25 F. Taxi to Orly approx. 150 F, to Roissy approx. 200 F.

Camping. 60–120 F for four persons with tent, 50–110 F with caravan (trailer).

Car hire (international company). *Renault 5 GTL* 206 F per day, 2.80 F per km., 2,314 F per week with unlimited mileage. *Renault 11* 242 F per day, 3.40 F per km., 3,150 F per week with unlimited mileage. *BMW 320* 413 F per day, 4.77 F per km., 5,685 F per week with unlimited mileage. Taxes included.

Cigarettes. French 4.50–7 F per packet of 20, foreign 7–10 F, cigars 17–48 F per piece.

Entertainment. Cinema 30–35 F, admission to discotheque 70–120 F, casino admission 55 F, cabaret 150–350 F.

Guides. 550–790 F for half day, 85 F for each additional hour.

Hairdressers. *Man's* haircut 80–180 F. *Woman's* haircut 80 F and up, blow-dry/shampoo and set 90 F and up, manicure 50 F and up.

Hotels (double room). ****L 1,000–2,500 F, **** 650–1,200 F, *** 450–600 F, ** 260–380 F, * 160–250 F.

Meals and drinks. Continental breakfast 15–70 F, tourist menu 50–75 F, lunch/dinner in fairly good establishment 120–200 F, coffee 5.50–10 F, whisky or cocktail 25–60 F, beer/soft drink 8–16 F, cognac 27–60 F, bottle of wine 40 F and up.

Museums. 10–20 F.

Youth hostels. 40–60 F per night.

PUBLIC HOLIDAYS

January 1	*Jour de l'an*	New Year's Day
May 1	*Fête du Travail*	Labour Day
May 8	*Armistice 1945*	Victory Day
July 14	*Fête nationale*	Bastille Day
August 15	*Assomption*	Assumption
November 1	*Toussaint*	All Saints' Day
November 11	*Armistice 1918*	Armistice Day
December 25	*Noël*	Christmas Day
Movable Dates:	*Lundi de Pâques*	Easter Monday
	Ascension	Ascension
	Lundi de Pentecôte	Whit Monday

These are French national holidays, inevitable sources of traffic jams on the eve. When a holiday falls on a Tuesday or a Thursday, the French often take the Monday or Friday off, respectively, to make a long weekend, called *le pont*.

R RADIO AND TV *(radio; télévision)*
The principal TV channels are TF1, A2 and FR3. Canal Plus is available only on subscription. All programmes (except for a few late-night foreign films, usually on Fridays and Sundays) are in French. The news is broadcast at 1 p.m., 8 p.m. and around 11 p.m.; films usually start at 8.30 p.m.

You can easily tune in to BBC programmes on short or medium-wave radios. In summer, the French radio (France Inter) broadcasts news and traffic information in English, usually at 8 a.m., 1 p.m. and 7 p.m.

RELIGIOUS SERVICES *(office religieux)*
France is predominantly Roman Catholic. Times of mass are always posted at church entrances, and on green roadside signboards at the entrance to towns and villages.

Hotel receptionists, policemen and tourist office personnel can supply further information.

Where is the Protestant church/the synagogue?	**Où se trouve le temple/ la synagogue?**
What time is mass/ the service?	**A quelle heure commence la messe/le culte?**

236

RESTAURANTS

Eating well is one of the most important aspects of life in France. **Breakfast** *(le petit déjeuner)* usually consists of a big bowl of milky coffee (chocolate for the children), with flaky *croissants* or slices of fresh *baguette*, butter and jam. The French often dunk their *tartine*—bread, butter, jam and all—into their coffee. **Lunch** *(le déjeuner)* is served between noon and 2 p.m. It can be a lengthy affair, with *hors d'œuvre*, main dish, salad (just lettuce and dressing), cheese and dessert. **Dinner** *(le dîner)*, served from 8 to 10 p.m., resembles lunch but can go on for hours. Children usually have a snack *(le goûter, le quatre-heures)* at 4 p.m. to fill in the gap.

There are many types of places to eat and drink. **Cafés** serve wine, beer and spirits, soft drinks, tea and coffee. Some of them sell snacks, such as ham or cheese sandwiches—substantial affairs made from half a *baguette*. In the morning there is usually a basket of croissants on the table; you can help yourself, then tell the waiter how many you've taken when you pay. A **bistrot** is a small café-restaurant serving simple meals, usually "dishes of the day" *(plat du jour)* placarded outside in whitewash on a blackboard. Beware of the sign "Steak frites" which is usually a passport to indifferent food. A **brasserie** is a larger café-restaurant, with copious local dishes. In the country you will see **auberges** (inns), **hostelleries** and **relais de campagne**; they serve full meals, and often superb food. Prices vary, but the menu, complete with prices, should be posted outside. **Restaurants** are classified by travel agencies, automobile associations and gastronomic guilds with a variety of codes—stars, knives and forks, chef's hats and so on. Look at the number plates on the cars in the car park—if they're mostly local, you can suppose that it's a good restaurant. An empty dining room with waiters lolling around suggests that there may be something wrong. **Rôtisseries** specialize in grilled meat; they may be quite expensive. On motorways you'll see the sign **Restoroute**; table and/or cafeteria service is available in these establishments. A **relais routier** is roughly equivalent to a roadside diner, often frequented by lorry drivers. The food here can be excellent, if you hit on the right place.

To help you order...

I'd like to reserve a table for 2/3/4.	**J'aimerais réserver une table pour deux/trois/quatre personnes.**
Do you have a set menu?	**Avez-vous un menu du jour?**

Deciphering the menu...

à l'alsacienne	with sauerkraut and pork
à l'ancienne	with wine sauce, carrots, onions and mushrooms
à l'andalouse	with green peppers, aubergines and tomatoes
à l'anglaise	boiled
à la bigarade	with brown sauce flavoured with orange, sugar and vinegar
à la bordelaise	with wine sauce, shallots, mushrooms and marrow
à la bourguignonne	with mushrooms, pearl onions and red wine sauce
à la broche	spit-roasted
en croûte	in a pastry crust
en daube	casseroled
à la dieppoise	with white wine sauce, mussels and shrimps
à la Dubarry	with cauliflower and cheese sauce
aux duxelles	with minced mushrooms, white wine, herbs
à la flamande	cooked in beer
à la forestière	with mushrooms, potatoes and bacon
à la hongroise	with paprika and sour cream
à la lorraine	braised in red wine with red cabbage
à la lyonnaise	with onions
à la Mirabeau	with anchovies, olives, tarragon
à la nage	simmered in white wine
à la niçoise	with garlic, anchovies, olives, onions, tomatoes
à la nivernaise	with carrots, onions, potatoes
à la normande	with butter and fresh cream or apples and cider
Parmentier	with potatoes
printanière	with spring vegetables
à la provençale	with garlic, onions, herbs, olives, oil and tomatoes
à la vapeur	steamed

TIME DIFFERENCES

France follows Central European Time (Greenwich Mean Time + 1). In spring the clocks are put forward one hour, and back one in autumn. If your country does the same, the time difference remains constant for most of the year.

New York	London	**Paris**	Sydney	Auckland
6 a.m.	11 a.m.	**noon**	8 p.m.	10 p.m.

What time is it?	**Quelle heure est-il?**

TIPPING

A 15% service charge is generally included automatically in hotel and restaurant bills. Rounding off the overall bill by a few francs helps round off friendships with waiters, too. It is considered normal to hand bellboys, doormen, filling station attendants, etc. a coin or two for their services. The chart below gives an indication of what to leave.

Porter, per bag	4–5 F
Hotel maid, per week	20–40 F
Lavatory attendant	2 F
Waiter	5–10% (optional)
Taxi driver	10–15%
Hairdresser/barber	10%
Tour guide	10%

TOILETS *(toilettes)*

Public conveniences in France range from the fly-infested squalid "footpad and hole-in-the-ground" to luxury three-star facilities, which you can usually predict by the general cleanliness of the establishment. It's best to use the toilets in cafés, which are generally free. A saucer with small change on it means that a tip is expected. In some out-of-the-way places, you may be given a big iron key or even a detachable door handle, to open the door. If you insist on luxury, look for a major hotel and glide past the reception desk as if you owned the place.

If there is no light-switch, the light will usually go on when you lock the door. Women's toilets are marked *Dames*, and men's either *Messieurs* or *Hommes*.

A recent innovation is the *Sanisette*: a cream-painted, cylindrical metal contraption, looking something like a telephone booth. You insert a 1-franc piece in the slot to open the door. When you come out, the whole thing is swilled, scrubbed and polished, ready for the next person. Don't let young children go in there alone, they might not be able to open the lock to get out.

Where are the toilets please?	**Où sont les toilettes, s'il vous plaît?**

TOURIST INFORMATION OFFICES *(office de tourisme/syndicat d'initiative)*

French national tourist offices abroad can help you plan your holiday and will supply you with a wide range of colourful, informative brochures and maps. They do not, however, book holidays.

Australia	BNP House, 12, Castlereagh Street, Sydney, N.S.W. 2000; tel. (612) 231-5244
Canada	1840 Ouest, rue Sherbrooke, Montreal, Que. H3H 1E4, P.Q.; tel. (514)931-3855 1, Dundas Street W, suite 2405, P.O. BOX 8, Toronto, Ontario M5G 1Z3
United Kingdom	178, Piccadilly, London W1V OAL; tel. (01) 493-6594
U.S.A.	610, Fifth Avenue, New York, NY 10020; tel. (212) 757-1125 645, N. Michigan Avenue, Suite 430, Chicago, IL 60611; tel. (312) 337-6301 9401, Wilshire Boulevard, Room 840, Beverly Hills, CA 90212; tel. (213) 271-6665 Post Street, Suite 601, San Francisco, CA 94108; tel. (415) 982-7272

On the spot, each sizeable town or tourist goal has its own *syndicat d'initiative*. They are invaluable sources of information, from maps to local hotel lists and other miscellaneous items. The personnel (often English-speaking) are extremely helpful. They don't recommend restaurants or make hotel reservations (unless there is an *Accueil de France* service). *Syndicats d'initiative* are usually found near the town centre, opposite the main church, and often have a branch at the railway station. Opening hours vary, but the general rule is 8.30 or 9 a.m. to noon and from 2 to 6 or 7 p.m., every day except Sunday.

The main tourist office in Paris is at:
127, av. des Champs-Elysées, 75008 Paris; tel. 47.23.61.72.

TRANSPORT

Buses *(autobus, autocar)*. Large towns and cities have urban bus services—a particularly good way to get around and sightsee as you go. Inter-city bus services are efficient, comfortable, inexpensive and fairly frequent. Terminals are often situated close to the railway station, where you'll find timetables and other information.

Taxis. In large towns, there are stands at the stations as well as in the centre, or you can hail a cab in the street. They're available only when their "Taxi" sign is *fully* lit up. Taxis can be called by telephone everywhere—local tourist brochures give the phone numbers. Rates vary from place to place. If you have a good distance to go, ask the fare beforehand.

Métro. Paris's underground (subway) is one of the world's most efficient and fastest, and a lot cleaner than in London or New York. Express lines (R.E.R.) get you into town in about 15 minutes, with a few stops in between. Buy a book of 10 tickets *(carnet)*, available for first or second class, if you plan to take the *métro* several times. There are also special tourist tickets, called *Paris Sésame*, for two, four or seven days, allowing unlimited travel on bus or 1st class *métro*.

Trains. SNCF *(Société nationale des chemins de fer français)*, the French national railways, run fast, clean and efficient trains. They have excellent regular services everywhere, often backed up by a network of SNCF-operated bus and coach services. (See also p. 230.)

Planes. France's principal domestic airline, Air Inter, and other short-haul carriers fly between Paris and 28 regional airports, and link some provincial cities directly with each other. The number of flights is increased in the summer.

single (one-way)	**aller simple**
return (round-trip)	**aller-retour**
first/second class	**première/seconde classe**
I'd like to make seat reservations.	**J'aimerais réserver des places.**

W WATER *(eau)*

Tap water is safe—and sometimes even tasty—throughout the country, except when marked *eau non potable* ("not safe for drinking"). The French drink mineral water; it's a good thirst quencher and helps to digest meals. Keep a bottle in the car. A wide variety can be found on sale everywhere. You pay a deposit *(consigne)* on glass bottles, refunded when you take the empties back.

a bottle of mineral water	**une bouteille d'eau minérale**
fizzy (carbonated)	**gazeuse**
still (non-carbonated)	**non gazeuse**
Is this drinking water?	**Est-ce de l'eau potable?**

WEIGHTS AND MEASURES

France uses the metric system. For fluid and distance measures, see p. 226.

Temperature

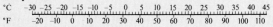

Length

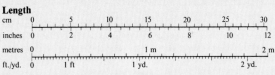

Weight

```
grams    0   100  200  300  400  500  600  700  800  900  1 kg
ounces   0    4    8    12  1 lb.  20   24   28  2 lb.
```

Y YOUTH HOSTELS *(auberge de jeunesse)*

There are about 200 youth hostels in France, well scattered over the country, with varying facilities. Your national youth hostel association can give you all the details, or contact:

Fédération unie des auberges de jeunesse,
6, rue Mesnil, 75116 Paris; tel. 45.05.13.14

USEFUL EXPRESSIONS

yes/no	**oui/non**
please/thank you	**s'il vous plaît/merci**
excuse me	**excusez-moi**
you're welcome	**je vous en prie**
where/when/how	**où/quand/comment**
how much	**combien**
yesterday/today/tomorrow	**hier/aujourd'hui/demain**
day/week/month/year	**jour/semaine/mois/année**
left/right	**gauche/droite**
up/down	**en haut/en bas**
good/bad	**bon/mauvais**
big/small	**grand/petit**
cheap/expensive	**bon marché/cher**
hot/cold	**chaud/froid**
old/new	**vieux/neuf**
open/closed	**ouvert/fermé**
here/there	**ici/là**
free(vacant)/occupied	**libre/occupé**
early/late	**tôt/tard**
easy/difficult	**facile/difficile**
Does anyone here speak English?	**Y a-t-il quelqu'un ici qui parle anglais?**

beach	**la plage**	*path*	**le chemin**
bridge	**le pont**	*river*	**la rivière**
church	**l'église**	*road*	**la route**
cliff	**la falaise**	*sea*	**la mer**
garden	**le jardin**	*shop*	**le magasin**
hill	**la colline**	*square*	**la place**
house	**la maison**	*station*	**la gare**
lake	**le lac**	*street*	**la rue**
market	**le marché**	*town*	**la ville**
mountain	**la montagne**	*village*	**le village**
museum	**le musée**	*vineyard*	**le vignoble**

Sunday	**dimanche**	*Thursday*	**jeudi**
Monday	**lundi**	*Friday*	**vendredi**
Tuesday	**mardi**	*Saturday*	**samedi**
Wednesday	**mercredi**		

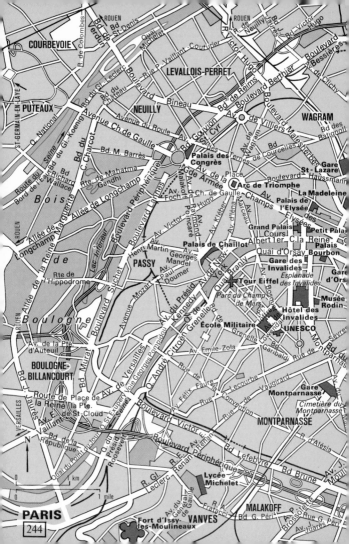

PARIS

244

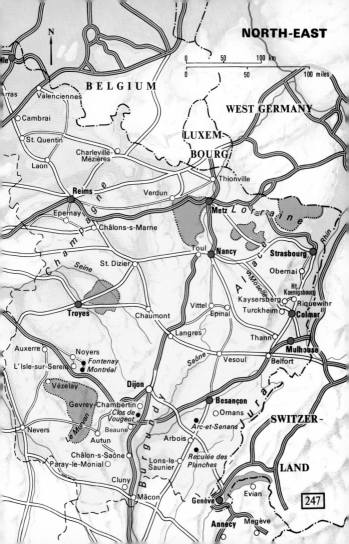

NORTH-EAST

N

0   50   100 km
0   50   100 miles

BELGIUM

WEST GERMANY

LUXEM-
BOURG

rras
Valenciennes
Cambrai
St. Quentin
Charleville-
Mézières
Laon
Reims
Epernay
Châlons-s-Marne
Verdun
Thionville
Metz
Lorraine
Toul
Nancy
Strasbourg
Obernai
Ht.
Koenigsbourg
Kaysersberg
Riquewihr
Turckheim
Colmar
Thann
Mulhouse
Belfort
Vittel
Epinal
Chaumont
Langres
Vesoul
St. Dizier
Seine
Troyes
Auxerre
Noyers
L'Isle-sur-Serein
Fontenay
Montréal
Vézelay
Gevrey-Chambertin
Clos de
Vougeot
Beaune
Nevers
Le Morvan
Autun
Dijon
Besançon
Ornans
Arc-et-Senans
SWITZER-
Châlon-s-Saône
Lons-le-
Saunier
Arbois
Reculée des
Planches
Paray-le-Monial
Cluny
Mâcon
Genève
Evian
Annecy
Megève
LAND
Saône
Jura
Burgundy
Champagne
Alsace
Moselle
Rhin

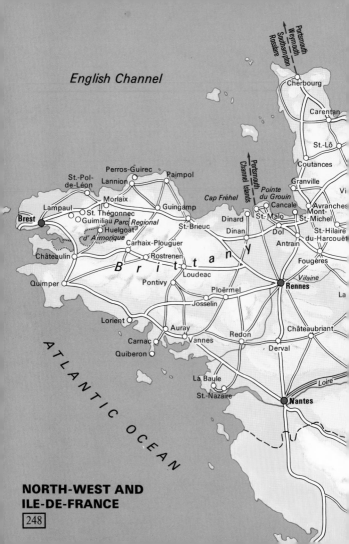

English Channel

Portsmouth
Weymouth
Southampton
Rosslare

Cherbourg

Carentan

St.-Lô

Coutances

Granville

Vi

Portsmouth
Channel Islands

Pointe
du Grouin

Cancale

Avranches
Mont-
St-Michel

Cap Fréhel

St. Malo

St-Hilaire
du-Harcouët

Perros-Guirec

Paimpol

Lannion

St.-Pol-
de-Léon

Morlaix

Dinard

Guingamp

Dinan

Dol

Lampaul

St. Thégonnec

Brest

Guimiliau

Parc Regional

St-Brieuc

Antrain

Huelgoat

d' Armorique

Fougères

Châteaulin

Carhaix-Plouguer

B r i t t a n y

Rostrenen

Quimper

Loudeac

Vilaine

Pontivy

●**Rennes**

La

Ploërmel

Josselin

Lorient

Auray

Redon

Châteaubriant

Carnac

Vannes

Quiberon

Derval

Loire

La Baule

St.-Nazaire

●**Nantes**

A T L A N T I C   O C E A N

**NORTH-WEST AND
ILE-DE-FRANCE**

248

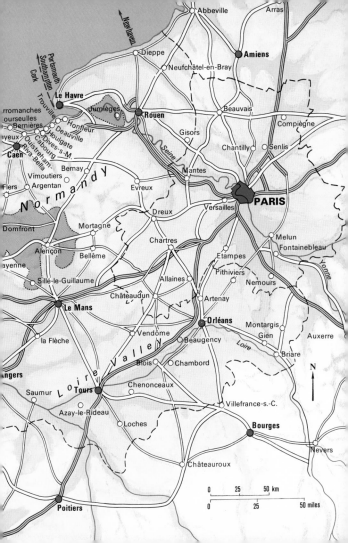

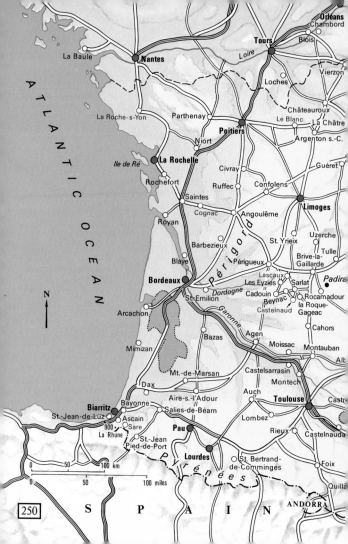

INDEX

An asterisk (*) next to a page number indicates a map reference. Where there is more than one set of page references, the one in bold type refers to the main entry. For index to Practical Information, see also pp. 216–217.